# Spey Flies & Dee Flies

## Their History & Construction

## John Shewey

# Spey Flies & Dee Flies

## Their History & Construction

### John Shewey

**Frank Amato**

PORTLAND

# ACKNOWLEDGEMENTS

A great many people lent their selfless assistance to the completion of this project, among them many fine fly dressers. I am especially indebted to David Barlow and Rich Youngers of Salem, Oregon; David Burns of McCall, Idaho; Gary Grant of Richland, Washington and Philip Glendinning of Aberdeen, Scotland. My friends within the fly tying and fishing community graciously supplied many of the beautifully dressed flies appearing herein. Among them are the following: Dec Hogan, Scott O'Donnell, Paul Rossman, Joe Howell, Clark Lucas, Dave Tucker, Bob Arnold, Walt Johnson, Tony Smith, G.S. Scoville, Paul Ptalis, Steve Schweitzer, Scott Peters, Jon Harrang, Bob Newman, Brad Burden, Joel Stansbury, Bob Petti, Roger Plourde, Jean Paul Dessaigne and Chuck Moxley. With luck, I've not excluded anyone from that list. Also, thanks to Jennifer for her unwavering patience and support with this project.

Philip Glendinning also helped immeasurably by providing me valuable details about William Garden and other Deeside historical figures. I am likewise indebted to Graeme Wilson (Local Heritage Officer at Elgin Museum) and Iain Russell (The Heritage Works), for aiding my research and to Timothy McCann, Assistant County Archivist for West Sussex and Kathryn Bellamy, Curator's Assistant at Goodwood. Thanks as well to Miriam Johnson at the Salem Public Library for tracking down many rare books. I also wish to thank Mrs. A. H. Mitcalfe of Moray, Scotland, the great granddaughter of Major James Grant, for allowing me permission to use photographs of the Major herein and to Yvonne Thackeray of Chivas Regal for providing these photographs.

I must also express my gratitude to Dave McNeese for it was his fascination with Spey-style flies that led to my own addiction to the style. Moreover, Dave's skill and creativity in designing and dressing Spey-style patterns served as my initial vantage point on the discipline. Dave has never received his due credit for his role in furthering the popularity of the Spey fly, yet as early as the mid-1970s he was experimenting at the vise with these remarkable dressings. It was shortly thereafter that I embraced the style as well, studying Dave's work in all its creative genius.

During the first decade of McNeese's Fly Shop, we could indeed watch the growth in popularity of these flies, first on the Steelhead Coast and then across the country as a whole. In retrospect I feel fortunate to have been a part of it all, yet it took the musings of several of Washington State's most talented tiers to allow me to realize fully the impact that the "McNeese's Fly Shop era" had upon the steelhead-tier's art: At different moments during the 1990s, Glenn Wilson, John Olschewsky and Steve Broco—three highly talented fly dressers from Washington all expressed to me how influential that era had been on their own tying, and the steelhead and Spey-tier's discipline in general.

**©2002 by John Shewey**

ALL RIGHTS RESERVED. No part of this book may be reproduced in any means without the written consent of the publisher, except in the case of brief excerpts in critical reviews and articles.

Published in 2002 by Frank Amato Publications, Inc.
P.O. Box 82112, Portland, Oregon 97282
(503) 653-8108
www.amatobooks.com

Softbound ISBN: 1-57188-232-4   Softbound UPC: 0-66066-00486-4
Hardbound ISBN: 1-57188-233-2   Hardbound UPC: 0-66066-00487-1

Endpaper maps for Hardbound edition: ©Bartholomew Ltd.
Reproduced by Kind Permission of HarperCollins Publishers www.bartholomewmaps.com

All photographs taken by author unless otherwise noted.
Title page photo of steelhead: Scott Ripley

Book Design: Tony Amato

Printed in Singapore

3  5  7  9  10  8  6  4  2

# Contents

# INTRODUCTION

Among the great salmon rivers of Scotland are the famed Spey and Aberdeenshire Dee, whose storied pools and sea-bright salmon inspired generations of anglers and fly dressers. So strong are the traditions on these waters that the Dee and Spey are afforded the unique luxury of having an entire class of salmon flies named for each of them. The Spey flies and the Dee flies originated and evolved in the valleys through which these rivers flow, but across the globe, fly dressers emulate the fashion of such flies, calling them "Spey-styles" and "Dee-styles."

No other salmon or steelhead streams enjoy such noteworthy traditions. No other waters have inspired styles of flies recognizable as belonging to a particular river's legacy, as is the case with the dressings originating Speyside and Deeside. Here in the New World, we certainly do not hear of "Miramichi-style" flies or "North Umpqua-style" flies. The closest we come to associating a river with a style of fly is on Oregon's Rogue, where small doubles were once quite fashionable. But the Rogue and its doubles rank as a now-extinct and rather short-lived local phenomenon, not a global fly-tying obsession.

For on salmon and steelhead rivers across the land, including those aforementioned, anglers tie and fish Spey- and Dee-style flies. During the height of Victorian salmon-fly dressing in the late 1800s, virtually every Scottish salmon river had its attendant flies designed by its local anglers. Yet even at that time only the traditional flies deriving from the Spey and Dee—and for a time perhaps from the Tweed and Tay—could be readily identified as such by the learned salmon fisher.

The legions of gaudy, complex flies and certainly the simpler flies dating much earlier might well find individual members assigned to superior effectiveness on a particular river by high-minded fly dressers. Hence there were the Findhorn flies, the Ness flies, and so on. But generally only the fly's inventor and its strong adherents would recognize it as belonging to a particular river. The same holds true on North America's West Coast steelhead streams.

Yet save for the Dee and Spey flies, none of these river-specific design peculiarities evolved into widely recognized styles of tying. By the latter decades of the 19th century, salmon anglers throughout the British Isles could recognize those flies tied for the Spey and Dee in the unique styles that developed on the two rivers.

Indeed, classic Spey flies are easily recognized by their thin bodies wound lengthwise with hackle from the Spey cock or heron, their multiple ribs and their low-set wings of bronze mallard. The particulars of the Spey cock and its hackle I will address in the second chapter.

From a stylistic standpoint, Spey flies are defined by their simple elegance; yet this elusive quality is the very thing that many fly dressers struggle to perfect. Part of the difficulty lies in the techniques and in the choice of materials; more significantly, it is the concept itself—simple elegance—that proves the undoing of many a Spey-style fly, especially in this age of the re-birth of the Victorian full-dress salmon fly.

During the past two decades, new heights of design and craftsmanship have been realized in the world of dressing these fanciful salmon flies. Yet the same fly dressers whose full-dress flies approach perfection and elicit due praise sometimes struggle in achieving a comparable level of expertise in the tying of simple Spey patterns. Often the fault lies in overdressing the flies. Perhaps such artists, trained in the intricacies of the complex Victorian full-dress styles, cannot resist the temptation to add a little flair, some hint of their preferred flies that exhibit all manner of exotic feathers.

In this regard, my observations are hardly unique. In his classic but rare work titled *The Angler's Companion to the Rivers and Lochs of Scotland* (1847), Thomas T. Stoddart espoused with classic eloquence upon the inherent divergence between dressing salmon flies indigenous to Scotland and dressing the gaudy salmon fly:

*"First of all, as to the dressing of the Scotch salmon-fly. It is generally imagined that, because of its sober, if not homely look, the fabrication of this lure is a matter of no difficulty in comparison with the fabrication of an Irish killer, such as the Doctor, or any other well-known magnet. I admit that the materials are not so costly, nor, in many cases, nearly so numerous; still there are points in the dressing of the former, which, in order to make it please the eye, require more nicety of execution, as well as the exercise of more taste and discrimination than are necessary to be employed in the construction of the latter."*

Indeed, accomplishing that feat of elegant, somber simplicity eludes many a would-be Spey tier. Certainly, Spey flies are easily overdressed. Tiers guilty of over-dressing the Spey fly need only understand the history of these flies: They are products of ghillies, anglers and fly dressers of centuries past in the Spey Valley, or Strathspey to use the indigenous vernacular—pragmatic men who used materials easily found Speyside. Hence their flies were adorned with wools and tinsels, heron and cock hackles, widgeon and teal flank, and of course the characteristic strip wings of bronze mallard.

Certainly modern fly dressers have expanded the definition of Spey flies and Dee flies, so much so that many contemporary patterns retain only subtle hints of their storied kin. Often the words "Spey-style" or "Dee-style" seem more appropriate labels for these new designs. Regardless of their label, however, the modern Spey flies and Dee flies derive from those dressed on the legendary Scottish rivers during the 19th century and perhaps earlier.

With that fact in mind, it matters little to me whether we call the newcomers "Spey flies," "Spey-style flies," "pseudo-Speys,"

or whatever, so long as we seek and retain some understanding of their roots. Hence I have striven herein to produce the most complete record compiled to date regarding the history of these flies.

We should also appreciate the fact that 19th century fly dressers catapulted their art to newfound heights and in doing so devised techniques and methods that remain frequently used today. Certainly new materials have forced upon modern tiers the need to devise new fly-dressing tricks; but for every such new technique I suspect there is an old method now largely lost to the contemporary fly dresser.

Likewise many a modern fly dresser lacks a fundamental appreciation for the "fishability" of the old Spey and Dee flies. Too many expertly dressed modern flies end their days framed under glass and not enough of them swim the rivers, meeting

retirement only after being worn threadbare by the teeth of steel-head or salmon. I say this not to be insulting, for I am duly impressed by and indebted to the supremely talented fly dressers who have driven the current rage in perfecting the art of dressing classic salmon flies and contemporary steelhead flies.

Remember, though, that these flies bear a hook point at one end. They are lures. The next time you sit down at the bench to dress a salmon fly, whether it be a simple Lady Caroline or Akroyd or a fanciful Jock Scott or Highlander, dress the gut loop for fishing and take the fly for a swim. Admire its sleek lines and watery flow. Beach a salmon or steelhead on this fly and I can assure you that your appreciation for the salmon-tier's art will attain new heights. Indeed, you will likewise appreciate and accept unfailingly my contention that a steelhead is too fine a game fish to be insulted with ugly flies.

# Chapter 1

# History of Spey & Dee Flies

*". . .the Spey, too, is a pleasant and instructive fellow-traveller,
and the Dee a positive poet, who embues the dullest
weight with some of his own imagination."*

—Rev. G. Gordon

Of the famed River Spey, Eric Taverner, writes, ". . .she is a river of great power, which is said to have caused the creation, in past days, of a special type of fly."

Further, Taverner marvels that ". . .there is something about the Spey-fly that makes me think it is dressed in the most rational way yet achieved of simulating life struggling beneath the surface of the water."

Indeed, the flies developed Speyside exhibited characteristics unique to them. They featured a style of hackling seen nowhere else: namely a rooster side-tail or saddle hackle, or perhaps a heron's hackle, wrapped in the reverse way to the rib or ribs. In other words, the rib material was used to lock down the hackle stem. The flies featured wings of brown mallard, set low over the somber-colored body. The usual mixtures of dubbings and mohairs or, later at least, strands of fine wool comprised the bodies on these flies. The finished package resembled nothing else and by the mid-point of the 19th century, the learned salmon fisher could readily identify a fly tied in this style as belonging to the River Spey.

Not yet fully and abundantly distributed during the first half of the 19th century, were the fanciful exotic feathers procured through England's dynamic world trade and largely destined for the prolific Victorian millinery industry. By the second half of the century—thanks in a large measure to the industrious William Blacker and then the incomparable (and perhaps incorrigible) George Kelson, amongst others—salmon flies would blossom into their full Victorian elegance and regalia. But the comparatively drab Spey flies predated the gaudy, complex dressings that eventually came to define the salmon tying tradition.

Of course, the Spey held no monopoly on somber-colored flies. Indeed, prior to the insurgence of the Irish influence, all of the major salmon rivers of the British Isles (and many of the minor flows, too) had their own salmon flies developed by the local anglers during the 18th and 19th centuries. These were nearly always of quiet tones and earthly shades. Sir Herbert Maxell reminds us in 1904 that, ". . . favourite locally indigenous flies are nearly always dull in colour, because bright feathers and materials were not easily obtained by those who invented them a hundred years ago."(1)

Amongst these indigenous dressings are styles differing only in subtle degrees. Certainly the Tweed had its unique flies, as did the Tay, Findhorn, Garry, Dee and Don and many others, yet finding differences between them would have proven tedious even for the most accomplished anglers of the

**ABOVE:** Major James Grant, long-time owner of Glen Grant Distillery, ranked amongst the notable 19th Century fly designers living Speyside.

**Facing Page:** Classic Dee flies as dressed by Gary Grant: Gardener, Moonlight and Glentana.

AMONGST THE EARLIEST RECORDED SPEY FLIES ARE THOSE LISTED BY THOMAS TOD STODDART IN
*ANGLER'S COMPANION TO THE RIVERS AND LOCHS OF SCOTLAND* (1846).

time. The traditional Spey flies, however, exhibited a style quite unique even when compared with the salmon flies from nearby rivers.

The anglers from the Spey Valley dressed these flies in a particular, peculiar and identifiable style, with thin, fully-hackled bodies. The unusual hackles were generally wound in the opposite direction to at least one of the ribs and over all was a pair of low-set wings dressed of sections from mallard scapulars, or what we know today as "bronze mallard."

For any Scottish salmon river, codified lists of patterns are few in number prior to the second half of the 19th century. And for the Spey flies, only a few of the old dressings are mentioned in period literature. A reasonably inclusive list of pattern descriptions was probably never assembled until the 1872 work of Arther Edward Knox, whose quaint little title, *Autumns On the Spey,* included dressings for 16 of the "old Spey flies." In all likelihood, some of these patterns, and certainly the unique style exhibited in them, date to the early 1800s and perhaps earlier.

Until the publication of Knox's book, Spey flies received mention in only a precious few historical texts from the period. Thomas Tod Stoddart, in *Angler's Companion to the Rivers and Lochs of Scotland* (1846), listed two Spey flies, one a rather typical rendering of the Spey style, partaking in the plumage of the grey heron (*Ardea cinerea*). The second pattern from Stoddart offers evidence that by the 1840s the old flies were beginning to

compete Speyside with patterns increasingly adorned with more exotic feathers. Regardless of the invading gaudy flies, Stoddart notes that, amongst the Scottish flies, "the most favourite ones are those which are winged with the brown mottled feather taken from the back of the mallard—and having a long-fibred hackle, generally one of those which depend from the breast of a male heron, brown or dun-coloured dubbing, and a strip of fretted tinsel, wound, not too closely, around the body."(2)

Stoddart records that a "soft, long fibred hackle or side feather from barn-fowl cock or hen is sometimes employed instead of heron hackle." Dressings as follows (Stoddart listed the dressings in tabular format; I have chosen to present them in the contemporary style):

## SPEY FLY, NO. 1

| | |
|---|---|
| *Wings:* | Brown mottled feather taken from the back of a mallard |
| *Body:* | Black and brown mohair, or pig's wool mixed; hackle taken from pendant breast feathers of male heron, broad gold or silver lace, lapped on widely |
| *Tail Tuft:* | Yellow or orange |

## SPEY FLY, NO. 2

| | |
|---|---|
| *Wings:* | A pair of crest feathers taken from golden pheasant |
| *Body:* | Black mohair; black hackle, silver tinsel |
| *Tail Tuft:* | Yellow |

Significantly, Stoddart relates of the first dressing that ". . . until recently, this, or one similar to it, was held as the only true Spey hook. But the fishers in that quarter have, of late years, greatly augmented their stock, discovering that others of a very different fabric are quite as killing."

Stoddart's observation reinforces the notion that the old Spey fly patterns, however many existed, differed only by subtle degrees while retaining their characteristic style. Likewise, Stoddart provides us empirical evidence that by the 1840s the brighter, more complex flies—generally of Irish origins—had appeared Speyside and on most of the other notable Scottish salmon rivers. The exotic feathers used to dress the Irish flies had similarly spread across the land, albeit rather sparingly at first. For example, Stoddart records the fly found effective for trout in Loch Awe by "Professor Wilson" when the latter fished these waters in 1845-46: ". . .one of the most killing flies is winged with mottled feathers taken from the bustard. . ."(3)

Regional experts of the time reported to Stoddart that on the Shin River, "The favourite for salmon is a large hook with a mixed wing, red, blue, and black hackle; with jay feathers for the shouldering, crest of golden pheasant for the tail, and silver tinsel."

Gaudy flies were likewise in use on the Ness and Garry and on the Kirkcudbrightshire Dee. For the grilse and sea trout of the Eachaig, Stoddart relates that "small, gaudy flies, like those used on the west coast of Ireland, seem the favourites."

Of the Irish salmon flies, Stoddart lists dressings for the Parson, the Doctor, the Childers, the Butcher, Dundas Fly, the General and Lascelle's Golden Fly. Obviously, then, by the 1840s, the gaudy flies were widely distributed and at least reasonably well known throughout the Scottish salmon fly-fishing community. Indeed, as Stoddart says, the Irish gaudys ". . .gradually, of late years, have been adopted by our fishermen, and become of common use throughout Scotland."

Meanwhile, William Blacker, whose *Art of Fly Making* first appeared in 1842, reports therein that:

*I had a fly sent to me some years past, by McPherson Grant, about the size of C or drake size, with which he killed a salmon, twenty pounds weight, on the Spey. The body of the fly was made of yellow silk, red cock's hackle, toucan tail ribbed with gold, jay at the shoulder, a neat gaudily mixed wing, feelers of blue and yellow macaw, and a small black head. It was one of my flies, which, if made on large size hooks, will kill anywhere.*

Sir John MacPherson Grant, 2nd Baronet of Ballindalloch, was no stranger to the Spey and its flies, for he was, in fact, one of the primary landowners along the river. The family's Ballindalloch Castle included the famous Pitcroy Beat. In his brilliantly detailed 1899 book *The Salmon Rivers of Scotland*, Augustus Grimble lists MacPherson Grant amongst the Spey's "chief proprietors between Grantown and Fochabers." Indeed, even today Ballindalloch Castle and Pitcroy Lodge remain the properties of the family that has owned them for more than four centuries.

In any event, such gaudy salmon flies as described by Blacker had appeared Speyside by the 1830s and perhaps earlier, for John Younger, around 1840, suggests that Irish flies were first introduced in Scotland around 1810.(4)

In fact, the introduction of gaudy flies occurred on virtually all the salmon rivers in Scotland before the mid-1800s. Such intrusions generally began with a single angler and perhaps a singular angling feat. The incomparable and sadly short-lived Charles St. John wrote in the 1840s of the Findhorn: ". . .but here you have a well-equiped and well-accoutred follower of the gentle craft in waterproof overalls, and armed with London rod and Dublin fly, tempting the salmon from their element with a bright but indefinable mixture of feathers, pig's-wool, and gold thread. . ."(5)

St. John also describes a fly deriving from his own hands, likely during the 1840s (his book was first published in 1849) when he lived on the Findhorn. The fly's wings included, ". . . bustard, from India; a stripe or two of green parrot; a little of the tippet of the gold pheasant. . .a bit from the argus pheasant. . ."

So even before 1850, the gaudy flies with their exotic feathers had permeated the salmon-fishing scene throughout Scotland. On most rivers the Irish invaders met with some resistance by local anglers. Stoddart writes:

*I am only, reader, stating a well-known fact, when I afirm that, in the time I allude to, the salmon-fishers on Tweedside not only held what is called the Irish fly in absolute ridicule, but actually forbade use of it on those portions of the river they individually rented; and this they did, not because they deemed it too deadly for everyday use, but solely because they conceived it acted as a kind of bugbear to the fish, scaring them from their accustomed haunts and resting-spots. And indeed, it is only gradually that, in the lower part of the district I allude to, a complete change has been affected in the matter of flies. Not absolutely discarding the old standard and local lures, modern anglers have introduced into their stock at least a thousand-and-one other varieties.*

IN HIS 1867 BOOK TITLED *A BOOK ON ANGLING*, FRANCIS FRANCIS RECORDED DETAILS ABOUT SEVERAL OLD SPEY FLIES.

Indeed on the Tweed and elsewhere, the trend was set in motion. Within a few decades, the gaudy flies would largely supplant virtually all of the local styles on the salmon rivers of Scotland.

The growing popularity around mid-century of the Irish flies certainly underscores the unique character of the traditional Spey flies. For had the Spey flies not been so unique in design nor so popular in general use Speyside, they would have succumbed much earlier to the Irish influence—as did the Tweed flies and many other river-specific designs. Indeed, no one today hears much of "Tweed Flies" and "Tay Flies." Yet of the former, Stoddart provides an unique and valuable record. Without question Stoddart was predisposed to favor the Tweed, for it was his home river and as such we should imagine that his two listed Spey flies were but a sampling of the flies actually in use on the Spey at that time.

In 1867, long after the publication of the books by Stoddart and St. John, Francis Francis enjoyed the release of his immortal work, *A Book On Angling*, the first edition of which "sold more rapidly than any other angling book produced in the last quarter of a century." (6)

"The Spey flies are very curious productions to look at," writes Francis, "it being customary to dress them the reverse way of the hackle, and to send the twist or tinsel the opposite way to the hackle."

Francis records dressings for several standard Spey patterns, including the Green King, Purple King and two variations on the Spey Dog. Dressings for and samples of the Kings, says Francis, were submitted to him by his "friend Mr. C. Grant of Aberlour." Francis includes a letter from Grant in which the latter describes two further flies, the Green Dog and the Purpy. "They are well-known standard flies on the Spey," says Francis.(7)

Mr. Grant of Aberlour (not to be confused with Major James Grant, who devised the Glen Grant pattern) relates to Francis that, "In spring the Purple King is of less red colour than one used at present. The Green King at that period is more green, but, as the season advances, more red is used in both, and redder feathers."

"The dubbing of the Green Dog," continues Grant, "is the same as Green King, feather a little lighter, with gold-colour spate and pea-green thread at equal distances on the body of the hook or fly. The Purple, or 'Purpy,' a thirty-second cousin of the Purple King, has a hackle somewhat redder than that of his progenitor; dubbing, dark blue and stone red, with gold spate and purple thread on body of fly at equal distances."

As so clearly enunciated by other authors of the period, the old Spey flies exhibited innumerable varieties and of no small concern amongst anglers Speyside was the infinitesimal difference between two outwardly similar patterns. Augustus Grimble, for example, relates that "the natives place great faith in the tinsel used, and it is common enough to hear one ghillie say to another after a study of the clouds and the light and the river, 'Well, I'm just thinking it will be a 'gold day,' or a 'silver day,' according to his observations."

Knox likewise addresses the subtleties of dressing in the old Spey flies:

*"Notwithstanding the subdued tone and apparent simplicity of all these Spey flies, and a certain family resemblance, if I may use the expression, that pervades them all, yet after a little practice they may be easily distinguished from each other, and however trifling and insignificant these minute differences may appear to the uninitiated, yet in the eyes of the experienced native fisherman they are of considerable importance, and when salmon are shy, success is frequently supposed to depend upon their due appreciation."*

Mr. Charles Grant's dressings for the Green King and the Purple King, as recorded by Francis, are as follows. In a 1920 reprint of *A Book On Angling*, editor Sir Herbert Maxwell included color fly plates, one of which includes a beautifully dressed rendition of the Purple King.

The Purple King—Body, a light purple mohair; hackle, brownish black with light blue dun tip; tinsel gold and silver and silver twist over hackle as before; teal shoulder, and two strips of grey mallard wing with brown tips.

The Green King—Body, orange and olive-yellow mixed mohair; hackle brown with grey tips; the rest of the fly as before.

The aforementioned Spey Dog and Green Dog, meanwhile, include traces of golden pheasant plumage, but otherwise adhere quite strictly to the typical form of a classic Spey fly. His dressing for the Spey Dog—a fly recorded only by Francis (until later decades)—follows the parenthetic style of Blacker, et al. and is worth quoting for Francis' description of the fly's construction as follows:

*"This is usually dressed large for the spring, the long-shanked Dee hooks being preferred. Body, black pig's wool; up this is then wound some broad silver tinsel in widish rings; over the tinsel is laid on a large black feather (it can hardly be called hackle) with a lightish dun tip, taken from the side of the Scotch cock's tail. The feather is dressed the wrong way, so that the hackle stands out abruptly, and is carried round the opposite way to the tinsel, as some of the tinsel crosses it; over this hackle is wound some gold tinsel, not side-by-side with the silver, but quite independent of it. This aids in the glitter of the fly, and strengthens and keeps the hackle secure. At the shoulder a teal hackle; wing, a good wad of gold pheasant tail, with two long strips of grey mallard with brownish points over it. The fly can be varied by using a brown hackle and turkey instead of gold pheasant tail; add also orange silk between the tinsels."*

A few years later, the substantive list of patterns recorded by Knox was derived from sample flies given him by a single source, George Shanks. Knox says, "To every fisherman on the river it will be sufficient to say that the descriptions are taken from specimens tied by that accomplished artist, Shanks, of Craigellachie . . ."

Christened at Aberlour on June 5, 1828, George Shanks became a famed fly dresser and was the ghillie at Craigellachieat until around the turn of the century. He tied the flies for Castle Gordon and often served as ghillie to royalty when they visited the Spey, even attending King George (Duke of York at the time of his first visit to Gordon Castle in 1899). Grimble wrote of Shanks' fly-tying ability that "there is no better exponent of the art."

WITH HIS NOTATION OF THE MALLARD WING, WILLIAM BLACKER'S REMARKABLE HAND-COLORED PLATES FROM *ART OF FLY MAKING* (1842) REVEAL A SUBTLE CLUE ABOUT SPEY FLY DESIGN.

In fact, for "more than half a century Mr. Shanks was engaged by the present Duke of Richmond and Gordon and his two predecessors as fisherman at Gordon Castle, and every autumn he was there for about eight weeks fishing with the noblemen and gentlemen who came there from far and near to ply the rod on the famous Castle Gordon water at Fochabers."(8)(9).

"Geordie" Shanks, as he was known, died at Walton House, Craigellachie, on June 19, 1915. "No man knew more of the lordly salmon and his ways," says Shanks' obituary. His memorial services were "very largely attended" and out of respect, all businesses in the village ceased operation during the proceedings.

Shanks' contribution to the history and evolution of the Spey fly remains elusive beyond the simple fact that his long tenure as ghillie to Gordon Castle and his highly-reputed skill make him perhaps the foremost Speyside angler in the river's history. Likely only the great John Cruickshank enjoyed equal repute during the latter decades of the 19th century (see Chapter 8). No doubt the regular visitors to the Duke's fishings on Speyside coveted any opportunity to fish for salmon under the guidance of Shanks, the head ghillie. In 1892, Gordon Castle's "Poet Chronicler" wrote:

"Breakfast o'er, with dread misgiving
That the rumor must be true,
Out we go in search of 'Geordie'
To the well-known 'rendezvous.'
See that row of solemn faces
Crowned with caps of Bismarck style,
As they sit in stony silence;
Could a jester make them smile?
Patiently they wait the verdict
Uttered by their worshipped chief.
See! he comes with lagging footsteps,
And a face of utmost grief.
'Worse and worse she's always gaining;'
Now the 'pinnie's' out of sight;
Not the smallest chance of fishing,
No not even nearer night. (10)

In fact, with nothing beyond circumstantial evidence to support such an assertion, I might suggest that Shanks probably devised the famous Lady Caroline—for many years now the single most popular classic Spey fly. The late British angler and author John Ashley-Cooper tells us this fly was named for "Lady Caroline Gordon Lennox, daughter of the Duke of Richmond and Gordon of Gordon Castle on the Spey in the last century."(11)

The Gordon-Lennox family, beginning with the 2nd Duke of Richmond, included no less than four "Lady Carolines," spanning five generations. Sir Herbert Maxwell, the prolific turn-of-the-century author, relates in 1913 that the Lady Caroline fly was "named after a lady still with us." Lady Caroline Elizabeth Gordon Lennox, daughter of the 6th Duke of Richmond and Gordon, Charles Gordon Lennox, died in 1934. She was the sole "Lady Caroline Gordon Lennox" that was "still with us" in 1913.

Furthermore, Caroline Elizabeth Gordon Lennox survived a sister named Lady Florence Augusta Gordon Lennox, who died in 1895. Although the dressing remains lost to antiquity, the "Lady Florence" pattern is listed by Grimble, alongside "Lady Caroline," "Lord March," and "Miss Elinor." The title

GEORDIE SHANKS SERVED AS GHILLIE AT GORDON CASTLE FOR NEARLY 50 YEARS. PHOTO FROM MURIEL BECKWITH'S *WHEN I REMEMBER* (1936).

"Lord March" refers to the first son of the Duke of Richmond and Gordon before the son inherits the Dukedom from his father. In this case, Lord March was Lady Caroline's brother Charles, who in 1903 became the 7th Duke of Richmond and Gordon. So this family of flies derives its individual names from the family of the 6th Duke of Richmond and Gordon, who, like his predecessor, had employed Shanks as head fisherman and fly dresser.

Without question, Shanks enjoyed a close, personal friendship with the 6th Duke and his family, including the grandchildren. Lady Muriel Beckwith, daughter of the 7th Duke of Richmond and Gordon, talks fondly of Shanks in her 1936 book, *When I Remember*:

*Fishing! What memories it brings back! We began very young, and Geordie Shanks, the head ghillie, instructed us all in the art. He was the dearest old man of his day, and under his care I killed my first salmon when I was eleven. I think this was the most thrilling moment of my life.*

*Geordie Shanks was a friend to the whole family, and was known far and wide as a great old boy. Whatever the weather he always wore a bowler hat, and his rules were as strict and rigid as his head-gear. He strongly disapproved of any slacking, a state of iniquity from his point of view, but which we often found*

GEORDIE SHANKS (LEFT) ATTENDS CHARLES GORDON-LENNOX, 6TH DUKE OF RICHMOND AND GORDON. PHOTO FROM AUGUSTUS GRIMBLE'S *THE SALMON RIVERS OF SCOTLAND* (1899).

*preferable to flogging the same pool again and again when the fish were not taking.*

*Under good circumstances it was quite another story, and there was much despondence when, coming to my grandfather's room to report on the Spey, he would sometimes announce: "There is no fishin' the day; she's risin' fast—not a bit of use."*

*On these occasions we used to collect in what we called the "Shankery," a large room where waders were dried, fly-books sorted, reels oiled, etc. etc. Here we made toffee, over the fire, to console ourselves for the disappointment. . ."*

Likewise held in high esteem, Lady Caroline was Muriel Beckwith's aunt, but also served graciously as Beckwith's guardian, mentor, friend and confidante. Beckwith recalls of "Aunt Lina" that "her memory was fresh and her wit keen, her appreciation of contrast shrewd. I wish it was in my power to put before this generation something of the loveliness and charm she represented, and which those who read this book and who knew her might expect, being aware of the innate part she played in our lives and the immense sympathy and understanding she showed to us, the devoted family of children she brought up."

Lady Caroline also selflessly served the community at large and was highly and widely regarded throughout British high-society of the time. For example, *The Northern Scot*, on November 3, 1900, reported that "Lady Caroline Gordon Lennox made her annual visit to Bellie Public School on Thursday and gave the pupils their usual treat of buns. . ." How fitting that the fly named in her honor has survived to become the most famous and popular of all the Spey flies.

In any event, it's upon the shoulders of this circumstantial evidence I base my contention that George Shanks invented the Lady Caroline. The close-knit bond he enjoyed with the Duke's family seems especially convincing when taken in conjunction with his reputation as one of Strathspey's foremost fly dressers and with the fact that, for many years apparently, he tied all the flies for Gordon Castle.

Remember also that just as Knox had consulted Shanks for the 16 dressings included in *Autumns on the Spey*, so too, apparently, did Grimble consult Shanks, at least in part, for the list of flies appearing in *The Salmon Rivers of Scotland*. Of his visits to Gordon Castle during the 1890s (and perhaps earlier) Grimble relates, "Geordie Shanks at Aberlour ties all the Gordon Castle flies, and there is no better exponent of the art, and several pleasant mornings have I passed with him in getting hints while chatting and looking through Lord March's fly-book—the biggest and the fullest I have ever seen."

I might add further that, while some writers have passed along the unfounded wisdom that the Lady Caroline ranks amongst the very old Spey flies (12), I hasten to disagree based on several prominent facts: First, Lady Caroline was born October 12, 1844 and her sister, Lady Florence, was born in 1851.(13) Second, the 6th Duke (Lady Caroline's father) did not inherit the Dukedom until 1860 and his first-born son (born 1845) then held the title of Lord March until 1903 when he inherited the Dukedom. In this latter fact I am presuming (with strong historical evidence to support this contention) that the "Lord March" fly mentioned by Grimble would have taken its name for Caroline's brother and not from her father (who would likewise have held the title Lord March until his father died in 1860).(14)

Third, the earliest mention of "Lady Caroline" comes in Kelson's book (1895), which was compiled largely of articles appearing between 1884 and the mid 1890s in the journal *The Fishing Gazette,* wherein the fly is mentioned at least once. Meanwhile, Hardy's, in their earliest available catalog from 1888, lists only the Spey Dog, Purple King and Green King for the Spey. By 1900 they had expanded the list to include the Black King, Silver Riach and Gold Riach. If there exists validity in my presumption that Shanks coined the Lady Caroline, he most likely did so some time after Knox's work appeared, for otherwise I suspect at least one member of this family of flies would have appeared therein.(15) I suspect these dressings, including the Lady Caroline, date no earlier than the mid 1870s.

Sadly, nowhere are the dressings recorded for the remaining patterns named for the Duke's family, all of which perhaps derived from the skilled hands of Shanks. If each was so timelessly and beautifully designed as the Lady Caroline, then we must indeed regret that no one chose to print their dressings.

The Duke's Gordon Castle fishings would prove, over the course of half a century, a major influence on the history of salmon fishing on Speyside. Indeed, during the latter years of the century, the Gordon Castle waters extended for nearly ten miles, from the famed Boat o'Brig at the bottom of Delfur to the sea and, says Ashley-Cooper, "it was normally fished by nine or ten rods. . .some of the best salmon fishing ever known."

"Presumably," continues Ashley-Cooper, "fishing started somewhere between 9:30 and 10 a.m. after a comfortable breakfast, and it would certainly be stopped by 5:30 p.m. in order to enable the fishermen to be back and changed into evening clothes in good time for dinner. . .all things considered, one could well envy the Duke and his guests."

Geordie Shanks, for many years, oversaw the fishing as head ghillie. His influence permeated all aspects of salmon angling at Gordon Castle, so much so that by the late 19th century, the tackle room had taken on the title of "The Shankery" and the other ghillies emulated Shanks in that they "invariably wore bowler caps, a form of headgear occasionally adopted by the rods also."(16)

A frequent visitor to Gordon Castle, Knox does not indicate whether he himself was a fly dresser. In fact, Knox offers little evidence as to how many of the 16 dressings enjoyed widespread or even modest popularity Speyside. It seems clear that the Kings and Riachs bathed in the spotlight of popularity. Kelson says, ". . .the best Spey fly among the old hands is a plain, flimsy, ragged-tailed 'Riach'. . ."

But what of the Speals, the Carron and the Culdrain? Did Shanks faithfully reproduce 16 popular Spey dressings or did he

CLASSIC SPEY FLIES: THE GOLD REEACH AND THE SILVER REEACH AS DRESSED BY JOHN SHEWEY.

intermix some well-known patterns with those no longer in general use on the river? This was, after all, the late 1860s or early 1870s and the gaudy flies, adorned with exotic feathers, had by then certainly become a well-known entity on the Spey. How much popularity the new full-dressed flies enjoyed is another matter, but their presence had long since been felt.

For the purposes of recording them for posterity, did Knox purposefully solicit the old Spey flies from Shanks? Did Knox himself hold little regard for the fanciful newcomers and therefore ask that Shanks supply him with the old dressings? Perhaps it was Shanks who held the interlopers in low regard. Certainly by 1872 when Knox's book was published, some of those "Old Spey Flies" were travelling the lonely path to obscurity. Perhaps Knox and Shanks, realizing this, elected to preserve for posterity the old Spey flies.

Certainly, however, there exists evidence beyond the empirical variety to support the contention that the flies described by Knox remained popular Speyside during the 1860s. Most telling is the fact that *Autumns on the Spey* was compiled from field notes kept and letters written by Knox during his autumn visits to Gordon Castle. Assuming he kept these

THE GOLD HERON AS DRESSED BY JOHN SHEWEY.

notes out of habit and not, initially at least, with the intent of compiling them in book form, Knox likely conspired with Shanks to assemble a list of dressings commonly used on the extensive Gordon Castle waters and elsewhere on the river. (17)

Knox and Shanks were certainly well acquainted, as Knox was a "privileged friend of the Duke of Richmond and Gordon" and "a frequent visitor in autumn to Speyside, where he made successful forays amongst salmon, deer, and grouse. . ." (18). He must have ranked among the privileged guests who enjoyed the pleasure of hunting over the Gordon setters, reputedly developed at Gordon Castle during the early 19th century and recognized by the British Kennel Club as an official breed in 1862. (19)

The personal friendship between the accomplished Knox and Charles Gordon-Lennox, the 6th Duke of Richmond and Gordon, was apparently a close bond. Indeed Knox dedicated his book to the Duke. Further, as one of England's foremost ornithologists, Knox had assembled a voluminous collection of mounted birds. Upon "breaking up his establishment at Trotten," Knox gave the entire collection to "his friend the Duke of Richmond and Gordon, to be preserved at Goodwood House." (20)

In any event, we must exercise caution in determining what can be deduced from Knox. We cannot decipher his intentions or motivations nor those of his source for the 16 flies, Geordie Shanks. Given Shanks' formidable reputation as a master fly dresser and ghillie, I suspect he contributed to Knox 16 of the old Speyside favorites and likely those he himself preferred.

We can of course ascertain the basic elements of the 16 patterns—their color and general design. But even to suppose anything related to actual construction would be presumptuous. Certainly Knox's reputation as both an ornithologist (he wrote two books on the subject) and a salmon angler inspires confidence in his recording of the plumage used in the flies.(21)

Even among those Spey patterns that were perhaps standardized throughout the valley, the evidence suggests that much variation occurred in the dressings. Without the aforementioned historical anecdotes, such a deduction might certainly stem from simple empiricism: Examine the traditional steelhead flies in use on the Pacific Coast today and you will find precisely codified patterns like the Brad's Brat, Max Canyon and Golden Demon tied in many different styles utilizing numerous choices in materials and proportions. These flies and their endless variations are products of the rivers on which they were popularized. Local tiers used materials at hand to arrive at the proper color scheme.

Imagine a similar scene Speyside. Local tiers, most of them serious salmon anglers or at least catering to their salmon-fishing clientele, use locally available materials to arrive at particular dressings. Some of these dressings become Speyside favorites and their recipes are passed along as anglers trade flies amongst themselves, scribble notes to one another, share an afternoon of fly dressing, and swap stories streamside. The development of the old Spey patterns probably occurred in much the same way as the subsequent development of the old steelhead flies. Try to find a book or article from the early 1900s that records steelhead dressings and you face a difficult task indeed. Most of the old dressings are recorded in later writings.

This same problem confronts the historian who wishes to codify the old Spey flies and if not for Knox, we would have precious little to aid in our search. Most of the pattern descriptions subsequent to Knox came a decade or more later and perhaps borrowed from *Autumns on the Spey*. Thankfully, the works of Francis Francis and Stoddart afford us the luxury of comparative analysis when taken in conjunction with Knox's book. These mid-century texts offer ample evidence of a firmly established style of fly on the Spey. What's more, Knox and Francis derive their sample patterns from different fly dressers, yet both offer the Purple and Green Kings, allowing us some confidence in the assertion that these were, at the time, popular flies.

Yet the dressings for these two flies vary between Knox and Francis, or, more correctly, between their respective submitters, George Shanks and Charles Grant. Indeed then, even without the benefit of empiricism derived subsequent to the development of the old Spey flies, one need only refer to the classic salmon literature to deduce that great variation occurred in the specific construction of these dressings. T.E. Pryce-Tannatt says that "there was no such thing as constant dressing for any Spey fly, for the reason that every dresser had a different rendering for each pattern, and, moreover, subjected his own rendering to considerable variation." (*How to Dress Salmon Flies*, 1914).

Perhaps more intriguing than the individual variation of dressing among the Spey flies is the general evolution of the style of both these and the somewhat similar Dee flies. How tantalizing it is to dream of a time when angling historians discover some long-lost document recording the first Spey-side fly dresser ever to tie a lure comprised of the elements we commonly associate with the Spey-style fly. Someone tied the first Spey fly, yet his name, his flies and his thoughts are lost in the endless void of unrecorded history. Nonetheless, this man, whomever he was, began the tradition, no doubt combining and building upon still earlier concepts in fly design.

Without question the earliest development of salmon flies Speyside occurred in relative isolation and in that respect might find a parallel of sorts in the initial development of steelhead flies in northern California, southern Oregon and northwest Washington. Without benefit of easy travel between these three regions, early steelhead-fly evolution proceeded for several decades on more of a river-by-river basis than on a region-wide front. Not until the 1930s did patterns and tying ideas begin to converge throughout the Northwest. Until then, an Eel River steelhead fly might seem quite foreign to a tier from Seattle. As isolation yielded to improved transportation and communication up and down the steelhead coast, patterns became more standardized and by the 1950s most serious steelheaders would recognize a Thor, Golden Demon or Purple Peril.

Spey flies evolved in an even more profound state of relative isolation, in part explaining not only their unique, peculiar and particular nature but also their continued ascription to the river on which they were born. For the first half of the 19th century, travel in northern Scotland remained a rather circuitous adventure. Sir Herbert Maxwell wrote in 1914 that ". . .eighty years ago there was neither railway nor anything that a pampered

LADY CAROLINE ELIZABETH GORDON LENNOX
(FROM MURIEL BECKWITH'S *WHEN I REMEMBER*)

modern tourist would recognize as a road. In the early 'thirties access to the heart of Sutherland from London required about as much expenditure of time and money as would now suffice to carry one to Bagdad."(22).

Strathspey certainly shared in the relative isolation of the rest of northern Scotland, for the railways there were barely complete by the early 1860s, by which time Highland Railway, Great North of Scotland Railway and several smaller rail companies had succeeded in finally bringing rail infrastructure to the region. In 1852, Morayshire Railway opened northern Scotland's first line between Lossiemouth and Elgin; In 1856 Great North connected Aberdeen and Keith and by 1858 Morayshire had laid tracks to Rothes and then Dandaleith.(23)

With the railways came dramatically increased mobility for travelers, including of course, salmon anglers. "Today," writes Dick Jackson, "it is almost impossible to realize the impact made by the arrival of the railway on a rural area such as Speyside."(24)

GORDON CASTLE GHILLIE A. SHIACH POSES WITH A WOODEN
REPRODUCTION OF A "SMOKING ROOM FISH."

Adventurous angling souls had years earlier introduced gaudy salmon flies to the Spey and most other Scottish rivers, but the railways brought increasing numbers of anglers from near and far. They carried with them all manner of exotic flies and the feathers used to dress them. In earnest now arrived the insurgence of the gaudy complex salmon flies and while I think it inaccurate to say that the new arrivals doomed the old Spey flies to anonymity, the explosive fervor over the former no doubt occupied the hands, hearts and minds of a generation of fly dressers.

Through it all, a few of the old flies clung precariously to their former popularity Speyside, but how could they compete for the attentions of anglers in the face of the fanciful designs of Blacker and Kelson and others? Ireland had invaded and then permeated the British world of salmon flies, and the obsession with exotic flies, with their attendant regalia of exotic feathers, left in their wake the drab and simple—and deadly efficient—original designs from the Spey Valley and from other rivers.

The old Spey flies were hardly forgotten; they were simply overshadowed. Authors continued to give them their due and even offer instructions in the dressing of the flies. However, if not for the 16 old flies recorded by Knox, I fear we would have but precious little detail on a mere handful of old Scottish dressings.

*Blacker's Art of Fly Making,* published in 1842 and revised by him in 1855, essentially spear-headed the forthcoming Victorian obsession with the so-called gaudy salmon fly. Blacker, an Irishman by birth but operating a tackle store in London, became the leading proponent of the colorful, intricate salmon fly. Sadly, he died in his 40s. Among the patterns recorded in his book was "#3," of which he says, "This is another of the Spirit Flies that kill so well in the rivers of Scotland, particularly the Spey and the Tweed."

*"The wings are made of the following mixtures of feathers, each side of the wings to be alike: Brown mallard, bustard, and wood-duck; a topping, scarlet macaw, teal, golden pheasant neck feather, a strip of yellow macaw, and feelers of blue and yellow tail; a head of black ostrich; the tail to be a topping, mixed with green and red parrot tail; the body is composed of joints, first a tip of silver, a tag of morone floss, a tag of black, a joint of brown, green and brown-red hackle, puce and red, green and yellow, blue and orange, with a tip of gold tinsel at every joint, a very small red hackle, and two red toucan feathers round the shoulder, and blue kingfisher's feather on either side of the wings. The hook No. 6, and No. 10 for grilse."*

As previously noted, the exotics—or gaudys—had already begun to invade the River Spey before the halfway mark of the 19th century. Kelson notes that feathers from the jungle cock were introduced in the Spey Valley in the 1850s (they had appeared long before on the Irish flies). So while the exotic flies might well have met with a resistant local audience Speyside, they were nonetheless in use there by mid-century. Tellingly, Knox (1872) reports that, "It is true that, of late years, some of these showy strangers have been introduced here. . ."

THE CRANE, A TAY FLY, AS DRESSED BY PAUL ROSSMAN.

Kelson's book, meanwhile, which he compiled primarily from two decades worth of his writings in the periodicals, includes well over 200 dressings. Amongst them, he records a few of what he terms the old standards on the Spey. Featured are the Carron, Gold Riach, Green King, Purple King, Black King, Red King and Lady Caroline. (the latter two being unrecorded by Knox). Kelson says, "There are several of these curious old standards on the Spey. Amongst others, the 'Secretary' and the 'Green Riach' find some supporters; but they resemble other flies so closely that I have thought it unnecessary to add them to the present list."

Surely I reside in the company of other Spey-fly aficionados in lamenting Kelson's exclusion of the "Secretary," while the Green Riach likely was co-specific with the Gold-green Reeach *and* Silver-green Reeach listed by Knox.

A few years later, Grimble says that there "are literally hundreds of variations in these flies; the best known, however, are the Purple (the 'purpy' as they call it), Green and Black Kings, Gold and Silver Heron, Black Dog, Gold and Silver Riach, Gold Green, Silver Green, Lord March, the Dallas, Lady Caroline, Lady Florence and Miss Elinor—the three last names indicating clearly enough that lady anglers are numerous on the river, more so, I think, than any other. . ."

Again, we find included on the list several flies whose specific patterns are apparently lost to antiquity. At the risk of dwelling on the subject, how wonderful indeed it would be to have a companion fly to the popular Lady Caroline—to have at hand the recipe for the Lady Florence or the Lord March. The Black Dog listed by Grimble may well be a progenitor of the Spey Dog and not the more complex pattern deriving from the Tay.

In any case, Kelson likely regarded the Spey flies as inferior to the full-dress flies he championed and for that matter I suspect he held in low esteem many patterns whose history excluded his skilled hands and verdant mind. He wrote, "In choosing a long-hackled fly, select, from the sort you want, one with the feather having the most life in it. This holds true on all rivers, exclusive of the Spey, and I fancy the cheesy, inanimate 'Spey-cock,' though worshipped locally, will soon be superseded by others which are more mobile and never 'drone' or 'droop.' There is. . .more life, in fact, in any hackle—those of the 'Eagle' class excepted—than in the fluffy butt of a 'Spey-hackle."

With his inimitable sense of self-importance, Kelson lends his hand in the furthering of the Spey fly. He includes, for example, his "Green Queen," saying that he prefers this pattern to the "Green King" and in his brief discussion of John Cruickshanks' "Rough Grouse," he suggests that Crown Pigeon hackle renders the fly more effective than the usual gray heron hackle. "The pattern," says Kelson, "can be varied for other rivers when it may have either 'mixed' or 'built,' wings and an ordinary Cock's hackle where Heron's do not serve faithfully."

Despite Kelson's apparent disdain for the less-splendid flies, he nonetheless provides not only a record of several old Dee and Spey patterns, but also provides instructions for tying them. Still, his general theme of the superiority of fancy flies and of his methods for dressing and fishing them permeates his work, underscoring his role in the advancement of the gaudy Victorian flies that overwhelmed the older, simpler flies, most of whom would never again fill the salmon-fisher's fly box. Indeed, not only does he insist matter-of-factly that the built- and mixed-wing flies are "vastly superior" to strip-wing styles, but even suggests that Blacker's work "is only valuable as a literary curiosity."

No doubt Kelson's deft handling of fur and feather was second to none and his inarguable contribution to dressing salmon flies extended to his inclusions regarding Spey and Dee styles, despite his assumption that the superior gaudy flies would no doubt prove the eventual undoing of the simpler styles. Amongst his own Spey dressings is the aforementioned Green Queen.

THE BLACK DOG, ANOTHER TAY PATTERN,
AS DRESSED BY DAVID BARLOW.

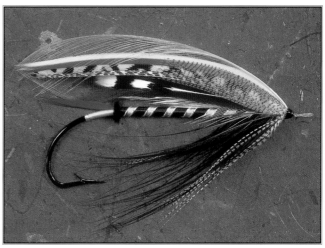

MAJOR JAMES GRANT (RIGHT) AND HIS MOST FAMOUS FLY, THE GLEN GRANT AS DRESSED BY RICHARD YOUNGERS.
(PHOTO COURTESY MRS. A. H. MITCALFE AND CHIVAS REGAL).

Kelson's own contributions at least retained a few of the basic components of the classic Spey fly. Likewise, the flies devised by Major Grant, while retaining some basic elements of the old Spey flies, nonetheless featured materials and styles derived from the newer gaudy flies. The new flies often featured more exotic plumage and brighter colors; the old-timers were dressed in somber shades with mallard wings and flowing hackles from the Spey cock and heron.

Naturally, the fly dressers from Speyside and from Aberdeenshire Dee held no monopoly on flies tied with the long, flowing hackles wound through the body, characteristic though they were. Francis Francis lists an Irish pattern dubbed "The Crane" and featuring a body hackle of gray heron. Likewise, the Black Dog, as it was dressed by Kelson and by Francis Francis, features a heron hackle through the body (Kelson) or at the throat (Francis). Kelson attributes the Black Dog to his father, but another, simpler fly of the same name predates Kelson's version, although the two may share only a name and no common lineage. The earlier Black Dog is mentioned by Mackintosh in his *Driffield Angler* (1808). Kelson's Black Dog has been described as a Spey fly, but its roots are from the Tay.

Stoddart, meanwhile, notes that the "flies used on the Findhorn for salmon-fishing differ considerably from those employed on the Spey, and are more assimilated to the Tweed hooks. Long-fibred hackles, however, are generally in esteem, and heron feathers, both for wings and legs, in great requisition."(25)

Certainly the Spey held no monopoly on the use of heron hackles; they were rather widely employed in Scotland and elsewhere. The hackles deriving from the Spey Rooster, however, were indeed unique to the river and its flies. These we will discuss in the next chapter.

In any event, by the time Kelson's book arrived in 1895, the old Spey flies clung precariously to their former popularity. They shared time astream with many of the gaudy flies of Irish tradition, the latter having swept over the British salmon-angling community. Naturally, the Speyside fly dressers lent a hand in designing increasingly fanciful flies—patterns that incorporated new exotic feathers and new designs while still maintaining elements found in their predecessors.

Fine examples of the "modern" Spey flies included Turnbull's "Pitcroy Fancy" as recorded by Kelson (sometimes spelled Pitchroy) along with those patterns dressed by the aforementioned Major James Grant, such as the "Glen Grant." This latter fly features the typical Spey-fly body and hackle, but the wing makes conspicuous use of showy jungle-cock eyes (see Chapter 8). (Kelson lists this fly as an "old standard" on the Spey, but in this case "old" becomes rather relative considering that the fly's inventor was born in 1849 and that Kelson himself says jungle cock was not introduced to Speyside until the mid-50s.)

Kelson lists additional dressings by Major Grant, including the "Mrs. Grant" and the "Glen Grant Fancy." Both flies feature complex wings and prominent use of exotic feathers. Major Grant's "Glen Grant" may indeed pre-date these latter two flies, but likely not by too many years. Kelson also lists a fly called "Miss Grant," attributing this pattern to "John Shanks."

My research on this matter has led to a dead end concerning John Shanks, but I suspect this to be an editing mistake on Kelson's part or his editor's part (given the rapidity with which Kelson prepared his book, such mistakes might be expected). He may have meant John Cruickshanks, the well-known Speyside salmon angler of the time or may have transcribed the name of the aforementioned George Shanks (26). This latter possibility seems most likely to me: Shanks was well acquainted with the Grant family. Iain Russell writes me that Grant had a considerable beat near his home on the Spey at Rothes. "We believe," notes Russell, "that this beat was obtained from the Duke of Richmond and Gordon, every September." Shanks, of course, was the head fisherman at Gordon Castle. Moreover, The Major appeared on the abbreviated list of attendees at George Shanks funeral in 1915.(27)

By the time Major Grant died early in the 20th century, countless of the old Spey flies had disappeared Speyside. A few remained and anglers still fished them, but for the most part the Spey style survived chiefly in the literature of the period, including the 1914 classic by T.E. Pryce-Tannatt titled *How to Dress Salmon Flies*. Pryce-Tannatt relates, "The Spey fly is a somewhat unique production. It is not every salmon fisherman who has used a Spey fly, or who even knows what it looks like. . ."

"Although," continues Pryce-Tannatt, "beyond the limits of Spey-side, one never hears much mention of Spey flies, nevertheless, Messrs. Farlow tell me that they sell a great number every season for use elsewhere than on the Spey, so it would seem that they enjoy a certain measure of general popularity."

Obviously Pryce-Tannatt possessed no first-hand empirical knowledge as to the relative popularity of the Spey flies and that fact alone offers some evidence of their fading light. Certainly they had their adherents, but by the early 1900s British salmon anglers enjoyed countless choices in fly pattern and style. Luckily, Pryce-Tannatt masterfully recorded the details of the classic Spey fly, noting that "They are out of the ordinary in every respect." (See Chapter 8).

Pryce-Tannatt obtained sample Spey patterns from William Brown's company in Aberdeen. These samples, he says, were "actually tied by Spey-side ghillies. . ." The color plates in the re-print of *How to Dress Salmon Flies* feature four classic Spey flies in the Carron, Grey Heron, Green King and Purple King. The text offers further dressings for the Black King, Gold Riach and Lady Caroline.

The Spey flies received further treatment in Eric Taverner's 1931 book titled *Salmon Fishing*. Taverner summarized rather concisely the evolving nature of salmon flies in the British Isles, writing, "From 1840 onwards, a rivalry was set up on many English and Scottish rivers between the old patterns and the new gaudy invaders from Ireland, the usual result of which was the defeat of the native flies, or at least their partial supersession."

Even after the heyday of Kelson-inspired late-century explosion of full-dress gaudy flies, the old local patterns remained doomed to obscurity. Certainly they had their adherents, as they had throughout the invasion of the Irish flies. But by the early 20th century, simpler—though still colorful—feather-wing varieties along with increasingly popular hair-wing flies proved the choice of most anglers.

## THE REBIRTH: SPEY FLIES IN NORTH AMERICA

In British Columbia, Roderick Haig-Brown found success catching steelhead with the Lady Caroline. He may well have been the first North America angler to fish the classic Spey fly; very likely he was the first to cast these flies for steelhead. Later, in his 1950 classic simply titled, *Flies*, American author J. Edson Leonard offered a brief description of the Spey fly along with dressing for three classics. Leonard offers no indication of his source, other than saying, "The fly patterns listed throughout the following pages are the product of years of compilation and correspondence."

Leonard relates that the Spey style ". . .is recognizable principally for its thin, smooth body and long, sparse hackle. Some fly dressers claim that Spey flies are traditionally without tail fibers. This seems to be borne out by the majority of dressings."

As we might expect, given the variation in recipe of any given classic Spey fly, Leonard's dressings differ from those offered by sources prior to his book, especially in the case of the Black Heron. Interestingly, however, the three patterns given by Leonard represent three of the four most popular classic Spey flies in use on the Pacific Coast of North America. The Carron Fly being the fourth. Whether Leonard's recording of these three flies helped cement their subsequent modest popularity on the Steelhead Coast I cannot ascertain; I suspect, however, that sheer coincidence may be a more likely culprit simply because Leonard's book appeared long before Spey flies came into widespread use in North America.

Leonard's dressing for the Black Heron varies from the original (e.g. Knox) rather dramatically, but the label "Black Heron" has been assigned to a fair number of divergent American Spey-style flies. Besides, considering the reasonable degree of accuracy in his dressings for the Lady Caroline and the Purple King, we must allow for the possibility that Leonard simply mis-wrote the dressing. A more typical dressing would include yellow wool for the butt and black wool for the balance of the body, a dressing that was often called "Gray Heron."

J. Edson Leonard's dressings from *Flies*:

## BLACK HERON

| | |
|---|---|
| *Tail:* | Gold pheasant crest |
| *Body:* | Yellow wool |
| *Rib:* | Gold |
| *Hackle:* | Large black |
| *Wing:* | Brown mallard |

## LADY CAROLINE

| | |
|---|---|
| *Tail:* | Gold-pheasant red body feather fibers |
| *Body:* | Olive-brown dubbing |
| *Rib:* | Oval gold |
| *Hackle:* | Large light gray dun, teal face |
| *Wing:* | Brown mallard |

## PURPLE KING

| | |
|---|---|
| *Body:* | Blue and red mixed wool |
| *Rib:* | Gold and silver alternating |
| *Hackle:* | Spey cock Palmer crossing over body ribs |
| *Wing:* | 2 strips mallard tied split |

About the same time that Leonard's book appeared, Syd Glasso was experimenting with the Spey style for his steelhead angling in Washington. Consequently, Spey flies old and new now enjoy widespread popularity and Syd Glasso deserves most of the credit for sparking interest in this style of fly. A schoolteacher, angler and extraordinary fly dresser from Washington's Olympic Peninsula, Glasso adopted the Spey-style fly for steelhead angling starting in the 1950s. He tied his flies in the bright colors popular with steelhead enthusiasts; his contemporaries—Dick Wentworth, Walt Johnson, Pat Crane and others—were quick to follow suit and a new class of steelhead flies was born of the Spey traditions.

In 1970, Joseph D. Bates, Jr. and Stackpole Books collaborated on the release of *Atlantic Salmon Flies and Fishing*, which would soon become a must-have reference for dressers of all manner of salmon flies. On the subject of Spey flies, Bates largely deferred to Geoffrey Bucknall, the English expert. Bucknall had written, the previous year, an article on the subject for England's *Trout & Salmon* Magazine. Bucknall notes that "the Lady Caroline is, perhaps, the most popular of the family."

At the time Bates' book was released, Spey flies remained something of an enigma in North America. Nonetheless, the seeds had been planted by Syd Glasso and his contemporaries on the rivers of northwestern Washington, where annually, around mid-century, there assembled on the North Fork of the Stillaguamish River a collection of steelhead enthusiasts that reads like a who's-who of the history of the sport. With so many dedicated angling minds assembling in one place, it should come

as no surprise that amongst its devotees, many innovations occurred on the banks of the Stilly in the art of designing and dressing flies for steelhead.

Meanwhile, the Inland Empire Fly Fishing Club, based in Spokane, Washington, published in 1965 a small paperback volume titled, *Flies of the Northwest*. For the first time, the remarkable works of Glasso and his protégé Wentworth were found in print form. Unfortunately, the original 1965 version was the only edition of this book that included the Glasso and Wentworth contributions. In fact, the 1974 edition contains no Spey or Spey-style flies.

Likewise, none of the other mid-century steelhead books offered any mention of Spey or Spey-style flies and that list includes such noteworthy titles as Clark C. Van Fleet's *Steelhead to the Fly,* Claude Kreider's *Steelhead,* Enos Bradner's *Northwest Angling*, and the well-traveled Canadian John Fennelly's *Steelhead Paradise.*

Nonetheless, Spey flies had quietly gained a following in northern Washington. British Columbia's Bob Taylor and Washington's Craig Shreeve and Pat Crane, influenced by their respective associations with Glasso, joined in the small but growing fraternity of Spey-fly enthusiasts.

Then, in 1971, Frank Amato Publications and Washington writer Trey Combs collaborated on a little softbound volume titled *Steelhead Trout*. An insightful book, *Steelhead Trout* included a black-and-white photo of Glasso's Spey-style steelhead flies.

Still, not until Combs released his second book, titled *Steelhead Fly Fishing & Flies,* did a wider fly angling audience admire for the first time the remarkable designs of Syd Glasso, Dick Wentworth and Walt Johnson. Spey-style designs from all three anglers appeared in full-color. I've written before that the fly dressing community owes a debt of gratitude to Trey Combs for his laborious effort at researching and recording a history of the flies and anglers that shaped the art of steelhead fly angling and fly tying.

Not long before the release of Combs' book, the incorrigible and spectacularly talented Dave McNeese developed an interest in the Spey style of fly. He too had seen Glasso's flies in Combs' earlier work and had enjoyed correspondence with Glasso for several years. McNeese's Fly Shop opened in downtown Salem, Oregon in 1977, it was to become the epicenter of the West Coast obsession with Spey-style steelhead flies by the mid-1980s. During those years, McNeese employed both myself and Deke Meyer, along with Brad Burden and Forrest Maxwell. During those fly-shop days, McNeese, Meyer and myself all published several articles on the subject of Spey and Spey-style flies. The first of these appeared in a 1979 issue of *Fly Tyer Quarterly* and featured two flies beautifully dressed by McNeese.

In fact, each of McNeese's several articles appeared in *Fly Tyer*, owned and published in those days by its founder, Dick Surette. While McNeese's articles focused on unique hackling methods, Walt Johnson contributed, in the August 1980 edition, an article about his Deep Purple Spey, writing that this fly "has rewarded me with more steelhead over the years than any fly I have ever used."

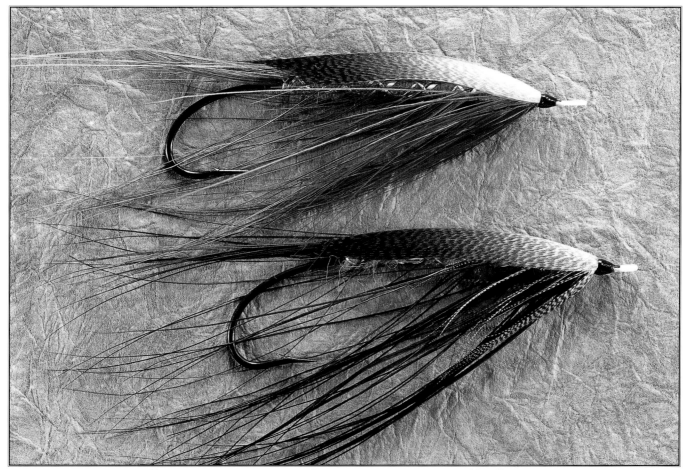

TWO OF THE CLASSIC AND POPULAR SPEY FLIES FROM THE MID TO LATE 19TH CENTURY:
LADY CAROLINE (TOP) AND CARRON FLY. DRESSED BY JOHN SHEWEY.

In 1983, southern Oregon's Al Perryman broke new ground for *Flyfisherman* Magazine with his article titled "Speys For Steelhead." Obviously, the West Coast floodgates had fully opened with regards to Spey-style flies for steelhead, all of it inspired by the innovative genius of Syd Glasso.

Despite the explosive popularity of the "steelhead Spey fly," the old Scottish classics remained little known even as Glasso's influence spread up and down the steelhead coast. The Scottish roots were recognized, but not the Scottish flies. In 1980, Larry Borders wrote a concise piece for *Fly Tyer Quarterly* titled, "Salmon Flies from the Past." He described two old Spey flies, the Spey Dog and Green King.

Borders reminded us, "Spey flies originated long ago on the big Spey River in Scotland. Most fly tiers know of at least two dressings, the Purple King and the Lady Caroline, which are, perhaps, the most famous. But there are, literally, hundreds of variations, and many were recorded in the works of popular angling writers of the last century."

Indeed, in 1980, knowledgeable American fly dressers would likely recognize on sight a Lady Caroline and perhaps a Purple King. But many flies quite well known just two decades later—the beautiful Carron and the striking Glen Grant, for example—remained in obscurity even during the first half of the 1980s.

With the 1978 release of Poul Jorgenson's *Salmon Flies*, a new generation of fly dressers enjoyed step-by-step instructions

for tying a classic Spey fly. Several years would pass, however, before Jorgenson's book reached a wide audience as a renewed interest in classic salmon flies gained steam during the 1980s. In part because of this rising popularity in tying full-dress salmon flies and in part owing to the West Coast momentum started by Glasso, old Spey flies would soon enjoy newfound popularity. For that resurgence, McNeese's Fly Shop also deserves some measure of credit.

Thanks to McNeese's predilection to providing customers with rare materials for salmon flies and with our shop-wide dedication to selling only well-tied steelhead flies dressed by our own hands, salmon and steelhead tiers from around the country soon came to recognize McNeese's Fly Shop as a premier source not only for feathers and flies but also for ideas and innovations regarding both. With two outdoor writers in his employ, McNeese could hardly have asked for a better public relations ploy.

Erstwhile, the aforementioned Brad Burden went on to approach perfection in the dressing of his sleek Spey-styles, his flies appearing in significant books, such as Randy Stetzer's *Flies: The Best One Thousand*. Maxwell, my fishing partner and also a talented fly dresser, cemented his legacy as the single most prolific steelhead killer in the history of our local river. In the late 70s, Keith Mootry's Purple Spey became an early favorite in the region. McNeese featured the fly in his 1979 article for *Fly Tyer Quarterly*. By the mid-1980s, the spectacularly talented

William Chin Jr. frequented the shop, often wowing us with his adeptness at bronze mallard wings (and any other technique involved in the art).

At different times during the mid to late 1980s, McNeese invited out-of-state tiers to teach classes in the art of dressing salmon flies. Among them were two of the fine Spey and Dee tiers from the East Coast, Bob Veverka and Mark Waslick. Naturally, even prior to the McNeese's Fly Shop days, there were other West Coast fly dressers delving into the art of the Spey and Dee flies. Virtually all of them would have to credit Syd Glasso with some level of inspiration. McNeese's simply provided a wellspring of ideas, materials and talented tiers that served and influenced not only the region, but to some extent the entire nation.

Thus during the 1980s, interest in tying and fishing Spey and Spey-style flies became a region-wide and then nationwide passion, if you will. Pacific Northwest fly dressers carried the style to new heights of design creativity. Among them—just to name a few—were John Farrar, Bob Aid, John Olschewsky, Glenn Wilson, Joe Rosutto, Dec Hogan, Mike Kinney, Scott O'Donnell, Joe Howell, David Burns and the incomparable Steve Gobin. The obsession continues, the most recent development being a renewed interest in the oldest classic Spey flies and Dee flies.

One can hardly overstate the West Coast contribution to the rebirth of interest in Spey- and Dee-style flies. During the 1980s, it was the steelhead angling community that drove this obsession to new heights and pushed it onto the national scene. Published in 1992 by Dick Stewart and Farrow Allen, the pattern guide *Flies for Steelhead* included no less than 33 Spey- and Dee-style flies, along with another nine marabou flies. Meanwhile, *Flies for Atlantic Salmon*, published a year earlier, offers only seven such patterns.

Great Lakes steelheaders emulated the westerners. By the mid-1980s a handful of dedicated fly dressers dared suggest that classic techniques and beautifully dressed flies could take steelhead from the Great Lakes tributaries. At first, these men followed a lonely path and even as late as 1992, Stewart and Allen wrote, "although Spey flies are popular among west coast steelheaders, it is rare to find them in use on the rivers of the Great Lakes."

Nonetheless, the seeds had been planted in the Midwest, and well-schooled fly dressers like Fred Vargas and Bob Blumreich embraced the Spey-style dressings designed in the Pacific Northwest. Soon they found their own designs quite effective on their local waters.

Indeed, by the last decade of the 20th century, the steelhead waters of the Pacific Northwest had produced legions of anglers and fly tiers dedicated to the art of dressing Spey-style flies. With Syd Glasso's legacy still fresh and vibrant, West coast steelhead tiers plunged headlong into the world of Spey flies and Dee flies. The rest of the country followed suit as the unique style of these flies found widespread appeal among fly dressers already versed in the dressing of salmon and steelhead patterns.

# A BRIEF HISTORY OF THE DEE FLIES

The archetypal Dee flies offer a similar history. They originated on a particular river and exhibited a unique style. No one knows who dressed the first fly featuring a "Dee-style" wing combined with the characteristic long hook, slim body and long heron hackles. The originator invented a style all his own and his style eventually became specific to the Aberdeenshire Dee, primarily for the spring fishing. Patterns were codified in the old literature, but the originators of the oldest Dee flies are unknown to us.

The Dee absorbed a more rapid and explosive insurgence of visiting anglers than did the Spey, largely owing to the bustling port city of Aberdeen, whose population alone exceeded that of Strathspey in its entirety. Thus the Deeside anglers no doubt enjoyed widespread opportunity to share ideas and tying styles with fly dressers from all quarters. In part, this may explain some of the characteristics of the Dee flies.

These Dee flies likely post-date the "old" Spey flies. The best evidence to this effect lies in their prominent use of bright colors. However, the evolution of the Dee fly seems more closely linked to other styles prevalent in Scotland during the 19th century. Whereas the lineage of the Spey flies appears a local evolution, the Dee flies may have been modifications deriving from the old Tweed flies and similar strip-winged patterns.

Certainly the old Tweed flies shared the strip wings, paired, and dressed more-or-less V-shaped atop the fly. The best evidence to the winging method of the Tweed flies comes from Stoddart's *Angler's Companion*, which includes a beautifully painted fly plate showing six Tweed salmon flies. These plates clearly show flies whose wings are dressed in a horizontal set and which derive from turkey tail, silver pheasant tail, mallard, teal and guinea.

At the very least, these old Tweed flies—now essentially lost to antiquity,—provide that the wing itself hardly defines the Dee fly. Likewise, the Dee fly held no monopoly on the long, flowing heron hackles. Of course they were used on some Spey flies and certainly found themselves dressed upon flies from other rivers. John Kirkbride, for example, noted the use of long, black heron hackles on Tay flies, a fact born out in the Black Dog.(28)

Rather, the Dee fly was identified by its combination of characteristics: the long, unusually slim body dressed on large, long-shank Limerick hooks, the long-fibered heron hackle, the strip-wings, and often the artfully designed tips, tags and tails reminiscent of the gaudy flies.

There would seem no sure way of determining whether the Tweed flies or flies from some other Scottish river contributed their characteristics to the Dee style. The similarities might well prove coincidental. Certainly by the time Francis Francis' book arrived in 1867, the Dee-style fly was established both in form and in pattern. He says of them, "The flies used are peculiar, and the local ones are of little use on any other river in

Scotland, save perhaps, a small size of the Gled Wing, or the Tartan, which may be used for the Don. The flies are usually large, but slenderly dressed, being meant to catch the salmon's eye, I presume, in the deep rough water, which a small fly would not, and not to frighten him, which too gross (grosse) and imposition perhaps might do. . .The Dee flies are dressed upon hooks specially made for them: these are very long in shank, with the Limerick bend."

Kelson credits William Garden of Aberdeen with several of the Dee flies included in *The Salmon Fly*. Indeed, one such fly bears the originator's name (Gardener). Likely, the Gardener was devised some time in the late 1870s, subsequently earning a reputation as one of the more popular patterns on Deeside. In his 1884 article for *The Fishing Gazette*, William Murdoch reports that, "Last autumn a friend of the writer's landed within two days twelve fish averaging 18 lb. They all rose to the same fly—a gardener, dressed by Milne, Aberdeen."

Unfortunately, Murdoch didn't specify the Milne in question, for a Peter Milne apparently enjoyed apprenticeship under Garden and may well have been in the latter's employ for many years. More likely, however, the fly in question came from William Milne, who operated a tackle shop in Aberdeen, located on Silver Street. Details on both Milnes are few, but if the Gardener used by Murdoch's friend derived from William Milne, then obviously the fly enjoyed so much popularity that competing tackle shops were compelled to offer Garden's pattern.

Among the other patterns that Kelson attributes to Garden (it remains unclear whether Garden invented these flies or simply dressed them for Kelson's writings) are flies that have survived the ravages of obscurity visited upon other members of their tribe. Garden's Balmoral and Glentana, for example, enjoy a reasonable degree of popularity with fly dressers and, in some quarters, with anglers. Harry Lemire, the legendary Washington steelheader who years ago brought us the Grease Liner, ranks among the contemporary champions of the classic Dee flies.

Scotland's Philip Glendinning, whose work appears herein, says that details about Garden are few. "Mr. Garden was from Aberdeen," says Glendinning, and "served his apprenticeship in Aberdeen with a gun & fishing tackle merchant. He then moved to Inverness for about 10 years, then returned to Aberdeen. Apparently Garden opened a fishing tackle shop on Belmont Street but soon moved his shop to 122-1/2 Union Street. He was born in 1846 and died March 29, 1906 at 60 years. He was married with two sons and two daughters. At time of death his home address was 38 Gray Street, Aberdeen."

Garden seems never to have set pen to paper. Glendinning reports that Murdoch, also of Aberdeen, seems to have sent Garden's patterns to Kelson for inclusion in *The Fishing Gazette*. In *The Salmon Fly*, Kelson credits to "W. Murdoch" a well-known pattern called The Dunt, of which Kelson quotes Murdoch as writing, "There is not a better all-around fly of the plain sort than the Dunt put upon the Dee in Spring or Autumn." Again, we

cannot be certain whether Kelson's attribution indicates that Murdoch invented the fly or just submitted it to Kelson.

Murdoch, born in 1851 near Aberdeen, worked as a bank teller in the city for many years and, in addition to his contributions to *The Fishing Gazette*, penned a book titled *Moonlight On The Salmon*. Upon retirement, Murdoch moved to Banchory. He died in 1925. His 1884 articles in *The Fishing Gazette* provide a rare record of dressings for several Dee flies—dressings which tend to differ from those recorded in the salmon-fly tying books (see Chapter 9).

Garden's was just one of many tackle sellers in Aberdeen. Indeed the famed William Brown Company enjoyed continual operation for many decades, beginning on George Street in 1835 and then later on Belmont Street until they closed just a few years ago. Aberdeen, in fact, boasted some 28 tackle shops during 1900. Competition must have been fierce. Likewise, all manner of flies and feathers likely found themselves circulated throughout the region.

Naturally, the winds of change had blown across the waters of the Aberdeenshire Dee and by Kelson's time, the river's salmon were subjected to a generous variety of fanciful flies. Garden himself seems to have embraced both old and new, as the tackle dealer from Aberdeen devised in his Lady Grace what might be viewed as a "mixed-media" dressing, encompassing elements from the older strip-wing Dee styles and from the newer gaudy styles. Kelson notes that Garden's Lady Grace (beautifully reproduced here by David Barlow) was a "famous low water fly on the Dee."

## LADY GRACE
(W. Garden, as per Kelson) (Dressed by David Barlow)

| | |
|---|---|
| *Tag:* | Silver twist |
| *Tail:* | Red breast feather of golden pheasant (point) |
| *Body:* | Light orange, red-orange, claret and blue Seal's furs |
| *Ribs:* | Silver tinsel |
| *Hackle:* | Gallina dyed yellow, from claret fur |
| *Throat:* | Light orange hackle |
| *Wings:* | Two strips of swan dyed yellow |

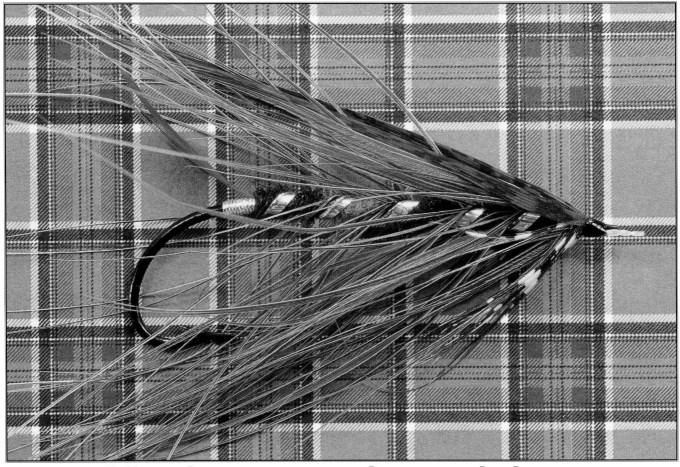

THE MINISTER OF DRUMOAK, A LONG-FORGOTTEN CLASSIC DEE FLY AS DRESSED BY PHILIP GLENDINNING.

More rapidly than on the Spey it seems, the invading full-dress salmon flies were adapted and relegated to general use on Deeside. However, the old Dee flies, such as the Tartan and Gledwing, likely date no earlier than mid-century; their deveopment and popularity occurred almost side-by-side with the

A 19TH CENTURY AKROYD
FROM THE COLLECTION OF DAVID MCNEESE.

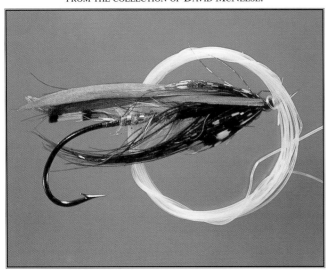

fanciful newcomers. As previously noted, the major port city of Aberdeen no doubt assured a more ready and accessible market for new ideas and for visiting anglers than could be possible on the more remote waters of Strathspey.

The typical old Dee fly differs from the old Spey flies not only in the wing, but also in the complexity of the fly in general. Dee flies tend to include more of the elements found on Victorian-era salmon flies. Thus many of the more complex Dee flies, such as those so beautifully crafted by Garden, certainly arrived on the scene somewhat contemporary to the increasingly gaudy Irish flies rather than preceding them as do the old Spey flies. At the very earliest, the older Dee spring dressings almost certainly date no earlier than the early period of full-dress flies. These Dee flies include tags, tips, tails of golden pheasant crest, jungle cock cheeks and multi-colored bodies. Their hackling resembles that of some Spey and Tay flies in the use of heron feathers.

Although less popular than Spey-style flies today, Dee flies nonetheless enjoy popularity among both salmon and steelhead tiers. Like the modern Spey-style flies, Dee flies have been re-tooled to arrive at many variations on the old patterns. In fact, many contemporary patterns blur the line between Dee- and Spey-style flies, although some would argue (myself included) that whether modern or antiquated, the Dee fly is defined by a combination of its long-shank hook, sparse and colorful body, long hackle and strip wings.

## End Notes

1. From *British Fresh Water Fish*, 1904.
2. The 1861 book *Halcyon*, by Henry Wade, offers the same two Spey flies listed years earlier by Stoddart; upon even casual inspection of the two books one must conclude that Wade simply copied from the accomplished Stoddart. Thus *Halcyon* offers nothing new save a sense of awe that Wade could borrow so liberally from Stoddart and offer no form of attribution whatsoever.
3. This is the Professor John Wilson of Edinburgh, who wrote under the pen name "Christopher North" and whose "Professor" wet fly remains in use to this day.
4. From *River Angling for Salmon and Trout*, by John Younger, 1840.
5. From *Wild Sport and Natural History of the Highlands*, by Charles St. John and first published in 1849 (see bibliography).
6. From Francis' introductory note to the second edition of *A Book on Angling*.
7. Likely this "Mr. C. Grant" was the same "Charles Grant" mentioned thus by Grimble: "Perhaps the most extensive collection of flies ever owned by one man was formed by the late Mr. H. Grant of Wester Elchies; they were tied by himself, Mr. Charles Grant, and Cruickshanks, and many hundreds were kept in a large box made from timber of the Old Gean Tree of Elchies, the trunk of which had a diameter of four feet." With apologies to the reader, I have been unable to ascertain further details about Charles Grant.
8. From the obituary of George Shanks in the June 25, 1915 edition of *The Elgin Courant And Courier*.
9. Shanks was thus first employed by the 5th Duke of Richmond & Gordon sometime prior to 1860.
10. This is just a short excerpt from a longer poem recorded by Grimble in the first edition of his book, *The Salmon Rivers of Scotland*, published in 1899. The first edition was a massive set of four large volumes. The later editions, compiled into single volumes, did not include some of the materials found in the first, including this poem.
11. From *Trout & Salmon Flies*, by Sutherland and Chance.
12. Frodin, for example calls the Lady Caroline "one of the oldest. . .in the Spey family" and the learned Terry Hellekson says it is "one of the oldest Spey patterns known."
13. Timothy J, McCann, Assistant County Archivist for West Sussex, writes me, "I am afraid that the peerages do not give the dates of birth of the 6th

Duke's two daughters. . .though I believe that Lady Caroline was born in 1844.
14. Grimble, in 1899, writes, "Geordie Shanks at Aberlour ties all the Gordon Castle flies, and there is no better exponent of the art, and several pleasant mornings have I passed with him in getting hints while chatting and looking through Lord March's fly-book—the biggest and the fullest I have ever seen."
15. Admittedly, this latter assumption is highly arguable in that any number of reasons might explain the exclusion of the Lady Caroline et al from Shanks' contribution to Knox's book.
16. From *The Great Salmon Rivers of Scotland*, by John Ashley-Cooper.
17. From: *A Bibliography of British Ornithology from the earliest times to the end of 1912 including biographical accounts of the principal writers and bibliographies of their published works* by W. H. Mullens and H. Kirke Swann, 1917.
18. (ibid)
19. From *The Gordon Setter Page*, a website by Magnus Lilja.
20. (ibid No. 17 above)
21. Rare and hard to find, Knox's other works were *Ornithological Rambles in Sussex* and *Gamebirds and Wildfowl*.
22. From the "Editor's Preface" to the 1927 edition of Charles St. John's *Natural History & Sport in Moray*.
23. Sources: *Speyside Railways*, by Burgess & Kinghorn. *The Speyside Line*, by Dick Jackson.
24. From *The Speyside Line* by Dick Jackson.
25. From Stoddart's *Angler's Guide to the Rivers and Lochs of Scotland*
26. John Cruickshank was certainly well known to Kelson, as the latter relates a story in which he watched "Cruiky" dressing a Green King. Hence, I doubt Kelson would have mistakenly transcribed the name of Cruickshank, for the two were apparently aquainted. Nowhere, however, does Kelson indicate that he knew Shanks nor does he offer any indication that he fished the Gordon Castle waters. However, there may indeed have been a fly dresser named John Shanks living Speyside in the 19th century. My research has not uncovered him, but I would be most interested should another researcher confirm his identity.
27. Ian Russell, of the Heritage Works
28. John Kirkbride, *The Northern Angler*, 1837.

# Chapter 2

# Hackles for Tying Spey & Dee Flies

*"They are uniquely designed for effectiveness in fast
rivers. Indeed, they need a fierce flow to give them full play."*

*—Geoffrey Bucknall*

Paramount to the tying of Spey- and Dee-style flies is the procurement of the appropriate hackles. The original designers of salmon flies from The Spey Valley often used feathers from the rump, tail and neck of the so-called "Spey cock." There exists much confusion as to the exact definition of a "Spey cock." Over the decades, various writers have simply passed along the unresearched "wisdom" that the Spey cock was in fact a particular breed of rooster and that now this bird is essentially extinct.

The question is not whether such a fowl existed Speyside. The record is clear on that account. Giving us the most concise definition of the Spey cock, Augustus Grimble (1898) writes:

"...nearly all are hackled with the Spey cock—a big, long, non-descript feather, with lengthy fibers...from a cross between a Hambro Cock and an old Scottish mottled hen. Of course there is a breed at Arndilly, Wester Elchies, Gordon Castle, and a few other places on the Spey, but these are difficult feathers to get good elsewhere...they are not hardy birds, and thrive better in England than in the north, and do especially well at Goodwood."

Grimble states further that, "Although these birds are good layers, their sharp breasts make them bad for the table." If the birds were unsuited to the table, then why else would they be propagated? Obviously they were kept to produce the desired hackles for dressing the Spey flies.

Goodwood, I might add, is an English estate under ownership of the Duke of Richmond and Gordon, the aforementioned owners of Gordon Castle on Speyside. The Duke of Richmond and Gordon, beginning sometime around the middle of the 19th century, employed the famed George Shanks as head fisherman and fly dresser. So no doubt Shanks had at his disposal a ready and abundant supply of these coveted hackles, for the cocks were bred not only at Gordon Castle but also at Goodwood.

Thus there remains little question that fly dressers Speyside partook in the keeping and breeding of these birds to produce the hackles in question. Francis Francis, in *A Book On Angling* (1867) includes a letter written him by "Mr. C. Grant of Aberlour." Grant relates that these "hackles are got from the common Scotch cock, and lie on each side of the tail, at the tip of the wings. The cock is rarely met with except with Spey fishers, who breed them for the sake of their feathers."

Bear in mind, of course, that most of the classic authors delve only sparingly into the details of the bird kept for its feathers by Speyside tiers. Pryce-Tannatt, for example, says the hackles derive from "...a certain breed of domestic fowl known as the 'Spey cock.'" It is only from Grimble and Francis that we ascertain with some certainty that the Spey cock was anything more than a barnyard rooster whose feathers exhibited the correct attributes. Instead, this fowl found himself rendered to selective breeding. The extent of that breeding cannot be ascertained, but it would seem the roosters were nowhere abundant, but rather kept primarily by a handful of Spey ghillies and fishermen.

No doubt the plight of the Spey cock followed that of the classic Spey salmon fly to whom the bird contributed its hackles. The Irish gaudy flies had appeared Speyside prior to the mid-point of the 19th century and as the ensuing decades passed, the gaudy flies (and then other styles) drowned out the old native patterns. With fewer and fewer classic Spey flies being tied—especially after the turn of the 20th century—the once-prized Spey cock likewise faded from the scene.

By 1931, when Eric Taverner's *Salmon Fishing* was published, the Spey cock had indeed become a scarce commodity. "The latter feathers are difficult to obtain," wrote Taverner, "because the bird from which they come is very little bred..."

Contemporary authors have presumed the Spey cock extinct, but I consider such assertions somewhat in error if only because, given the vast store of domestic chickens running loose around the globe, the genetic material exists to produce birds with the desired feathers practically at the drop of a hat. Indeed, one reclusive tier from Idaho bred his own flock as late

FACING PAGE: SPEY-STYLE STEELHEAD FLIES DRESSED BY DAVID BURNS. THE FLY AT TOP FEATURES BLEACH-BURNED GOOSE SHOULDER FOR THE
HACKLE WHILE THE OTHER FEATURES DYED BLUE EARED PHEASANT.

as the 1990s. Dave Burns, who was acquainted with the keeper of these chickens, sent me a few samples and indeed they exhibited every desirable characteristic. Likewise, in an early issue of *Fly Tyer* Magazine (1981), Larry Borders writes, "While living in Scotland some years ago, I was fortunate enough to meet an old gentleman fly tier and angler, who still breeds his own birds for the hard-to-find feathers."

Thus, this presumed "extinction" may exist de facto only because demand has not reached heights sufficient to prompt anyone in the fly-tying business to "re-engineer" the Spey cock.

Certainly we can presume that the Speyside fowl breeders sought the same feather characteristics that we today also desire: namely slim, flexible stems and specific shades. Knox confirms the variety of feathers available, noting that the sample flies given him by Shanks were dressed with "red cock," "gray cock" and "black cock." Naturally, we need not lament the unavailability of the Spey cock and its feathers, for modern tiers have at their disposal all manner of rooster feathers. Pick through a large quantity of schlappen or coque (rooster tail

HACKLES FROM THE ASIAN PURPLE HERON, NATURAL AND DYED.

plumes) and one cannot help but secure a handful of hackles that would no doubt compare favorably to the original item.

Indeed, Henrik Strandgaard, in his appendix to the 1999 reprint of *Autumns on the Spey*, writes, "What the difference was between this fowl and an ordinary barnyard cock we may never know, but judging from the fair number of antique Spey flies that I have been fortunate to examine over the years there was probably little or none at all. One should recognize the possibility though, that the great importance of these hackles may have led to a local interest in the breeding of birds with particular feather characteristics, such as light stems, fibre lengths and different colors in particular."

As I have shown, such selective breeding certainly occurred. My point is that the feathers available to us today are close enough to get the job done. Dyed schlappen and coque are easily obtainable. More difficult to find are these feathers in the natural light brown ("red"). Of course they can be dyed to approximate this shade, which is required for a number of the classic Spey flies.

The aforementioned Taverner likewise recognized that ". . . occasionally, satisfactory substitutes can be procured from the common barn-door cock. There is a great deal of variation in their shades, from red-brown to iridescent green-black; but, as the fibres are all but opaque, colour matters far less than mobility upon which the effectiveness of the Spey-flies depends."(1)

Meanwhile, other old flies from the Spey and Dee rivers used the feathers of the heron, specifically the gray heron (*Ardea cinerea*) native to the region and not (initially at least) the similar great blue heron (*A. herodius*) indigenous to North America or other members of the tribe. The genus *Ardea* includes several similar herons including the aforementioned species and also the purple heron (*Ardea purpurea*), found in the Far East and central Europe—and in the British Isles, although not in breeding populations. All have similar gray back hackles, differing slightly in tone; the purple heron also features back hackles of an attractive rusty brown.

Without question, various Asiatic species of heron were used to dress salmon flies in Great Britain during the 19th century. In their monumental work titled *Rare and Unusual Fly Tying Materials*, Paul Schmookler and Ingrid V. Sils say of the purple heron that ". . .it has been called an 'accidental visitor' to the British Isles. As a result, its plumage was not regularly specified in salmon fly tying; however, in dressings that simply called for 'Heron,' it was up to the fly tier to select which species he used, and the authors have identified Purple Heron in numerous antique flies."

Kelson himself no doubt furthered the demand for some of his favorite exotics, such as the plumage of the Nankeen night heron (*Nycticorax caledonicus*), a small heron that breeds on southeast Asian islands. Nonetheless, the early development of salmon flies in Scotland largely pre-dated the Victorian-era infusion of exotic feathers from the far-flung corners of Asia and the New World. That fact—not to mention the relatively isolated development of the Scottish flies—suggests that the indigenous gray heron provided the feathers for the Speyside

THE GEORDIE, DRESSED BY JOHN SHEWEY.

tiers, at least until the Victorian millinery plumage trade exerted its influence throughout the Isles.

Once the plumage trade reached full stride, however, Spey tiers very likely began adorning their flies with feathers from non-indigenous birds. Indeed, feathers from the North American egrets and herons may well have found their way to the Spey Valley; certainly the Asiatic feathers adorned Spey flies prior to Kelson's writings. The large herons from Asia no doubt contributed feathers to the trade, amongst them *Ardea insignis* (white-bellied heron) and *A. sumatrana* (great-billed heron), both roughly equal in size to the gray heron, along with the world's largest heron, *A. goliath* (goliath heron).

Fly dressers in the United States suffer a severe disadvantage in the procurement, use and ownership of heron hackles: The great blue heron's status as a federally designated migratory bird assures that citizens cannot legally possess its feathers. On occasion, feathers from the gray and purple herons find their way into the U.S. fly-tying materials trade. In Europe and Canada, heron feathers remain available in the materials trade, though not necessarily easy to obtain.

Dave McNeese, during the 1970s, legally procured a large supply of gray heron hackles from England. Initially he sold and bartered rather conservatively in these hackles through his fly shop in Salem, Oregon, but the supply proved impossible to replace, so McNeese mothballed the spartan remnants of that lone shipment. Over the ensuing years, we used a few of these to tie our own flies. Otherwise we remained rather quiet about them lest someone mistake McNeese's prized stash of European gray heron feathers for illegal plumes from the indigenous great blue heron—both feathers are quite nearly identical in appearance.

A decade later, with the full legal backing of the U.S. Fish & Wildlife Service, Robert Borden of Hareline Dubbin' imported from Asia a large quantity of purple heron feathers. For about a year, Hareline Dubbin' wholesaled these feathers to a select few dealers in the United States. Upon making its next such acquisition of these feathers, however, Hareline received word from U.S. Customs that the importation would not be allowed.

In any event, During the 1980s the blue eared pheasant (*Crossoptilon auritum*) became the standard fare for imitating gray heron hackles. These large birds offer rump and body feathers whose color and texture lend themselves well to the job of hackling Spey- and Dee-style flies. Unfortunately, owing to their particular characteristics, blue eared pheasant hackles are of lesser quality than those they seek to replace. Unlike heron hackles, the pheasant plumes are brittle and their fibers softer; they are shorter and smaller than the large heron hackles often used to dress the largest Spey flies. Perhaps their greatest limitation is that the usable portion of the hackle, even on a large blue eared pheasant feather, allows but three, perhaps four palmered turns.

Nonetheless, these blue eared pheasant hackles comprise the best of the easily obtainable heron substitutes. A fly dresser never acquainted with the delight in tying with heron hackles will no doubt find great satisfaction in crafting Spey flies adorned with blue eared pheasant. Conversely, those of us who have designed, tied and fished flies bejeweled with heron hackle will forever lament its unavailability in many quarters.

Though reasonably common in the fly-dressing materials trade, blue eared pheasant can be difficult to locate and expensive when found. Check with retailers with a reputation for selling materials for salmon and steelhead flies. Typically, hackles from the blue eared pheasant are available in packets of individual feathers and as whole skins, these latter, as of this writing, retailing for as much as $200. So priced, these skins are a worthwhile investment only if they are of the finest grade, heavily feathered with large hackles, especially at the rump, from whence derives the largest and best hackles. Otherwise, hackles packaged by size tend to be the better deal.

The blue eared pheasant is but one of three distinct species and several inclusive races of eared pheasants. The other two species, the brown and the white eared pheasants (*C. mantchuricum* and *C. crossoptilon*, respectively), are afforded protection in the United States by their status as federally designated endangered species. Therefore, their feathers or skins,

THE MISS GRANT AS DRESSED BY RICHARD YOUNGERS.

THE BLUE EARED PHEASANT.

even if derived from captive domestic birds, are illegal to buy, sell or offer for sale, or so I am informed by agents from the U.S. Fish & Wildlife Service. During the early days of my feather business, I knew an aviculturist who raised rare pheasants, among them the brown eared pheasants. Of these, he had six that had been born club-footed and therefore he culled them from the breeding stock. I was set to purchase and then re-sell the skins from these birds, figuring I'd stumbled on a figurative gold mine, but luckily I checked with U.S. Fish & Wildlife first.

Fly dressers in other countries should check with their wildlife enforcement organization for pertinent laws regarding such feathers. Both the brown and the white eared pheasants have white rump patches offering heron-like feathers that are easy to dye. Likewise, heron feathers of various kinds remain legal to buy and sell in some countries.

Additional substitutes for heron hackles include rump feathers from the common ring-necked pheasant. These can be dyed various colors or even bleached and dyed. A pure white morph of the ring-necked pheasant is sometimes seen in collections or on gamebird farms—obviously its feathers prove ideally suited to dying. Don't purchase a pheasant skin straight from the rack; look through all that are available and choose those rooster skins offering the largest rump feathers. Sometimes the rump patches are available independently of the full skin and purchasing them this way makes sense if the remainder of the skin is not of particular interest in your tying needs. Hen ring-necked pheasants offer smaller, but equally attractive rump feathers well suited to small Spey-style patterns and eagle flies.

The gray flank feathers from the common coot ("mud-hen") serve as a nice heron substitute on smaller patterns. Unfortunately, U.S. federal law does not allow for the sale of coot plumage nor of plumage from gallinule and rails when these birds are killed legally during authorized hunting seasons.

You must legally shoot your own during the authorized season, in which case you may retain and tie with the feathers (even if adorning a fly, these feathers cannot be bought or sold). The same holds true for all migratory game birds except legally killed ducks, geese, brant and swans, whose plumage, according to federal law, may be purchased and sold for fly tying.

So-called "burnt goose" offers another alternative for hackling heron-style flies. Popularized by Deke Meyer, these are small "goose shoulder" feathers that are burned slightly in bleach to remove the rachies from the fibers, thus preventing the fibers from marrying together. They are then dyed various shades. These feathers tie a reasonable fly in the hands of a practiced tier, but are otherwise rather cumbersome owing to their thick stems. The stems, however, can be split to arrive at a more manageable feather. Directions for splitting and bleach-burning are included herein.

Still, having sorted through pounds and pounds of goose shoulder I can assure the reader that their exist but a few really superb Spey hackles in any given quantity of these plumes. Those precious few exceptional plumes, however, need no bleach-burning, for they exhibit a fine, flexible stem and clean, fine, long fibers. They come from the flanks of the large white geese. If more abundant, these feathers would prove almost as useful as eared pheasant hackles, but nowhere are they sold in bulk to the fly-tying trade.

Carefully-chosen turkey marabou forms yet another possible substitute for heron—not for the large gray hackles (which come from the heron's back) but instead for the soft, black shoulder feathers, which so beautifully dress a Black Dog or various other patterns. Such marabou plumes must be chosen with an eye for fine stems and fibers with little fuzz, especially near the tips. These are then dyed black to imitate heron shoulder (or any other color for all manner of so-called "marabou Spey flies"). These same marabou plumes are ideally suited to imitating the leg feathers from the golden eagle used in tying the so-called "eagle flies" deriving from the Aberdeenshire Dee.

Having said all of the above in regard to heron and its substitutes I should hasten to add that a majority of the classic Spey dressings use the feathers from the Spey rooster rather than from the heron. As previously noted, these feathers were nearly identical in form to typical "schlappen" and "coque."

Schlappen is the name given to the long, soft hackles found at the base of a rooster's tail, below the actual saddle patch; coque refers to the somewhat stiffer and longer hackles adorning the sides of the tail. Both, when chosen carefully, tie beautiful classic-style Spey flies and colorful steelhead flies that retain the basic form of the old Scottish dressings. The late Syd Glasso was the first West Coast tier to create steelhead flies using colored schlappen as the body hackle. Perhaps the foremost contemporary artist in this regard is Steve Gobin, whose elegant Spey-style steelhead flies retain the character of the classics while utilizing colors common to steelhead dressings.

Coque feathers—the side-tail feathers from the rooster—behave somewhat differently than schlappen, which they resemble

HACKLES FOR SPEY FLIES, LEFT TO RIGHT: DYED SCHLAPPEN AND DYED COQUE, BLEACHED AND DYED BLUE EARED PHEASANT, NATURAL BLUE EARED PHEASANT, RING-NECKED PHEASANT RUMP, MARABOU PLUMES.

in basic form. The stiffer stem on these hackles rarely presents a problem to the experienced fly dresser and coque tends to exhibit longer fibers, at least on the best plumes. In either case, the tier should exercise extreme selectivity in choosing coque and schlappen hackles for Spey flies because the best feathers create the best flies. Look for feathers with fine stems, long fibers and uniform fiber length. Both feathers come in myriad dyed colors along with natural shades, these latter being more difficult to obtain from fly shops (because they are less popular among tiers).

Having long tied flies with schlappen hackles, I received in 1991 a single specimen of rooster side tail, or coque, from Dave Burns. I was immediately convinced that this type of feather would adequately mimic the hackles originally taken from the Spey cock. I had previously seen several original Spey cock hackles, procured and saved years ago by Dave McNeese. Those antique Spey cock hackles differed from the typical coque only in stem width and color, the former exhibiting a deep reddish-brown center and slightly grayish fiber tips. Until the mid-90s coque was primarily an item used by the costuming trade. But recognizing its potential, I purchased a bulk lot of white, strung coque from a wholesale feather broker and was soon offering a dozen dyed colors through my catalog. As a

result, Hareline Dubbin' Inc., owned by ever-creative Robert Borden, decided to wholesale dyed coque to the fly shops, where it can be found on occasion to this day (especially in the Pacific Northwest).

Like certain other hackling plumes, coque and schlappen often benefit from a brief bleach-burning, which removes some of the rachies that cause fibers to cling together. A 4:1 mixture of water to bleach does the job, followed immediately by a rinsing bath. The rinse-water should include vinegar, which will neutralize the bleach reaction more immediately than plain water. Naturally, if you dye your own feathers, do so after the bleach-burning and not before.

Generally, rather than bleach-burning, I prefer to grade through enough schlappen or coque to find perfect hackles. The most difficult of these hackles to find are those of a natural red-brown shade. In the feather trade, however, "half-bronze" schlappen and coque refers to those feathers with a bronzy iridescent shade mixed with some natural brown. Pick through enough of them and you find plenty of pure red-brown hackles ideally suited to the classic Spey flies, such as several of those recorded by Knox. If you can't find these feathers in a fly shop, go in search of feather dusters, which often include half-bronze schlappens.

Many feathers used as hackles are best stripped of the fibers on one side, leaving the better side for use on the fly. The off-side fibers are easily peeled from the stem, but consider also the possibility of "splitting" the hackle to produce from thick stems a thinner, more workable one and/or to produce two hackles from one feather. One technique for splitting hackles is to use a blade to carefully sever the feathers down the middle of the stem. Another method is to "hand split" them, tearing off the fibers on each side along with the outer layers of the stem. Both techniques are addressed herein.

In many instances, Spey flies afford the tier the unique luxury of planning a fly's construction based on the characteristics of a particular hackle plume. The hackle can be wrapped in the normal direction or in the counter direction, which explains why the plume is stripped of its inferior side—the tier simply chooses the hackling method based upon which side of the feather is stripped of its fibers. Less pragmatic is the rather unimaginative option of always choosing hackles whose left or right side is better.

In any case, tiers interested in dressing classic-style Spey and Dee flies must procure schlappen and coque along with heron and/or its substitutes. However, thanks largely to Pacific Coast steelhead tiers, the array of contemporary Spey-style flies now includes patterns dressed with body hackles made from duck flank feathers, marabou and many other feathers. Of the former, large flank feathers from the mallard, gadwall, widgeon, pintail and shoveler allow for long flowing hackles. Gadwall ranks amongst my favorites owing to its size, shape and color, while the beautiful large flanks from the shoveler—though difficult to obtain—make rather striking hackles.

While many classic Spey dressings ask for hackles from the Spey cock, the Dee flies were predominantly tied with heron. Some flies from that river, however, were dressed with the hackle taken from the legs of the golden eagle and are hence

Dyed coque. The bottom feather has been bleach-burned.

Natural jumbo schlappen closely resembles the Spey cock hackle traditionally used on many classic flies, including the Red King (dressed by John Shewey).

termed the "eagle flies." In the U.S., possession of golden eagle feathers is illegal, of course, but marabou makes a fine substitute. The natural eagle "hackles" are of a brownish-gray shade, which can be readily imitated with marabou by the competent dyer.

In fact, tiers in the Pacific Northwest and in the Great Lakes region are chiefly responsible for the explosion of so-called "marabou Spey flies." The Spey label befits but few of these flies. Some resemble the eagle flies in basic form and others are more properly termed "marabou flies."

John Farrar and Bob Aid, both well-known steelhead anglers and guides from Washington, began experimenting with marabou-hackled flies more than 20 years ago. Each man created his own designs. Aid's method involved tying in the marabou plume and palmering it forward; Farrar devised a scheme for stripping the fibers from the plume and spinning them into a thread loop in the same manner as Dave McNeese had done with pheasant-tail fibers. The "Aid Marabous" and the "Farrar Marabous" (as Alec Jackson termed them), provided models for many other fly dressers and quite rapidly the so-called "Marabou Speys" exploded in popularity in the Pacific Northwest.

The evolution of these flies in the Pacific Northwest actually began decades ago with patterns tied for steelhead and for silver salmon; but early marabou flies featured full blood plumes or bunches of fibers tied in as wings. Farrar and Aid popularized the use of marabou as a palmered hackle.

Marabou flies tend to take full advantage of the brightly dyed colors in which marabou plumes are readily available. Although tricky to work with, marabou plumes dye easily and produce great-looking flies in the hands of even modestly skilled tiers.

Some years ago I began "tip-dying" individual marabou plumes. My intent, originally, was to create an imitation for the breast feathers of the great blue heron. These long-fibered hackles exhibit black edges contrasting with white along the stem. Initially I hand-colored the marabou tips with a black permanent marker. This proved laborious and less than satisfactory because

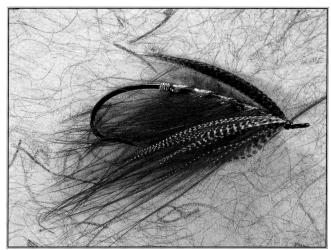

A PURPLE KING WITH MARABOU FOR THE HACKLE.
DRESSED BY THOMAS DUNCAN.

the ink caused the fibers to stick together, making them difficult to manipulate. I soon abandoned the ink-dying method. Some years later Bob Blumreich devised a simple and ingenious solution to separating the fibers after ink-dying (see page 39).

Taking my cue from Dave McNeese's hand-dipped two-tone hackles, I tried dipping the marabou plumes directly into a dye bath. After some experimentation, I arrived at reasonable results and soon began "tip-dying" all sorts of colors, reproducing the shades I had once dyed heron belly hackles. I would first dye the plumes in bright colors and then roll the tips through black or purple dye. The resulting two-tone feathers, colored along the stem but dark at the tips, spawned a host of new "marabou Spey flies." Once I had perfected the process to my satisfaction, I began offering these in my catalogs under the name Imitation Heron Belly.

A few seasons later, I recognized the obvious fact that my "tip-dye" jobs were not limited to black and purple. Indeed, so long as one uses complementary colors, virtually any combination is possible. By the late 1990s, the colors most popular with my customers included red tip/orange, red/yellow, green/chartreuse and royal blue/silver dr. blue along with the always-popular purple/pink and various black-tipped colors. I should add that I hesitate in completely claiming invention of these tip-dyed marabou plumes for I learned long ago that there remains little that has not been tried by ingenious fly dressers of decades past. However, the inclusion of these feathers in my product line no doubt hastened their ensuing popularity.

As previously stated, my earliest efforts at obtaining a suitable heron-belly substitute involved trying to color the tips with felt pens. I abandoned this method in favor of the acid dyes I now employ. But several other tiers continued to experiment with marking pens, among them the widely respected Wisconsin fishing guide Bob Blumreich, who solved the major difficulty inherent to this method. Bob's process for creating his marabou hackles is outlined herein.

RING-NECKED PHEASANT RUMP HACKLES.

JOHN SCHAPER'S AMETHYST.

One last trick for working with marabou is to spray the feathers with hairspray and then brush them with a toothbrush. The hairspray mats the fuzzy rachis down against each fiber and then the brushing frees the fibers. The result is a hackle that more closely resembles a heron plume.

Virtually any other hackling plume readily takes the dye from a permanent-marking pen. Simply color the tips as desired and if needed use a toothbrush to stroke the fibers after the ink sticks them together.

For the tier willing to go to what could be reasonably termed "extremes," there exist other avenues of hackling these flies. Among them is the use of fibers from the tails of golden and Amherst pheasants. The latter can be dyed brilliant colors, enhancing the striking black-and-white pattern of the natural feather. My first exposure to this concept came years ago from the creative mind of Dave McNeese.

McNeese used three different methods of hackling with pheasant tail. The first was what he termed "bunch hackling," wherein he simply cut the fibers from the tail and tied them in at several evenly spaced intervals along the body. The second method involved cutting the pheasant-tail fibers from the stem and then inserting them between two strands of silk, sealing the silk strands with Plio-bond to create a custom-made hackle stem. Lastly, McNeese also perfected the art of hand-stripping or blade-splitting the tail plumes to create workable stems.

Using these methods, McNeese demonstrated striking results by mixing the tail-plume fibers from several different species of pheasant. In many cases, McNeese first bleach-burned and dyed the pheasant tails. He was the first person to expose me to the idea of using bleach to burn off some of the rachies. His experiments in that regard date to the 1970s.

Another method for creating these custom hackles is to insert the feather fibers between two strands of silk and then twist the silk (or floss) to lock the fibers in place. The inherent advantage to these "built hackles" is that they need no bleach-burning because the tier controls the spacing between individual fibers.

Instructions for each of these methods are included herein. A few years after he and Keith Mootry devised the idea of "gluing" the fibers between silk (or monofilament strands), McNeese abandoned that tedium in favor of the spun-loop method.

# DAVE MCNEESE'S PHEASANT-FIBER SPEY HACKLES

Ever innovative in his fly-dressing skills, Dave McNeese was among the first Oregon tiers to embrace the Glasso-inspired tradition and it was McNeese who inspired several of his friends to explore the art of the "steelhead Spey fly." Almost immediately upon delving into the Glasso methods, McNeese recognized the need to find new and different hackle feathers to replace the increasingly scarce heron plumes. Some years earlier he had invested in a large quantity of imported heron feathers, but the supply was dwindling. McNeese obtained and sold small packets of blue eared pheasant hackles long before these feathers appeared in other shops. In fact, I recall these feathers being rather slow sellers—ample evidence that until the 1980s the Spey-style hadn't gained the widespread following it now enjoys.

In addition, McNeese began purchasing large quantities of rump feathers from the common ring-necked pheasant. We would grade through thousands of the feathers, selecting the best and then bundling these in lots of two dozen. Then Dave would bleach and dye the hackles. Within a few years we were selling them faster than we could produce them.

Years prior, though, McNeese had already devised his custom-built hackles made from pheasant-tail feathers. His favorites tail-plume fibers derived from golden pheasant and Lady Amherst pheasant, both of which offer bold markings. Usually he would dye the black-and-white patterned Lady Amherst tails to arrive at some striking and brilliantly colored hackles. From time to time McNeese also made use of ring-necked pheasant and Reeve's pheasant-tail plumes.

SCOTT O'DONNELL DRESSES THESE FLIES WITH SPLIT PHEASANT TAILS AS THE HACKLES.

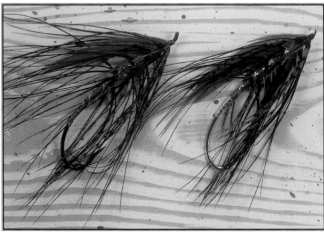

JOHN SHEWEY'S TRI-COLOUR RIACH.

His method of choice was "bunch hackling." McNeese would first treat the pheasant-tail sections with brief bleach-burning to prevent the individual fibers from clinging together. He would then dye them in various shades. Next, as he dressed the fly, he would tie small bunches of these fibers at three or four intervals along the fly, using his fingers to spin them around the hook shank. He would then lift the fibers out of the way when spiraling the rib forward—the most tedious task involved with this otherwise unique method.

Soon thereafter, McNeese began spinning the hackle fibers directly into thread or silk loops. In many regards, this proved the superior method as it still allowed McNeese to mix different colored fibers into the same hackle. Both he and local angler Keith Mootry experimented with literally gluing hackle fibers between two strands of silk, monofilament or oval tinsel. They would bleach and dye the pheasant-tail sections as before, but in this case they would then build the hackle ahead of time. The technique is tedious, but simple: Space the fibers carefully along a length of tinsel, mono or silk. Then coat a second strand with Plio-bond and lay this over the first strand. Use a small brush to press the fibers together and suspend the strand between two "bridges" of wood or cardboard until dry. If the strands are made in eight- to 12-inch increments, they can hackle half a dozen flies or more.

# BOB BLUMREICH'S PEN-DYED MARABOU
By Bob Blumreich

Many of the old Scottish Spey- and Dee-type flies called for materials that are now illegal under numerous state, federal and international laws. Other materials are available, but so expensive that they're not practical to use on fishing flies. As ethical tiers and anglers, we need substitutes that will maintain the character of the old flies, not break any laws, and not require a second mortgage to buy. Here's a little trick to imitating heron-belly hackles. The natural feather has a white center, with black tips on each flue. Dying the feather leaves the tips black and the center white part takes the color. Using a black permanent marker pen to stain the tips of a colored marabou feather creates a very natural looking imitation of heron hackle. The solvents in the ink burn the excess fuzz from the flue, and make it look very much like the real thing. The feather will get matted, so allow it to dry, and then brush it out with a piece of Velcro. Using colors other than black on the tips will give some "hot" combinations for steelhead flies. Consider the following:

## POLAR SHRIMP VARIATION

| | |
|---|---|
| **Hook:** | Any steelhead/salmon model |
| **Body:** | Hot orange SLF or similar |
| **Rib:** | Oval gold tinsel |
| **Hackle:** | Red-tipped orange marabou |
| **Throat:** | Red-dyed mallard flank |
| **Wing:** | Narrow strips of white goose |
| **Head:** | Red |
| **Hints:** | A right-handed tier will strip the left side of the body hackle before tying in by the feather's tip. Wrap the hackle close behind the rib, from the 2nd or 3rd turn of tinsel. This depends on how dense the tier wants the finished fly. Use a dubbing needle to pick through the hackle fibers while wrapping the counter rib. The wire is wound in the opposite direction to the rib and hackle, in order to bind the hackle stem down and reinforce it against bite-throughs. Throat hackles are usually two turns of doubled feather that has been tied in by the tip. Allow the wings to set slightly down on the sides, in order to keep a low profile. Use of a cauterizing tool permits close trimming of butt ends, without disturbing the wing's position. |

JOHN SHEWEY'S BOGUS CREEK RIACH.

THE AUTHOR'S TIP-DYED MARABOU PLUMES.

## JOHN SHEWEY'S TIP-DYED MARABOU

Although the exact year escapes me, some time during the early 1980s, Dave McNeese began dying what he called "two-tone hackles." Anyone possessing a mid-80s mail-order catalog from McNeese's Fly Shop will find these listed in several color combinations. Dave's idea was to create a feather that would allow for two-tone collars with a single hackle (in this case he used large white rooster neck hackles). Using these unique feathers one could collar a Skykomish Sunrise or Borden Special with a single hackle. The tip was one shade, the base another. The idea set me to thinking. Why couldn't I use the same dying technique to create an imitation for the hackles derived from the belly of the great blue heron? These feathers—illegal to possess in the United States—feature a white center with black tips on each fiber. The white portion of the feather takes dye readily.

My initial efforts relied on selected marabou plumes. For my earliest experiments, I first dyed the tips black and then dyed the color, but this immediately proved unsatisfactory and I suppose the reverse arrangement should have seemed obvious. So next I dyed the color and then the tips by carefully hand-dipping the feather in black dye. The process was tedious and soon I began experimenting with felt marking pens. These achieved the desired colors, but the ink clotted the fibers and I never took the next step, which would have been to figure out a method for un-sticking the fibers, such as Bob Blumreich does with Velcro. Bob's method is ideal for the individual tier not concerned with producing lots of feathers.

However, when Dave McNeese sold his fly shop, I began my own mail-order business for Atlantic salmon and steelhead materials and although the first few years comprised a period of painfully slow growth, my so-called "imitation heron belly Spey hackles" proved a big hit and remained a staple of my catalog offerings. Given the quantities involved, I had little choice but to perfect the dye-bath method of coloring the tips. All manner of colors, beyond the basic black tips, seemed possible so long as the base and tip shades were more-or-less complementary. Pink/purple worked; orange/purple did not.

After six or eight years of selling these feathers, several of the colors proved overwhelmingly popular here on the steelhead coast. Among these are purple/pink, purple/cerise, purple/light blue, red/fluorescent yellow, red/orange and red/fluorescent orange. Obviously these vibrant color combinations share little common ground with the heron hackles for which I originally created imitations. Yet the popularity of these bright colors offers testimony to the collective creative genius of the steelhead tying community. Atlantic salmon tiers likewise began experimenting with these feathers, creating some unique and striking patterns.

After these feathers—and flies tied with them—appeared in several magazine articles, the term "tip-dyed marabou" began floating about the Northwest. The name fits the process. The key is to use good acid dyes (I use Keystone), bring the dye to high temperature, add a drop of dishwashing soap to break the surface tension and then dip several (10-20) feathers simultaneously.

MANY FEATHERS CAN BE SPLIT TO FORM HACKLES.

# BLEACH-BURNING HACKLES

The exact ratio of bleach to water is relatively insignificant assuming the mixture is neither a majority bleach nor so weak as to render it ineffectual. Far more important is the amount of time the feather spends in the bleach solution: Too long and the feather is burnt beyond being usable; too brief a time and the feather remains relatively unaffected. A few practice sessions with throwaway feathers will reveal the precise amount of time needed to achieve the desired degree of burning. Of course these practice feathers should be of the precise type as those intended for actual use.

1. Begin by mixing a wetting solution of warm water and liquid dish detergent. Then mix a 4:1 solution of warm water to bleach. In a separate solution, fill a bowl with white vinegar. Place the three solutions side by side.
2. Immerse the feathers in the wetting solution, stroking them with your fingers to assure they are fully wetted.
3. Take each feather (or several at a time) from the wetting bath and dip them in the bleach solution, watching them carefully. Generally 20 seconds to one minute or so does the job.
4. Immediately immerse the feathers in the vinegar and agitate them vigorously and then rinse thoroughly with warm water.
5. Because bleach solutions tend to weaken the structure of the feather, some bleach-burned hackles can be soaked prior to use to render the stems more flexible.

# SPLITTING HACKLES

Most hackle plumes can be split to yield a thinner, more workable stem. Thick stems can be carefully split down the middle with a razor blade or the hackles can be split by hand. In the latter technique, you may wish to soak the hackle for several hours, rendering the stem more flexible and less prone to breaking. In my experience, most feathers can be split without soaking and either way, you must exercise extreme delicacy in the procedure. Also, you may wish to soak the resulting hackle prior to use to avoid breakage during the tying process and you should counter-rib the stem. If you intend also to bleach-burn the hackles, do so after splitting.

The advantage to the split-stem hackle is that the fibers, by necessity, stand out at abrupt angles to the stem. Such hackles hold their form in any flow and the rigid fibers offer maximum play when swinging through fast currents. Scott O'Donnell, the highly reputed steelhead guide from Washington's Stillaguamish country, ranks amongst the leading proponents of such flies. He splits his hackles without soaking the stem and prefers those made from pheasant tails.

Pheasant tails (from any species), turkey tails, goose shoulder and various other feathers are easily split. If you decide to soak the feathers ahead of time, first cut away the butt end of the stem so the feather more easily absorbs water. Soak the feather overnight in a mixture of hot water and hair conditioner. Remove the soaked feather and grasp the tip with both hands. Pull in opposite directions and gently split the hackle by pulling the fibers down toward the base of the feather. The same process works for un-soaked feathers. Experiment with both methods.

GOOSE SHOULDER FEATHERS (LEFT) CAN BE BLEACH-BURNED AND DYED TO MAKE NICE SPEY HACKLES. LIKEWISE, THESE FEATHERS ARE EASILY SPLIT.

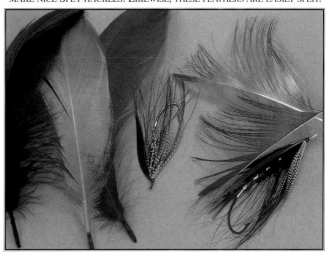

## End Notes

1. Taverner's later work (1942), was titled *Fly Tying For Salmon* and was largely taken from the fly-tying sections in his earlier and far more comprehensive work. Either title ranks among the most important books the dresser of salmon flies can add to his or her library.

# Chapter 3

# Materials for Spey & Dee Flies

*". . .the most favourite ones are those which are winged with the brown mottled feather taken from the back of the mallard—and having a long-fibred hackle. . .brown or dun-coloured dubbing, and a strip of fretted tinsel, wound, not too closely, around the body."*

—Thomas Tod Stoddart

## COLLAR MATERIALS

Frequently, duck flank plumage comprises the collar or throat of Spey and Dee flies. Historically, the flies from Scotland made use of widgeon flank (Eurasian widgeon) along with pintail and common teal. Steelhead tiers have expanded the use of various duck flank plumage. Syd Glasso adorned some of his flies with the rosy-brown flank feathers from the American widgeon (*Anus americana*) and later, at the prompting of Dave McNeese, began using the exquisite brown-and-black barred flanks from the stunning hooded merganser drake (*Lophodytes cucullatus*). Other useful flanks include those from the green-wing teal (*A. crecca*), gadwall (*A. strepera*), northern shoveler (*A. clypeata*), redhead (*Aythya americana*), ringneck duck (*Aythya collaris*), canvasback (*Aythya valisineria*), blue-winged teal (*Anas discors*), falcated duck (*A. falcata*) and, of course, the mallard. Options are further expanded for the tier who uses dyed flank feathers.

The classic salmon literature makes frequent mention of flank plumage from widgeon, teal and pintail, but in all likelihood, Victorian-era fly dressers also used imported exotics such as falcated duck, Baikal teal (*A. formosa*) and gargany (*A. querquedula*) amongst others. Note that in all classic salmon literature, the term widgeon does in fact refer to the Eurasian widgeon rather than the American widgeon. Flank feathers from the two birds are of an entirely different shade and are not interchangeable. Likewise, "teal" refers to the common teal of Eurasia, but this bird is now considered co-specific with the green-wing teal of North America.

Guinea fowl feathers likewise form the collar on certain Spey flies, especially some of the contemporary designs. These too can be dyed with excellent results, thus greatly expanding their range of uses. Generally, guinea fowl plumage is best purchased by the skin because the tier then has access to a full range of feather sizes and markings. On occasion, feathers from the Kenya crested guinea appear on Spey- and Dee-style flies. Rare and expensive, these plumes offer a distinctly striking pattern of small bluish dots on a black background.

## WING MATERIALS

Wing materials for Spey and Dee flies derive from a variety of birds. Bronze mallard plumes form the historical wings of choice on most classic Spey dressings. These feathers come from the back (scapular) of the drake mallard and vary somewhat

**ABOVE:** TEAL FLANK FEATHERS.
**FACING PAGE:** DEE-STYLE DESIGNS BY JEAN PAUL DESSAIGNE.

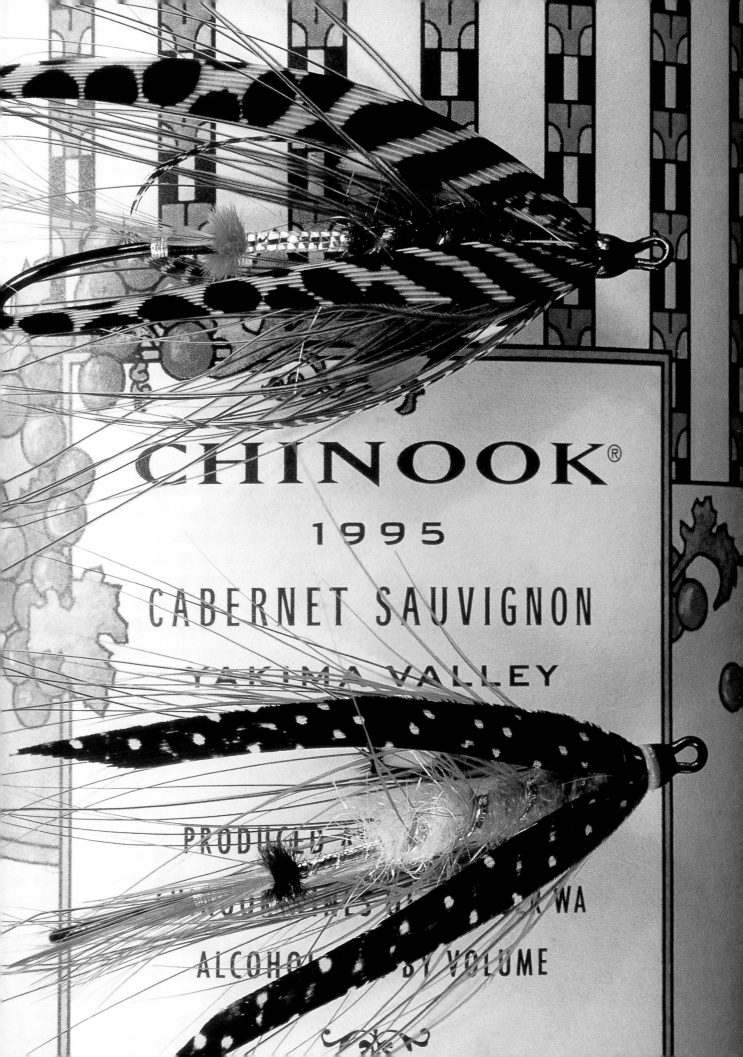

in specific shade. The best feathers offer fibers that are gray at the base and rich, cinnamon-brown across the outer half. Bronze mallard feathers are easily found in fly shops, but take care to purchase clean, well-matched feathers (you will need lefts and rights). If you hunt your own ducks, expect late-season mallards to produce the best feathers.

Contemporary Spey-style dressings sometimes call for wings of various other duck plumes. Among these are the terribly difficult-to-find hooded merganser flanks, the larger examples of which stretch to three inches in length and are elongated in shape, therefore making excellent wings on flies such as the Brown Heron or my own Number One. Likewise, the green-wing (common) teal drake offers several pairs of similarly elongated flank feathers, whose striking black-and-white barring makes for an exceptional wing (incidentally, these are the feathers best used to make the wings on flies such as the Black & Teal, a classic full-feather-wing salmon fly.)

Also, various duck flanks can be used like bronze mallard, with slips cut from left and right feathers. The gadwall, for example, offers large, dark-colored flanks featuring a fine, distinct barring pattern. When matched up and mounted as a Spey-style wing, these create a distinctively dark roof on the fly. Pintail,

AUTUMN BRONZE BY JOHN SHEWEY.

widgeon and falcated teal offer similarly structured flank feathers. Any of these feathers take dye readily. Dyed bronze mallard, in fact, lends a unique contemporary look to classic-style Spey flies (see page 46).

Dee flies generally require wings made from turkey tail plumes. Sometimes, various other feathers are used, including the vividly patterned quills from the great argus pheasant and the center tails from the golden pheasant and Lady Amherst pheasant. Old salmon literature often refers to wings made from the tail of the "Gled," which is the red kite (*Milvus milvus*) previously common in Scotland and now largely absent from much of its historical range in

NORTHERN SHOVELER FLANK.

HOODED MERGANSER FLANK.

NUMBER ONE BY JOHN SHEWEY.

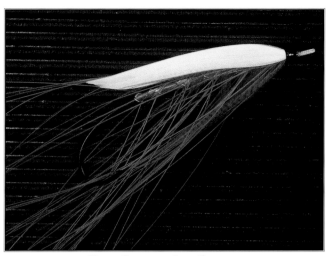

POLAR SHRIMP BY JOHN SHEWEY.

the Isles. The Gled Wing is one such pattern. Kelson excluded the Gled Wing (or "Glentana Gled") from his list, explaining, ". . .when the hawk died on Deeside the fly died too; or, in more staid language, the kite is now extinct in that neighbourhood, and, as far as regards any special distinction, so is the fly, for no imitation of its attractive wing-feather has proved of equal avail."

The red kite sports a long, rust-colored tail. So, despite Kelson's lament, cinnamon-colored turkey offers a fine substitute for these Gled tail quills, although good cinnamon turkey tails are by no means abundant. Various other turkey tail varieties, in their natural state, are useful for winging Dee flies.

Many contemporary Dee-styles and Spey-styles exhibit colorful wings of dyed turkey, swan or goose shoulder. Of those three, goose shoulder is easiest to obtain. Dyed white turkey tail, invaluable in building mixed wings on large salmon flies, has become increasingly scarce in recent years and dyed swan is difficult to find, but available from time to time from dealers who specialize in the Atlantic salmon materials trade. United States federal law allows for the sale of feathers from legally killed waterfowl, including swans, so tiers living in those few states offering swan-hunting seasons might consider checking with hunters. Otherwise, legal swan

TURKEY TAIL VARIETIES, LEFT TO RIGHT: LILAC AND PLAIN CINNAMON, DUN AND ZEBRA TURKEY.

DYED WING MATERIALS, LEFT TO RIGHT: SWAN, GOOSE SHOULDER, WHITE TURKEY.

quills derive from captive mute swans (the type commonly found in parks and aviaries).

Goose, swan and turkey differ markedly in structure and rigidity. Turkey tail sections are the stiffest of the lot and thus much preferred by Dee tiers, at least for large patterns. Goose shoulder is the softest of the three and is often tied "tent-style" on modified Spey- and Dee-style dressings. All three plumes—goose shoulder, swan secondary and turkey tail—dye rather easily, although some care must be taken in the drying process, after which the feathers may require grooming and steaming.

## DYED BRONZE MALLARD

Surprisingly, contemporary Spey tiers have only recently begun to embrace the use of dyed bronze mallard to add a little color in the wing of otherwise traditional-style dressings. During the mid-1980s McNeese's Fly Shop offered dyed bronze mallard in shades of hot orange and purple. They proved a slow seller and McNeese quit dyeing them after a season or two. However, flies tied with these feathers looked great, but another decade would pass before I decided to undertake the workload involved in adding dyed bronze mallard to my retail offerings. The dressing at right exhibits wings of dyed bronze mallard.

## PEACOCK SPEY
(John Shewey)

| | |
|---|---|
| *Tag:* | Flat silver tinsel |
| *Tail:* | Peacock sword |
| *Body:* | Peacock herl |
| *Ribs:* | Small silver oval, counter-wrapped |
| *Hackle:* | Blue eared pheasant, dyed claret (or similar) |
| *Collar:* | Mallard flank, dyed cerise |
| *Wings:* | Bronze mallard, dyed cerise or claret |

# BODY MATERIALS

For Spey- and Dee-style flies, the remaining components are straight forward: silk, dubbing, wool yarn and tinsels for the body and ribs; golden pheasant crests for use as tails; various other materials for specific dressings. In all manner of fur, feather, silk and tinsel, the dresser of salmon and steelhead flies is no better than his or her materials. Therefore, the tier should learn to grade materials and should then go to reasonable lengths to procure the very best materials available.

The body materials deserve some discussion: Classic Spey flies sometimes call for Berlin wool, which was a finely spun wool yarn originating first with Merino sheep of Spanish descent and then with the dying and distribution services in Berlin. Finely spun wool crewel yarns make excellent substitutes. A perusal of craft stores often leads to the procurement of the appropriate yarns. Likewise, the fine wool yarns now spooled for fly tiers make the perfect component for bodies on Spey flies. My favorites are the yarns sold under the label UNI-Yarn. Multiple-strand yarns can be separated into individual strands, but be sure to check the strength of the strands.

Seal fur dubbing, another traditional material, is rare and hard to find in the United States, where the Marine Mammals Act prohibits importation of marine mammal parts. Good substitutes include Angora goat dubbing and American opossum dubbing.

Angora goat dubbing must be cut to reasonably short lengths, otherwise the hair proves slick and troublesome. In some cases, the hair is fine right out of the package. If not, cut the fibers repeatedly and then re-blend the dubbing to arrive at a much more user-friendly body material. Dubbing from the American opossum might prove difficult to obtain despite the animal's abundance throughout much of the United States. From time to time, wholesalers offer "possum" dubbing under various labels. A tier adept at dying, however, can obtain skins through a fur dealer. These are shaved, the hair dyed and blended (bleaching may be required to dye light, bright colors).

As for tinsels, those made from varnished metal prove superior in all regards to the Mylar tinsels, which are prone to stretching as you work with them. The varnished metal tinsels

A WIDE VARIETY OF WOOL AND SYNTHETIC YARNS CAN BE USED AS BODY MATERIAL FOR SPEY FLIES.

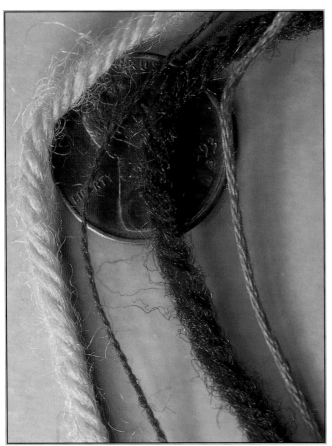

CLOSE-UP: LARGE WOOL YARN, UNI-YARN AND TWO DIFFERENT
SYNTHETIC YARNS (RIGHT).

## HOOKS FOR SPEY & DEE FLIES

Classic Spey and Dee flies call for long-shank irons, usually in light or medium wire weights. Thanks to Alec Jackson and Partridge of Redditch, such hooks are available now widely available in blind-eye form. Alec Jackson's Blind-eye Spey Hook (as of this writing), is available in Size 1.5 and features a long, slightly humped shank, a finely tapered eye and a beautiful black finish. The Partridge HE2, meanwhile, boasts an even longer shank and comes in sizes 1/0, 2/0 and 3/0. Partridge also makes a blind-eye version of its popular Bartleet hook, listed as Code CS10/3.

The blind-eye hooks, of course, require that you attach an eye of twisted silkworm gut or of some similar material. While the gut-loop eyes are nice for display flies, I prefer my fishing flies be built with a loop made from 30-pound Dacron backing material pre-treated with Sno-Seal (available at ski and outdoor shops). Any such loop-eye designed for fishing must be able to withstand the strain of a lengthy fight with a heavy fish. Thus great precision is required in attaching the eye to the hook shank (see Chapter 4).

Naturally, the eyed hooks offer the decided advantage in that you never need worry whether the eye will hold up during the heat of battle. Alec Jackson and Partridge both offer attractive "humped-shank" hooks that tie attractive flies and fish quite well. Best known of these is the Partridge "Bartleet" CS10/1 salmon hook. Originally, Dave McNeese contracted with Partridge to build this hook. A few years later, Alec Jackson likewise contracted with Partridge to produce his hooks, but today these hooks are manufactured by a Japanese company and are superior to the original Partridge design. In addition, many straight-shank hooks lend themselves well to the Spey and Dee flies, including the Partridge Code N Low-water hook.

come in many sizes and styles. For tying salmon flies, the most useful of these are oval and flat tinsels. You will need several sizes of each. Genuine French-made varnished metal tinsels are currently being sold under the label "Lagartun" here in the North America. Check your local fly shop.

CLOSE-UP, OF METAL TINSELS.

STEELHEAD SPEY-STYLES BY CLARK LUCAS.

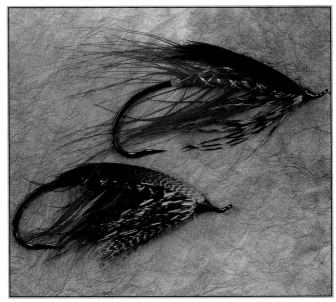

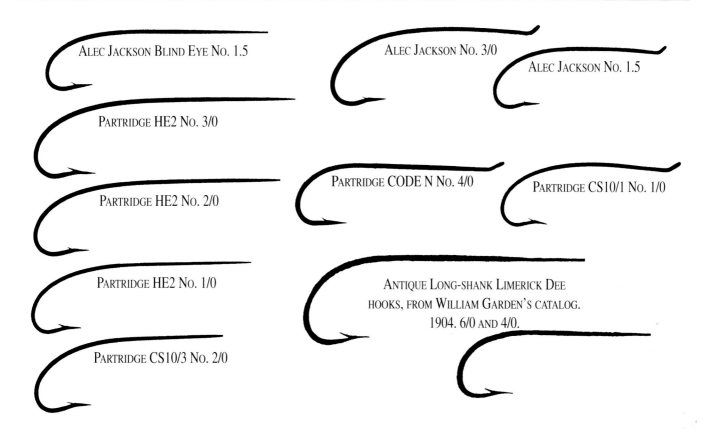

ALEC JACKSON BLIND EYE NO. 1.5

ALEC JACKSON NO. 3/0

ALEC JACKSON NO. 1.5

PARTRIDGE HE2 NO. 3/0

PARTRIDGE HE2 NO. 2/0

PARTRIDGE CODE N NO. 4/0

PARTRIDGE CS10/1 NO. 1/0

PARTRIDGE HE2 NO. 1/0

ANTIQUE LONG-SHANK LIMERICK DEE
HOOKS, FROM WILLIAM GARDEN'S CATALOG.
1904. 6/0 AND 4/0.

PARTRIDGE CS10/3 NO. 2/0

AN AKROYD DRESSED BY ANTHONY SMITH AND USING REEVE'S PHEASANT TAIL AS THE WING.

# Chapter 4

# Design Considerations:
# Tying a Durable, Sinkable, Fishable Fly

*"The ability to 'dress' a fly, even fairly well, enhances the pleasure of
Salmon fishing to a degree inconceivable to the uninitiated."*

—George M. Kelson

In general I think it a reasonably demonstrable observation that—despite our collective history of angling for both salmon and steelhead—we haven't the slightest clue as to why these fish grab a fly in the first place. Theories abound: aggressiveness during spawning runs, triggering latent feeding instincts, appealing to real feeding instincts, and so on. Yet none have ever been proved and if any predominant theory were proved, we would be well on our way to narrowing our list of effective patterns.

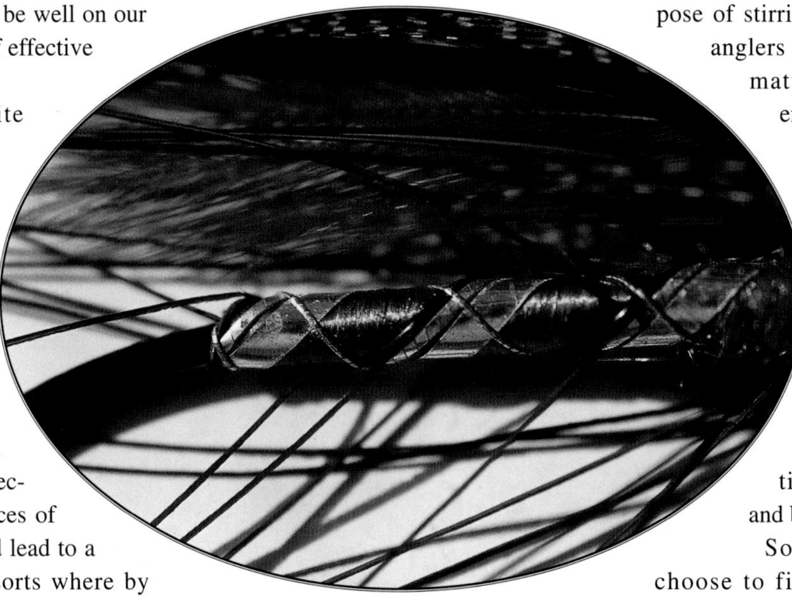

Instead, the opposite occurs: The number of patterns used to hook these anadromous fish continues to grow—ample proof of only one fact: That a salmon or steelhead is likely to eat just about anything when of a mind to do so. Indeed, if one particular pattern, style, size or color were more effective than all others, the forces of collective experience would lead to a convergent evolution of sorts where by now we would all be fishing such a lure.

Early in the 19th century, Thomas Tod Stoddart wrote:

*There is, I cannot help thinking, a great deal of prejudice, self-conceit, and humbug exhibited by salmon-fishers generally, with respect to their flies—a monstrous mass of nonsense hoarded up by the best of them, and opinions held, quite at variance with reason and common sense. I will not go so far as to assert, in relation to salmon-flies, that it would be expedient to greatly reduce their number, or establish, as I have recommended to be done with trouting-hooks, any limit to their variety. An innovation of this sort, if proposed, would, I well know, be treated with ridicule. Still, I have reason to believe that the salmon is not quite so finical in its taste as many angles represent it to be; that the fastidiousness is more on their part. . .*

I relate all of this not for the inevitable purpose of stirring controversy among fly anglers (although debate on such matters is both healthy and entertaining), but rather out of a need to establish a base of fundamental principles in tying and fishing Spey and Dee flies. Certainly these flies are effective in attracting and hooking salmon and steelhead, but so too are countless other styles, not to mention countless other lures and baits in general.

So why should the angler choose to fish Spey- and Dee-style flies? For many of us—including those whose works appear herein—the answer to that question derives in part from our appreciation for the elegant beauty of these patterns. We take for granted that these flies catch fish and remain fully cognizant of the fact that the Speys and Dees are no better or no worse than many other fly styles in their ability to attract salmon and steelhead. So we fish these flies because we are enamored with them. In a related vein, our love affair

**ABOVE:** A COUNTER-RIB LOCKS EVERYTHING NEATLY INTO PLACE ON THIS ORANGE HERON DRESSED BY JOHN SHEWEY.

**FACING PAGE:** SPEY FLY DESIGNS BY DAVID BURNS, BOTH BUILT TO WITHSTAND THE RIGORS OF FISHING: SHORT BODIES, HEADS SET SLIGHTLY AWAY FROM THE EYES AND COUNTER-RIBS.

with Spey and Dee flies compels us to believe that such flies befit the regal nature of our quarry and of the rivers in which they live.

Almost without exception, Spey- and Dee-fly aficionados adhere to the principle that the means with and manner in which they pursue their fish must at some level offer reverence to these steelhead and salmon, whose unique and unlikely life histories we barely comprehend. Even the angler among us who might on occasion fish deep with a leaded Bunny Bug or Comet-style fly will readily admit a greater level of satisfaction in hooking fish on a well-tied Spey or Dee fly.

Naturally, during his or her personal angling journey, the Spey-fly addict has developed a sense of extreme confidence in the use of these flies. The confident angler simply disdains any notion that failure to hook fish on any given pool or any particular day could in any way be ascribed to pattern choice: These flies with which we are so enamored will always hook fish—it's up to us to fish the fly in the right manner, in the right place at the right time.

As such, it follows that our duty then extends to tying our flies in a manner consistent with the way we expect them to perform. In doing so, we would be wise to study the simple wisdom of 19th century fly dressers, who tied their flies for fish-ability and durability. Modern pattern references remain wholly overstocked with Spey- and Dee-style flies that, quite frankly, have no business on the end of a leader. Many such flies are designed and dressed by some of the foremost salmon tiers in the world— people whose skills in the deft handling of fur and feather leave one ripe with wonder and admiration for such artistic endeavors. Nonetheless, beautiful flies don't always equate to good fishing flies, although good fishing flies should aspire to some level of beauty.

The divergence between fishing flies and artistic flies has precious little to do with the preferences of the fish themselves. As previously stated, salmon and steelhead are prone to eat just about anything when the mood strikes them or absolutely

VULNERABLE COLLAR HACKLES CAN BE REINFORCED WITH THREAD WRAPS TAKEN REARWARD BACK OVER THE HACKLE STEM.

nothing when another whim overtakes them. I personally have witnessed steelhead chasing and "eating" everything from the seed pods of the cottonwood tree to the yellow-tinged leaves dispersed in autumn by the red alder. I've watched steelhead rise like trout for tiny dry flies, as if to entertain themselves; I've seen them toy with skated dry flies with no intention of actually taking hold.

Hence a fly tied for display might fare equally well as one tied for fishing, but in today's fly-dressing world, there certainly exists a style of tying whose proponents produce salmon flies that could never withstand the rigors of fishing. Any learned angler can identify such flies at a glance and dismiss them immediately as belonging under glass on the den wall and not on the end of a leader. In such flies we find the divergence between art and function.

But fly anglers passionate about their salmon and steelhead flies seek a convergence of art and function. They consider themselves bound by pride to first expect a certain behavior and durability from their patterns and then to dress their flies in a manner consistent with their expectations. To do so requires an intimate knowledge of fly construction in relation to fly behavior under actual fishing conditions. The only way to acquire such knowledge is to spend time fishing—lots of time fishing—as the craftsmen included herein have done and continue to do.

In that it includes a combined wealth of experience, this volume, with luck, can save future anglers and tiers the many countless hours of experimentation required to discern exactly what constitutes a fishable and durable fly. Not that any angler should be discouraged from committing vast resources to the furthering of the art, for there always remain things to be discovered, theories to be tested, future generations to be enlightened. Besides, in the words of Forrest Maxwell, my long-time partner in outdoor pursuits, "Every day that you wake up and decide not to go fishing. . .is one less day you'll go fishing."

A STEELHEAD'S TEETH SEVERED THE HACKLE STEM ON THIS ORANGE HERON, BUT THE COUNTER-RIB HELD THE FLY TOGETHER.

## TYING FOR FUNCTION

Function in a Spey- or Dee-style fly relates primarily to how easily the fly sinks and to the manner in which it swims. All else being equal, heavily dressed patterns—those exhibiting a liberal application of materials—sink less efficiently than sparse dressings. Therefore, tiers must consider the effect of their dressing upon the relative "sinkability" of the fly. Classic Spey flies exhibited thin bodies of wool yarn and reasonably sparse hackles. They sank quickly and efficiently.

Such design elements are certainly not lost on modern tiers. On the Pacific Coast, steelhead anglers tend to rely on Spey-style flies more during the winter/spring runs than during the summer runs (during which classic hairwing flies predominate). Cold, swollen river flows dictate that flies be fished deeper in the water column, so sinkability does indeed remain a primary concern. Spey-style, Dee-style and marabou steelhead flies should be dressed sparse and clean; the weight of the hook, combined with appropriate line choice and line-control techniques, allows the fly to sink efficiently. Overdressed flies do not sink as quickly.

The problem is especially pronounced when floating lines are employed for fishing to winter-run steelhead holding in shallow runs and tailouts. In these cases, the fly must sink fast so that it will begin its swing at the deepest possible point in the water column. The taut line causes the fly to plane toward the surface, but a heavy-wire hook combined with a sparse dressing allows the

GRAY HERONS: A FULL-HACKLED VERSION BY DAVID BARLOW AND A SPARSE-HACKLED EXAMPLE BY AARON OSTOIJ.

DEE FLIES DRESSED BY WASHINGTON ANGLER BOB ARNOLD.

fly to regain depth each time the angler mends or slips line. Hooking winter steelhead on a floating line, using a classic swing, requires skill in line manipulation and ranks as perhaps the most rewarding method of hooking these magnificent fish. These angling methods are covered more completely in the final chapter.

Design elements also dictate the manner in which the fly "swims." Hackles tied in at their root and palmered forward tend to remain open and expressive in the water during the swing. Hackles secured by their tips and wrapped forward tend to collapse around the body of the fly, although this is not necessarily a negative effect. Again, the tier's expectation of the fly's performance should dictate the nature of its construction.

Dee flies offer a classic study in design elements that profoundly affect performance. When tied in the classic manner with stiff, scissors-shaped wings of turkey tail, these flies show a decided tendency to ride true in the water under tension from a taut line. Conversely, Spey-style flies often flip to one side or the other during the swing so that the hook bend faces left or right rather than down. The Dee-style wings produce a planing effect on the fly, working somewhat like an airfoil to keep the fly upright.

However, this planing effect works only on large patterns whose wings are long enough to encompass the roots of the turkey-tail slips. In other words, large Dee flies require long wings. Therefore, long slips must be cut from close to the turkey feather's stem where the fibers are thickest. These thick fibers assure that the wings are quite rigid at their base (front of the fly). Small Dee flies, wherein only the soft outer half of the slips comprise the wing, do not enjoy this planing effect simply because the wings lack the rigidity to brace strong currents during the swing. Likewise, if the Dee-wings are mounted to the sides tent style, the flies tend to flip to the left or right like many Spey flies.

This planing effect may be one of the reasons that Dee-style flies were tied on long-shank hooks. The other advantage of the long shank wires on classic Dees and Speys is that the extra shank length allows more room for the hackle fibers to play without hanging up on the hook bend. Furthermore, the long shanks offer more room to dress the body of the fly without impinging upon that portion of the hook that will likely be exposed to the fish's teeth.

The aforementioned tendency for flies to flip sideways during the swing may seem harmless enough at first glance, but consider the potential consequences: Most fish turn to chase the fly after the fly has swung past them. The fish pursues the fly to the left or right and therefore grabs the fly broadside, thus explaining the corner-of-the-mouth hook-ups that predominate. However, if the fly happens to be swimming sideways at the moment of the take, there exists every chance that the hook point will fail to connect with the tissue of the salmon or steelhead's mouth. I suspect some takes are missed for precisely this reason.

One way to combat this problem with tented wings (or with full-dress wings on salmon flies, for that matter) is to shred the wing into strands. Perhaps this seems a bit ludicrous to spend half an hour or so dressing a nice fly only to run a bodkin through the wing slips to—in effect—create a pseudo hair-wing fly. However, some anglers do exactly that. My own preference is to avoid wing styles that might contribute to flipping the fly over. Also, on many patterns I prefer heavy-wire hooks to help "keel" the fly so it remains hook-point down as much of the time as possible.

Regardless, I have spent quite a lot of time studying the way flies work in the water and I remain convinced that we cannot fully solve the problem of "side-riding" flies using single-point hooks. Any Spey-style fly is liable to flip to one side or the other, at least for brief moments, at any given time during the swing. They are quite simply at the mercy of the currents. Therefore, we must solve these problems partly through fly design and partly through our ability to manipulate the fly with line-control techniques. Spey flies exhibit this side-riding tendency most noticeably on a "hard swing," that portion of the presentation on the inner half of the river when the fly closes in on a direct downstream hang. Our ability to control the line and fly throughout the drift is paramount in allowing the fly to fish in the manner for which it was designed. Again, fishing techniques are covered in detail in the final chapter.

Double hooks offer an entirely different scenario. They swim true all the time owing to the balance and weight of the twin hook bends. Yet no recorded precedence, historically, exists for the widespread application of double-hook Spey flies. For the contemporary tier and angler, double hooks may seem an abstract concept because they cannot legally be employed on many fly-only waters. Even on waters where double hooks remain legal, they must be used judiciously in order to prevent undue harm to fish intended for release.

My home steelhead river, however, has afforded me the ideal scenario for fishing double hooks. Here the summer steelhead run is comprised entirely of hatchery-produced fish introduced to a river system historically devoid of summer steelhead. These fish do not reproduce and because they are a threat to dilute the spawning population of native winter steelhead, these summer fish are best removed from the river to the largest extent possible. Thus the fish and game department encourages anglers to keep them. Hence I enjoy frequent summer barbecues with fresh steelhead.

From many days fishing double hooks, I've concluded that they are, to be frank, deadly in their inherent ability to hook and hold fish. On countless occasions I've found myself resorting to pliers to remove a double-hook fly from a steelhead's jaw. Of course I'm fishing with barbed hooks. Double hooks, at least in small sizes, can be safely fished for wild fish so long as the barbs are removed. With the barbs smashed flat, double hooks slide out easily, yet still allow for solid hook-ups and for flies that balance and swim perfectly.

## TYING FOR DURABILITY

Many of the anglers whose work appears in this book share a common deficiency—a shortage of flies in their own fly box. This is a direct result of more time spent fishing than tying and of frequently offering samples to fellow anglers met on the river. All such anglers share a healthy respect for durable flies—flies that withstand not only the teeth of steelhead and salmon, but also the simple rigors of fishing.

The body hackle is of foremost concern in a Spey or Dee fly. The hackle's exposed stem breaks easily, even from the strenuous demands of casting. Brittle feathers such as blue eared pheasant and ring-necked pheasant are especially apt to come apart. The simple solution is to counter-rib the fly. In fact, regardless of how you choose to hackle the fly, a counter-wound reinforcement is indispensable and 19th century fly dressers recognized this necessity.

Kelson, for example, recommends a length of tying silk: "Along with the tinsels is fixed a length of tying-silk for binding the hackles at intervals of, say, 3/16 of an inch. This is done simply to protect the hackle from uncoiling if cut by the tooth of a fish."

Although a length of tying thread will suffice, oval tinsel or wire generally makes a more durable counter-rib. The only difficulty lies in tying off the counter, since it typically runs in the opposite direction of the tying thread. Techniques for counter-ribbing are forthcoming in Chapter 6.

An alternative to counter-ribbing can again be found in fly design: If you hackle only the forward half or third of the body, you reduce the chances of the hackle stem ever coming into contact with a fish's teeth. Still, I've seen too many body hackles break under the rigors of fishing to allow such leniency in my own flies, especially since I expect a single fly to last through several fish.

Another significant concession to durability is the actual length of the fly. A Spey or Dee fly whose body extends to or behind the hook point is prone to rapid destruction, probably by the first fish kind enough to take the fly. Conversely, a fly tied so that body ends ahead of the hook point stands a better chance of keeping its fur, feather and tinsel out of harm's way. In other words, leave plenty of bare hook for the fish to chew. This is perhaps the strongest argument for long-shank hooks on Spey and Dee flies: You can dress the body long and lean yet still end short of the hook point.

## ATTACHING GUT EYES FOR FISHING

Blind-eye hooks are rarely used by anglers these days for the simple reason that they offer no advantage over modern eyed hooks. When tying display flies on blind-eye hooks, modern tiers attach the gut loop at the foremost extreme of the taper. The idea is to reduce bulk, allowing for more precision in the application of the body materials. Such flies are rendered unfishable because the gut eyes could never withstand the strain of fighting salmon or steelhead.

However, some anglers derive a certain pleasure from the aesthetic appeal of fishing classic Spey and Dee flies dressed on blind-eye hooks. From time to time I count myself among those anglers, although I prefer to use 30-pound Dacron backing material for the eyes on such flies, as the Dacron seems better able to withstand the ravages of time and the elements. In any event, whether gut or Dacron or some other material is employed as the eye, the strands must be secured well back along the shank.

Use a hard thread (such as UNI 6/0) to bind down the material. In doing so, use tightly compacted thread turns while maintaining constant tension on the tag ends of the Dacron material. A drop or two of an adhesive like Super Glue or Zap-a-Gap completes the job (see instructions to follow).

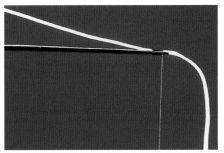

**Step 1:** Begin by attaching one end of the gut or Dacron (or whatever material you choose) to the far side of the shank, just behind the end of the front taper. Use half a dozen tight thread wraps.

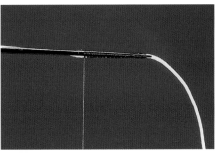

**Step 2:** Begin binding this first strand to the shank with neat, compact thread wraps, going back about a third or half the way down the shank.

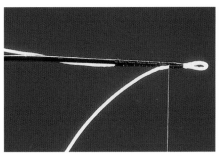

**Step 3:** Reverse directions and spiral the thread forward, and begin binding down the second strand on your side of the shank.

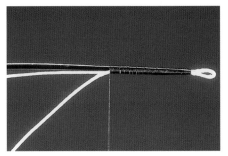

**Step 4:** Continue rearward with the thread, making tight, adjacent wraps of thread.

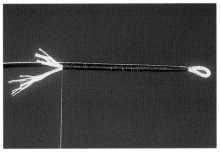

**Step 5:** Well back on the hook shank, fray the ends and stagger cut them as shown to create a smooth taper.

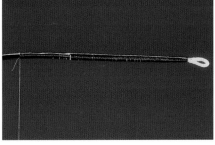

**Step 6:** Bind down the frayed ends again using neat, tight thread wraps.

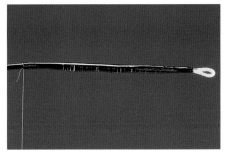

**Step 7:** Coat the wrappings with an adhesive and allow to dry. Test the loop for strength before dressing the fly.

# Chapter 5

# Tags, Tails & Bodies

*". . .it is essential, if aspiring to excellence, that the
artist be endowed with a tasteful and correct eye. . ."*
—*Thomas Tod Stoddart*

Spey flies generally exhibit simple bodies comprised of dubbing or yarns. Most of the classic Spey flies lack tails and tags of any kind. The Dee flies comprise a different matter. Virtually all of them include tags and tails and several of the Dee flies feature tags and tails boasting a complexity similar to the full-dress salmon flies.

For the uninitiated, frustration often accompanies the building of tags and the mounting of tails and, as in any part of a salmon fly, mistakes made during the initial tying steps tend to manifest themselves as the fly nears completion. In other words, mistakes tend to catch up with you. For that reason, these few lessons in dressing tags, tails and bodies might prove worthwhile.

The simplest tag is formed of a double layer of small, flat metal tinsel. Secure the tinsel the hook somewhere *forward* of the tail. The exact tie-in point varies with the style of fly. If, for example, the fly's body is comprised of silk or tinsel, the tag should be secured near the eye of the hook. A wool or dubbed body allows you the luxury of securing the tinsel just ahead of where the body will start. Yarn and dubbed bodies hide the slight lump created when you tie down the tinsel. Bodies of silk or tinsel, however, require that you maintain constant diameter along the entire length of the hook, thus allowing for a smooth, uniform body. Many full-dress salmon flies feature "joints" or butts of ostrich herl, which are used, essentially, to hide the tie-in points for other materials. In these cases (a rarity with Dee and Spey flies) you need not run the tinsel the length of the shank.

In any event, the flat-tinsel tag is formed as follows: Having secured it to the shank, wind the tinsel *rearward*, toward the bend of the hook. Keep each turn precisely adjacent to the previous turn, but do not allow any overlap. Upon reaching what will be the end of the tag, simply reverse direction and wind the tinsel forward, forming the double layer. Again, keep each wrap edge-to-edge with the previous wrap, with no overlap.

Several of the Dee patterns include a long tag of fine oval tinsel. To form this type of tag, first visualize its placement on the shank. Usually, the tag on a Dee fly is rather lengthy, beginning ahead of the hook point and extending back to a position just ahead of the barb. On the underside of the hook, attach the oval a thread turn or two ahead of the tag's forward-most point. Then, maintaining tension on the tinsel, wrap the thread rearwards in neat, tight spirals, keeping each wrap adjacent to the previous wrap. Make sure the tying thread remains flat, counter-spinning the bobbin when the thread begins to twist into round form.

Upon reaching the rear of the tag, you have two choices: You can begin winding the tinsel forward, simply pushing the thread ahead as you go or you can wind the thread forward ahead of time, again in neat, consecutive wraps. I generally opt for the latter arrangement. Wind the tinsel forward, keeping each turn snug against the previous wrap. Secure the tag on the underside of the hook, adjacent to and parallel with the initial tie-in point for the oval tinsel.

Among the Dee flies, the most complex tag and tail arrangements occur on patterns such as the Dunt, Gardener and Pryce-Tannatt's version of the Gledwing. This latter fly features a tag of silver oval and yellow silk followed by a tail comprised of golden-pheasant crest and breast feather. A tag/tail assembly of this kind is identical in construction to those often included on full-dress salmon flies. (Instructions follow).

In fact, most salmon flies feature a single golden-pheasant crest feather dressed for the tail. Generally, this feather is secured by its bare stem after the removal of the lower fibers. Steelhead tiers, however, often add additional color density to the tail by securing several such feathers, stacked together, as the tail or by trapping the lower fibers under the thread wraps to produce a slightly fuller tail (inset photo). In any event, instructions for dressing the tag/tail assembly on Pryce-Tannatt's version of the Gledwing follow on page 58.

FACING PAGE: THE GOLDEN GREED, DESIGNED AND DRESSED BY JOHN SHEWEY.

# DRESSING THE TAG & TAIL ON A DEE FLY

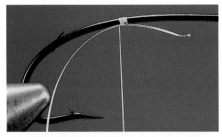

**Step 1:** Attach the thread at the rear of the hook as shown and then slip a length of small silver oval under the thread wraps positioning the tinsel so it is tied in on the underside of the shank.

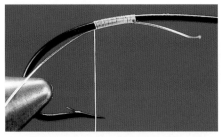

**Step 2:** Maintaining the tinsel's position on the underside of the shank, wrap rearward with thread. Keep each wrap of thread immediately adjacent to the previous wrap but do not allow any overlap. Maintain a flat thread.

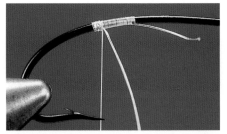

**Step 3:** Now wrap forward with the tinsel, pushing the thread along as you go. Make five turns and then secure the tag end on the underside of the hook with a wrap or two of thread.

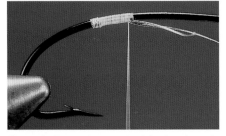

**Step 4:** Wrap forward with the thread. Make sure the tinsel remains on the bottom side of the hook shank, parallel to and adjacent to the strand already tied down.

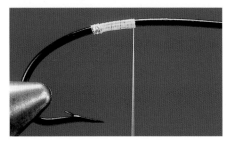

**Step 5:** Carefully cut away both tag ends of tinsel.

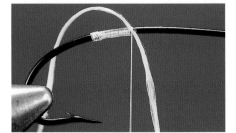

**Step 6:** Secure a length of yellow silk by pulling the strand underneath the thread wraps so that the silk is angled up and down as shown.

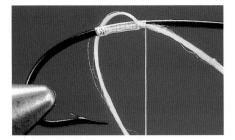

**Step 7:** Make four or five forward turns of thread to secure the silk.

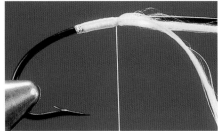

**Step 8:** Carefully wrap the silk rearward and then forward. When you reach the tie-in point, unwind the thread wraps used to secure the silk and wrap over the tag end.

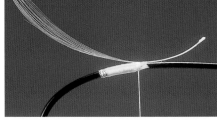

**Step 9:** Trim away the excess silk and then position a single golden-pheasant crest feather atop the hook, securing this tail with three wraps of thread.

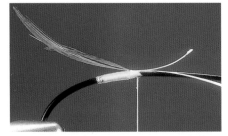

**Step 10:** Over the top of the golden pheasant crest, secure the tip of a small feather taken from the breast of the golden pheasant. This completes the tag and tail assembly on Pryce-Tannatt's version of the Gledwing.

# DRESSING THE TAG ON DOUBLE HOOKS

When tying double-hook patterns, a tag of oval tinsel is easily formed as follows:

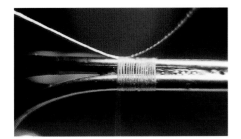  

**Step 1:** First create a platform of thread near the bend of the hook. Then slip a length of oval tinsel under the last thread wraps, securing it with several rearward thread wraps along the far wire.

**Step 2:** Then wrap the oval tinsel rearward in snug turns, each touching the previous. At the end of the tag, take the oval around the near wire and pass it down through the gap between the two hooks. Pull the oval forward and tie off the tag end on the underside of the hook.

**Step 3:** Viewed from below, you can see that the tag end holds the turns of tinsel firmly in place as it crosses over them.

# USING THE DUBBING HOOK

Coarse dubbing materials—seal, Angora, and opossum—are difficult to use without the aid of a dubbing twister. The easiest and most efficient dubbing twister is the hook devised by the ingenious Cal Bird, since copied by Dr. Slick Company.

 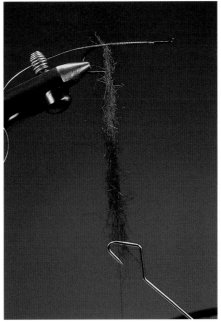 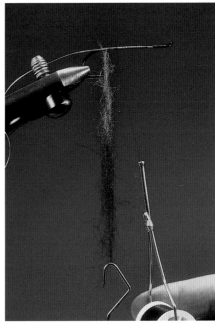

**Step 1:** Release a length of thread from the bobbin and gently spin the fur onto the thread. Don't try to spin the material on too tightly, as the coarse furs will resist your efforts to do so. Instead, just apply the fur to the thread so it stays put.

**Step 2:** Lay the hook over the top of the thread.

**Step 3:** Return the bobbin to the hook, making several turns to secure the loop just created.

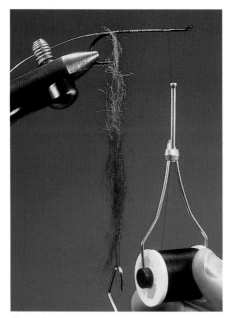

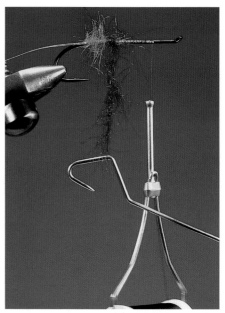

**Step 4:** Wrap the thread forward to the front of the hook.

**Step 5:** Spin the dubbing tool, binding the fur into the loop.

**Step 6:** Push the dubbing tool forward so that the thread slides into the second notch. So long as this notch remains pointed toward the fly as you wrap, the thread cannot slip off the tool. Using the long handle to maneuver around the bobbin, wrap the dubbing loop forward.

## MIXING WOOL STRANDS

Strands of wool yarn form the bodies on many old Spey flies. Specific shades are achieved through mixing several strands of different colors. Obviously, small-diameter wool yarn strands are more easily combined than large strands, allowing you to achieve the desired blended look rather than a "barber-pole" appearance. Multiple yarn strands can be combined in hand or by attaching them to the hook simultaneously and then brushing them slightly to aid in the blending of the colors as follows: To do this, choose the strands and then attach them as a unit to the front of the shank. Wrap the tying thread rearwards, binding down the wool yarns. Then hold the yarn strands taught in one hand while stroking and teasing them with a small brush or with steel wool. My favorite tool for this job is a .22 caliber bore-cleaning brush (a small, inexpensive cylindrical wire brush used to clean the bore on a .22 caliber firearm and available from gun stores). Having teased out the wool yarns, wrap them as a unit on the hook shank. The finished look is more a blending of colors than of a striped appearance.

## DEALING WITH MULTIPLE MATERIALS

Traditional Spey flies often feature two, three or even four rib materials. Take for example, the Dallas Fly or the Culdrain, both of which feature metal tinsels alongside various colors of silk. In addition to three or four ribs on such flies, there is the hackle and the body material, both of which must be secured to the hook shank alongside the ribbing materials. As a general rule, you should attach these materials in reverse order: The first material tied in along the shank should be the last one brought forward. This is not a hard and fast rule but rather a predominant and logical arrangement.

In the example shown, three tinsels, a hackle and a strand of orange wool yarn are all attached to the shank. Because the hackle and counter-rib (oval tinsel) are brought forward last, they are secured to the shank first, followed by the wool yarn and the remaining tinsels. In this case, the intent is to build first a butt of orange wool yarn and then a body of purple yarn. Thus the purple yarn need not be attached until the butt is in place.

First, however, we must consider the spacing between rib materials. In this case the main ribs are comprised of a strand each of wide flat silver tinsel and small flat gold tinsel. The two flat tinsels will spiral the body at equal distances apart from one another. In other words, the turns of gold tinsel will run between the bars of silver tinsel. In order to attain and then maintain this spacing in the main ribs, we must start each of them from different points on the body of the fly. A study of Figure 1 shows how this is accomplished: The small flat gold is attached in the normal position, secured at that point marking the back of the fly's body. The wide flat silver is then attached a fraction of an inch further forward (I have bent the tinsel forward to show the tie-in

FIGURE 1.

FIGURE 2.

FIGURE 3.

point), leaving space for two or three turns of the body material *between* the two tinsels at the rear of the fly. Notice also that I have trimmed down the tag end of the wide tinsel so it more easily secures to the hook and so that the first turn is seamless.

In the second photo (Figure 2), the butt of orange yarn has been completed, after which the tying thread is run forward along the shank to secure a length of purple yarn. Notice that the wide silver tinsel protrudes from the butt of the fly, with two or three turns of orange yarn behind it, and that its tapered end (where I trimmed the tinsel down) remains slightly exposed.

To complete the fly's body (Figure 3), I have wrapped the purple yarn forward, followed by the wide flat silver and then by the small flat gold. Notice that the two flat tinsels are spaced equally along the body of the fly, with the small gold appearing to run equa-distant between the bars of silver. Having dressed the main ribs, I then palmered the hackle forward in the opposite direction (more on this in the next chapter). The counter-rib, which locks down the hackle, comes last and, in this case, follows along the rear edge of the wide flat silver.

THE MAHONEY, DESIGNED AND DRESSED BY DEC HOGAN.

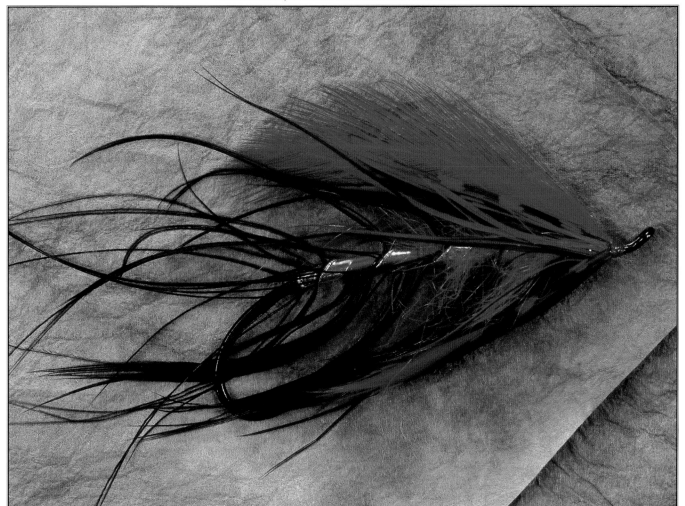

# Chapter 6

# Hackling & Ribbing Techniques For Spey & Dee Flies

*"The Spey flies are very curious productions to look at, it being customary to dress them the reverse way of the hackle, and to send the twist or tinsel the opposite way to the hackle."*

—*Francis Francis*

Spey-style flies, and to a lesser extent Dee-style flies, utilize a variety of feathers as body hackles. Each type of feather exhibits its own physical characteristics and in many cases (coque, heron, marabou) individual feathers of the same type vary considerably in the width and shape of the stem, length and density of fibers and strength of the stem.

Because each feather is different, tiers must familiarize themselves with a variety of hackling methods and then choose a method that best suits a particular fly and a particular hackle. Herein lies an important concept in dressing Dee, and especially Spey, flies: Versatility in method allows for greater control over the final results. Indeed, the classic literature on tying salmon flies reflects the advantages enjoyed by the Spey tier who keeps an open mind about hackling techniques.

The basic hackling techniques for Spey flies are as follows:

## BASIC HACKLING TECHNIQUES FOR SPEY FLIES

**Step 1:** The body material and two of the ribs are attached along the hook, leaving a space along the near side of the shank for the hackle stem. The stem has been stripped of its inferior side and attached at a slight upward angle as shown.

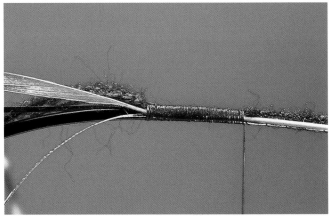

**Step 2:** The hackle stem is now locked down along the shank and a second length of flat tinsel is attached forward of the tie-down point for the other body and ribs materials.

---

**FACING PAGE:** THE ORANGE EGRET, BY JOHN SHEWEY.

**Step 3:** This top view shows the space left between the two flat tinsels on the far side of the hook. By attaching one tinsel slightly forward of the first, you create the spacing needed between the ribs on large, long-shank hooks.

**Step 4:** The body, ribs and hackle have been completed as follows: First the body material (purple wool) is brought forward, with the first turn or two being taken behind the flat silver tinsel. Then the ribs are formed of the flat tinsels. Next wind the hackle forward and lock it down with the counter-rib.

You can dictate the hackling method by learning to mount the feather with any of several slightly different options, which are discussed later in this chapter. Regardless of which method you choose, I suggest following the advice of Spey-fly angling enthusiasts past and present: Always counter-wind the hackle with a rib of oval or wire. Anyone who has spent considerable time fishing these Spey-style flies can certainly appreciate the added durability gained by the counter-rib, for typically the hackle stem is the most vulnerable part of the fly. The first fish often breaks the hackle stem, but even the rigors of casting and fishing the fly allows ample opportunity to weaken and break an already-brittle feather. Reinforced by a counter-rib, even a broken stem remains securely affixed to the Spey fly.

Though often lost on the contemporary tying community, the importance of the countering rib is well documented in the old salmon-fly tying literature. George M. Kelson, in his classic 1895 work *The Salmon Fly*, recommends a length of tying silk for this job: "Along with the tinsels is fixed a length of tying silk for binding the hackle at intervals of, say, 3/16 of an inch. This is done simply to protect the hackle from uncoiling if cut by the tooth of a fish."

The tying thread certainly does the job, but a length of oval tinsel generally proves more durable, especially considering that most contemporary fly dressers use extremely fine thread.

Indeed, the counter-rib makes the fly more durable and at the same time allows the tier more versatility in his or her method of hackling. Because a countering rib will always be the last rib wound through the fly, its mere presence—several inches of oval tinsel hanging beyond the back of the fly—allows the tier to wind the hackle in either direction starting from either end of the fly. Moreover, the choice in hackling method need not be set in stone. The tier sets in the materials with a certain method in mind, but once the hackle is secured to the fly, perhaps a slight twist in its stem dictates that this feather must be wrapped opposite the direction that had been planned. The counter-rib wraps just as easily in either direction, so the tier simply adapts rather than "forcing the feather."

Again the Spey tier well versed in the different hackling techniques never frets over the peculiarities of individual hackles. Kelson describes what might be considered a typical hackling process: "One side of the Spey cock hackle (which is wound from its root along the body) is stripped of its fibres, leaving the better side for use. If the tinsels are wound from you (a matter decided according to which side of the hackle is stripped), the hackle is brought *over* them towards you, and vice versa."

In other words, if the ribs are wound in the normal fashion, then the hackle is counter-wound over them. As Kelson notes, this task depends on which side of the hackle is stripped. Kelson's directions also introduce the idea of winding the ribs in the "abnormal" direction. Again, the skilled dresser of Spey flies is versed in all these techniques.

In short, there exist no hard and fast rules for ribbing and hackling the Spey fly. In *How to Dress Salmon Flies* (1914), Pryce-Tannatt notes that the hackles "are *sometimes* wound round the body in the reverse way to the tinsel."

Obviously, you can feel free to wrap the ribs and the hackle in either direction, often depending on which side of the feather is stripped of its fibers. Likewise, you might choose to reverse-hackle the fly as described so accurately by Eric Taverner in his classic work *Fly Tying for Salmon*.

Taverner also suggests that tiers utilize both sides of the plume, at least where heron hackles are concerned, rather than stripping one side. On this count there exists much debate, mostly centered on the concept of determining how much body hackle is too much. The Spey hackle is intended to allow for maximum life-like movement along with maximum sinkability. Overdressed flies fail on both accounts in contrast to the properly dressed version, but some feathers—heron and pheasant hackles to be sure—exhibit rather sparse fiber counts.

In regards to flies dressed with heron, blue eared pheasant, ring-necked pheasant and various similar plumes, I often find myself in complete agreement with Taverner. If I can dress the fly using the "doubled" hackle and only the best part of the plume, I believe the results produce a fly equally sinkable and even more mobile than an identical fly tied with a hackle stripped of its inferior side.

Moreover, the doubled or folded hackle offers the added advantage of allowing some of the fibers to stand at more rigid angles away from the body of the fly. This occurs when the folded hackle fibers are pinned by hackle stem against the body of the fly. The added rigidity allows the fibers more resistance to the force of the water currents, allowing them to remain full and expressive instead of being forced down against the body as the fly swings cross-stream.

Taverner relates his thoughts as follows: "I have discarded the old method of stripping from the heron hackle one complete side of fibres, because some excellent fibres were thereby lost and the weak lower fibres as well as a thick quill were retained. It is far better to keep the strong dark fibres near the top, double the feather and wind it with the quill next to the body, so that every fibre stands out from the body."

Certainly a fine line divides the fully hackled fly and the over-hackled fly. In private correspondence, Walt Johnson summarizes the concerns wrought by an over-hackled Spey fly, saying, ". . .I tie it considerably sparser in the hackle than most. I do this for a reason. First of all it allows the body to be more visible to the steelhead besides providing superior action to the flowing hackles when on the drift. . .I know many anglers hackle their flies too heavily, defeating the action as well as also somewhat hindering sinking capabilities."

On many modern dressings, of course, (and probably on many old ones) the feather is tied in by its tip at the rear and both sides of the feather are used to hackle the fly. When dressing a hackle using both sides of the plume, you are free to allow the feather to dictate the direction it is wound. When tied in at the rear of the fly, a hackle feather generally exhibits a propensity for one direction or the other. Should a given hackle decide it wants to wind counter-clockwise instead of clockwise, then by all means allow it to do so and then bind it down with an oval tinsel.

Versatility can also rescue the tier from a broken hackle stem. In teaching the Glasso Orange Heron in my classes, I typically introduce the use of blue eared pheasant hackles. Often these hackles lack the length needed to palmer an entire 2/0 body, so we attach the hackle by its tip at the joint between the rear half (silk) and front half (dubbing) of the body. Blue eared pheasant hackles are decidedly brittle and easy to break. On many occasions I have joked with students while tying the Glasso Orange Heron, saying that "if you break the hackle stem, just attach a hair wing and make a Polar Shrimp."

In reality, however, the countering rib waiting at the rear of the fly allows the tier to simply attach by its butt a new hackle at the front of the body and reverse-wind this feather through the fly. The counter-rib locks the hackle in place.

The hackle's direction also affects the aesthetic design and the functional design of the Spey fly. A reverse-wound hackle typically crosses over the main ribs while a hackle palmered in the normal direction follows along the same spiral as the main rib, generally trailing the tinsel or falling in between the bars of tinsel. With a reverse-wound hackle, the counter-rib winds in the same direction as the other ribs (in the normal direction). Conversely, a hackle wound in the normal direction requires a counter-rib that crosses over the main ribs. Obviously, many different combinations of hackles/ribs are possible.

From a functional standpoint, hackles tied in by their tip at the rear of the fly or by their butt at the front of the fly tend to exhibit a sleeker, more slender profile. Reverse this arrangement by tying the hackle in by its butt end at the rear of the hook, and the fly holds its shape better in the water because the hackle fibers at the rear protrude at a sharper angle. Thus if I want a Spey-style whose hackle fibers defy the forces of water current, I attach the hackle by its butt at the rear of the fly or by its tip at the front of the fly. Flies designed in this manner fish quite perfectly in fast flows, contrary to what has been written about modern Spey-style flies.

Along these same lines, a hackle stem can be persuaded to roll over on its own fibers when wrapped on the fly. In other words, the fibers need not necessarily protrude from the side of the stem facing away from the fly's body. Instead, you can dress the hackle fibers to protrude from the stripped side of the stem, forcing them into a more rigid position than is possible with the usual manner of hackling. Generally this arrangement is reserved for traditional-style flies dressed with schlappen or coque as the hackle.

**Step 1:** In this example, the hackle is stripped of its left-side fibers and then attached by its tip at the front.

**Step 2:** Next the hackle is wound rearward and locked down with a length of oval tinsel wrapped forward in the usual manner.

**Step 1:** In this example, a blue eared pheasant hackle is tied in by its root at the front of the fly, with both sides of the feather left intact.

**Step 2:** Next the feather fibers are folded rearward with strokes of the fingers.

**Step 3:** The hackle is wound rearward. Then a counter-rib of oval tinsel is wound forward to lock in the hackle.

**Step 4:** The completed reverse-wound body hackle.

As usual, strip one side of the feather and secure the hackle by its root at the rear. Then wrap the hackle in the reverse way from normal, with its bottom (dull) side facing forward instead of its top (shiny) side. This is the opposite of normal, but produces a unique effect as the hackle stem—with a little prodding from your fingers—rolls over on its own fibers, trapping them against the body of the fly and forcing them to stand up at rather rigid angles. In more exacting terms, strip away the fibers on the right side of the stem and then attach the hackle as usual (shiny side facing you), then wrap the hackle in the reverse way from normal. In the more usual method, you would wrap the hackle in the normal direction had you stripped away the fibers on its right-hand side. The more typical arrangement is further described below.

# PREPARING THE HACKLE: COQUE, SCHLAPPEN & NECK HACKLE

Before tying in the hackle, decide whether you want a sparse or full dressing. For the former, you can strip away one side of the hackle; for the latter you can "fold" the hackle as described later in this chapter. If you strip one side of the feather—the advisable practice with coque and schlappen feathers—you must first consider the direction in which the hackle is to be wound. Generally, if you tie the hackle in by its root and wrap in the normal direction, you will strip away the fibers on the right side of the hackle (the right side is on your right when you hold the feather upright with the glossy side toward you). The reverse arrangement is to strip away the left side and wrap the hackle in the reverse direction.

The basic construction of the fly, then, depends upon which side of the hackle is stripped. With so many methods of dressing Spey flies, you enjoy the unique luxury of examining each hackle and then stripping away the inferior side, whether it be the right or the left side. Your hackle then determines the direction in which the ribs are wound.

When tying with stiff-stemmed hackles such as bleach-burned goose shoulder or even coque, you might consider soaking the feathers prior to use. Add a drop of liquid dishwashing detergent or Synthropol to a dish of warm water. After preparing the hackle for use, submerse it in the water and allow the feather to soak for at least 30 minutes or so. Rinse before use, but wind the hackle while its stem is still moist. The softened stem is less prone to splitting.

# RIBBING AND HACKLING ARRANGEMENTS

These photos show three possible arrangements for ribs and hackles. The first is a Carron Fly showing ribs of wide flat silver and scarlet silk wound in the normal direction. The hackle stem, also wrapped in the normal direction, then follows along the leading edge of the flat tinsel and is bound down by a rib

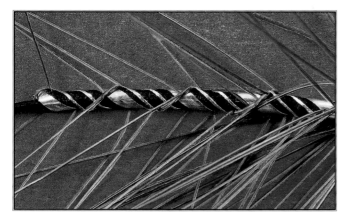

of fine silver oval wrapped in the counter direction. The second fly, a Black Heron, shows ribs of wide flat gold, small silver oval and small gold oval. The flat tinsel and the silver oval are wound on first in the normal direction. The hackle is then wound in the counter direction and bound down by the gold oval. In the third fly, a Gold Heron, the ribbing materials are wound in the counter direction, the last one (small gold oval) being wound on last, over the hackle, which is wound in the normal direction.

As noted in the last chapter, many Spey flies include two, three or even four ribs, requiring in such instances that these rib materials begin at different tie-in points so the spacing between the turns remains consistent. A common arrangement for example, might feature two flat tinsels and oval tinsel. On such a fly, one flat tinsel and the oval tinsel begin at the rear of the body, while the second flat tinsel begins slightly forward, with two or three turns of the body material behind.

Refer back to the photos at the end of Chapter 5: In the first photo, the rib materials, wool yarn and hackle have all been attached. I've bent the wide flat silver forward to show its tie-in point, which is slightly ahead of the other materials. The small flat gold tinsel is attached on the same side of the hook, but at the rear, while the oval tinsel is positioned on the far side. In the second photo, a butt of orange wool is completed, with the first two or three turns of yarn *behind* the wide flat silver. In the completed body (3), the flat ribs are properly spaced and the oval rib runs along the rear edge of the flat silver tinsel. The hackle has been wound in the reverse way so that the oval tinsel locks the stem in place.

You might also choose to attach all of the ribs at the rear of the body, but on opposite sides, thereby providing the initial spacing. However, where exact spacing is required, the better option is to begin the main ribs at different starting points as previously described.

# ATTACHING THE HACKLE

Any time you force a sharp bend in the stem of a hackle, you risk breaking or splitting the feather. Thick-stemmed hackles are especially prone to splitting, so coque and heron hackles are especially at risk. Soaking helps, but more important is your method of attaching the hackle to the fly. The first turn of the hackle is most critical. Make too radical a bend and you risk splitting the hackle stem. By forcing the hackle stem into a gradual bend rather than a sharp turn, you substantially reduce the risk of breaking the feather at its first turn.

Such concerns, of course, are relevant primarily to thick-stemmed hackles tied in by their butt ends at the rear of the fly. Many tiers simply alleviate the problem altogether by dressing flies whose hackles are tied in by the tips at the rear of the fly. However, the usual root-first arrangement produces a more functional and traditional Spey fly.

When tying in the hackle stem by its root, then, you can choose from two basic arrangements: Either run the bare stem the length of the hook shank or attach the hackle just by its angle-cut "nub" at the rear portion of the shank. Both methods offer their inherent advantages. By tying the stem along the shank you maintain uniform diameter in the underbody, which leads to uniform diameter in the body. In other words, no lumps appear in the finished fly. By angle-cutting the stem immediately below the usable fibers, however, you can attach the stem almost perpendicular to the hook shank, allowing for a less radical bend in the first turn of the stem.

Inherent to this latter method is the slight lump at the tie-in point, which must then be leveled with the body by layering the body material to cover the imperfection. On the other hand, if you run the stem along the entire shank, you can gradually force a curve into the feather as your thread wraps bind the stem down toward the rear of the hook. By creating this gradual curving of the stem you reduce the angle of the first turn of the hackle, thus reducing the stress on the stem.

As previously mentioned, soaking the hackle in water makes the stem more flexible and more forgiving. Moreover, when you wrap the pre-soaked hackle, the stem takes a set as it dries, allowing it to compress around the body of the fly, enhancing by subtle degrees the fly's durability. Another option, of course, is to split the stem, either in its entirety or just along that portion that will be bound down along the hook shank. Often, when using coque for hackles, I will use scissors to trim the butt end of the stem. The slimmer stem proves more manageable.

Schlappen hackles tend to boast slimmer stems than coque and are thus inherently less problematic. They require no soaking. Remember, however, that bleach-burning renders all stems more brittle and certainly some schlappen hackles will benefit from brief bleach-burning.

## FOLDING TECHNIQUES

In wrapping a body or collar hackle, you have the choice of either stripping away the "off side" fibers or folding these fibers backward so they join the "good side" fibers. Your decision here depends on the particular feather in question and on the style of fly you wish to produce.

Coque, schlappen and goose shoulder hackles, for example, generally tie better flies when one side is stripped of its fibers. Heron and pheasant hackles, however, often tie better flies when the off-side fibers are folded over rather than stripped away. Much depends on the relative sparseness of any given heron or pheasant hackle.

Folding techniques are especially beneficial for collar hackles. Duck flank and guinea, the most popular collar/throat hackles, are easy to fold and doubling them in this manner gives you twice the hackle fibers for half the wraps as compared with stripping one side of the feather.

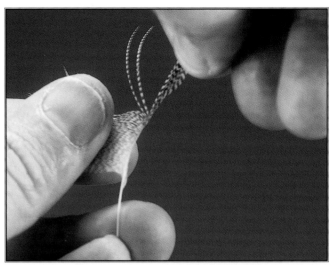

HAND-FOLDING DUCK FLANK (SEE TEXT).

Likewise, with heron and blue eared pheasant plumes, I prefer a slightly fuller look to my flies, so I frequently leave both sides intact and fold the off-side fibers, especially when I wrap the hackle tip-first from the rear of the fly. Like many tiers, I usually strip one side of the hackle when I wrap butt-end first from the rear of the fly or when I reverse-wrap from the front. Opinions vary considerably on this point, reflecting the individuality involved in dressing these flies.

In any case, hackle can be folded, or "doubled," with any of several techniques. I rely overwhelmingly on two easily learned methods. The first of these is simple "in-hand" folding and the second method is accomplished with a scissors blade after the hackle is attached to the fly. With just a little practice you can easily fold most hackles in hand as shown by securely gripping the butt end of the feather between the last two fingers on your left hand. Grip the tip of the feather in your right hand, holding the stem taught. Then use the thumb and middle finger on your left hand to pinch and fold the fibers towards your palm.

## COUNTER-RIBBING THE HACKLE

Fish Spey-style flies often enough and you will soon realize the importance of counter-ribbing most of them. The sharp teeth of salmon and steelhead easily sever exposed hackle stems. Moreover, the rigors of casting and fishing often prove the undoing of brittle hackles stems. Of course not all hackles are equal in the brittleness of their stems. Pheasant hackles are the weakest and most apt to break (including blue eared pheasant). Rooster-tail hackles are less brittle. Marabou and schlappen tend to be quite resistant to breakage, but still fail with regularity under duress from the fish's teeth.

If you intend to fish your flies, then build them to withstand any amount of rough treatment, at least if you expect more than one salmon or steelhead per fly. The design of the fly itself affects the durability of the hackle stem. Classic Spey flies tend to exhibit rather short bodies that end well short of the hook bend. Such a design keeps the fly out of harm's way because the fish's teeth don't make contact with the body of the pattern. Also, hackle stems can be buried rather tightly in a dubbed body and then followed closely by a wide rib.

Regardless of the design, a counter-rib—a rib wound in the opposite direction and crossing over the hackle stem—creates an indestructible fly. Should the stem be severed or broken, the rib prevents the stem from unwinding and you can continue to fish the fly indefinitely.

Small oval tinsels serve perfectly as counter-ribs. Other options include lengths of tying silk, wire or monfilament. Also the counter-rib need not necessarily run counter to the main ribs: If the hackle is wound in the opposite direction then the counter-rib is wound in the normal direction, thus being made to cross over the feather's stem. This latter arrangement also allows you to use one or more of the main ribs as the countering rib should you elect to do so. As with most avenues in tying Spey flies, there exists no hard and fast rule about counter-ribbing the hackle.

## USING DUCK FLANK AS A BODY HACKLE

Large duck flank feathers make attractive body hackles on Spey-style flies. Amongst the best are gadwall and mallard because both offer feathers with exceptionally long fibers. Pintail and widgeon (both species) offer some large flanks as well. You want the so-called "centers." These are the largest flank feathers whose left and right sides are balanced and they derive from the flanks immediately under the trailing edge of the wings. A little further down on the bird, around the legs, are found the "sides," these being the highly off-balanced flanks that are matched up as lefts and rights for use in making sides on full-dress built-wing flies. Generally, flank feathers should be tied in tip first and wrapped forward to the root of the feather. The largest gadwall and mallard flanks will fully hackle large flies; otherwise, start at the second or third turn of tinsel. I prefer to use both sides of the feather, but then I tend to do so with many other feathers used to hackle my flies. These flank feathers are easily folded with the scissors-method described below. Others might prefer to strip away the bad side.

## SCISSORS FOLDING

**Step 1:** Stroke the fibers backward so they stand at right angles to the stem. Then tie the feather in securely by its tip as shown, with the "shiny" side of the feather facing you.

**Step 2:** Open the scissors and hold them at the joint. Grasp the hackle by its butt end and hold it towards you so the shiny side faces forward and so that the stem remains taut. Then lay the sharp edge of the far scissors blade on the top of the stem, near the fly.

**Step 3:** Rake the blade toward you along the top of the stem, keeping the sharp edge upright so it grips each fiber. Do not allow the blade to slip behind to the "dull" side of the fibers. You will feel and hear the fibers being folded over as the blade "bumps" along the stem.

**Step 4:** Next use your fingers as shown to reinforce the fold.

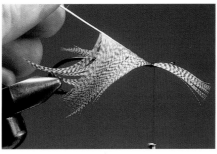

**Step 5:** The folded feather is now ready to wrap as a collar (or body hackle).

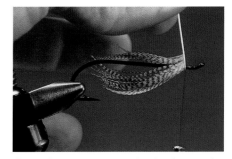

**Step 6:** As you wrap the feather, make sure all the fibers flow rearward.
*Note:* You can also grip the feather in hackle pliers and fold with the scissors using the method described.

# TWO-FEATHER TECHNIQUE FOR SHORT HACKLES

Some years ago, quite by accident, I arrived at what might seem a rather ingenious method for using notoriously short blue eared pheasant plumes to hackle the entire length of flies tied on the longest hooks. Unfortunately, no manner of ingenious thinking accompanied my stumbling upon this method: I simply forgot what I was doing at the tying bench and rescued myself with the first thing that came to mind.

I was tying an Orange Heron on a Partridge Code N, No. 4/0 and using a large blue eared pheasant rump feather for the hackle. This latter feather I tied in at the rear, intent on hackling this beast from back to front as I often prefer rather fully-hackled dressings for my own fishing. I then finished the floss butt, added the dubbing to the thread and finished the body. Only then did I realize my pheasant hackle would never wrap all the way to the front on such a long hook. Unwilling to begin anew, I unwrapped the dubbed portion of the body and added a second hackle, tied in by its tip at the middle of the fly. Then I re-wrapped the dubbing.

Next I ribbed the fly with the flat silver and then spiraled the first hackle through the butt of the pattern. Of course this first hackle ran out of fibers at mid-shank, so I took up the second hackle and used its first turn to wrap over and thus bind down the stem from the first hackle. I spiraled the second hackle through the front half of the body and counter-ribbed the works with oval tinsel. I realized I had just solved my problem of hackling with blue eared or even ring-necked pheasant the entire length of a very large hook.

**Step 1:** Secure at the rear a length of wide flat tinsel, a length of small oval tinsel and a pheasant hackle, secured by its tip. Then dress half the body with orange silk.

**Step 2:** At the mid-point, attach another pheasant hackle by its tip. Then dub the front half of the body with orange seal or similar.

**Step 3:** Spiral the flat tinsel through the body.

**Step 4:** The hackles can be folded as shown for a fuller fly; otherwise strip away the left-side fibers prior to attaching them.

**Step 5:** With your right hand, wrap the rear hackle along the path of the rib. When you reach the second hackle, take its stem in your left hand and cross over the stem of the first hackle. Continue with the second hackle along the path of the rib. Tie the stem off at the front.

**Step 6:** Now run the oval tinsel over the hackles in the opposite direction.

**Step 7:** A close look reveals the two stems crossing one another.

# THROATS

The terms "collar" and "throat" tend to be used interchangeably, but in essence they describe different elements. In the precise sense, the collar is the facing hackle, which is wound around the front of the body. A throat, traditionally, is comprised of hackle fibers protruding from the bottom half at the front of the body. A throat can be dressed in two ways, the first being to simply wrap the hackle (usually duck flank or guinea) as a collar and then remove the top fibers or bend them down along the sides of the body.

The other method is to actually tie the throat feather in at the bottom of the hook shank, its tip facing rearward, and allowing the fibers to envelope the materials immediately behind. This method is illustrated here.

# DRESSING THE COLLAR AS A THROAT

1. Wrap the collar as usual, first folding ("doubling") the hackle as described previously.
2. Next, pick out the fibers directly on top of the fly, being careful to remove them at their base either by hand or with the aid of tweezers.
3. Using your thumb and forefinger, stroke the remaining upper fibers downward along both sides of the hook.
4. Holding the fibers in that position, take one or two angled wraps of thread up and over the turns of collar hackle, effectively trapping the upper fibers in their downward-facing angle. These thread wraps should begin immediately in front of the collar and then pass slightly backward and over the collar so as to trap the fibers in place.

# DRESSING THE THROAT

**Step 1:** Select a feather showing perfect balance on both its left and right sides and cut the stem mid-way down the feather. Ideally, you should cut away enough of the tip so that no portion of the stem protrudes *behind* the thread wraps that will hold the feather in place.

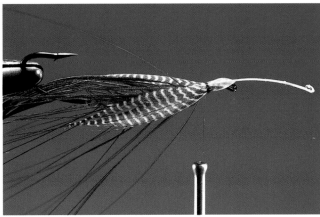

**Step 2:** With the fly upside down, gently press the feather against the underside of the hook, using your fingers to curl the fibers around both the left and right side of the fly. Purposefully mount the feather a little too long and secure it with three consecutive turns of thread.

**Step 3:** Now gently pull forward on the stem so the feather slides into the correct position. Then secure with additional thread wraps, none of which should over-lap.

**Step 4:** The finished throat.

# Chapter 7

# Winging Techniques For Spey & Dee Flies

*"But it is in respect of the wings that some
knowledge and much practice is needed."*

—*George M. Kelson*

---

Perhaps the greatest challenge in dressing Spey and Dee flies lies in the mounting of the wings. Virtually all of the traditional Spey dressings feature wings formed of bronze mallard while Dee patterns are defined by their unique wings made from turkey tail slips. The so-called "Dee-style" wings are mounted flat and v-shaped atop the fly.

Contemporary Spey- and Dee-style flies exhibit a wide range of wing styles. Syd Glasso designed many of his flies with wings formed of hackle tips and this style remains popular owing to Glasso's legacy. Simple strip wings made from goose shoulder adorn many modern flies and increasingly popular are built-wing styles.

Mounting wings on Spey and Dee style flies—and indeed on everything from full-dress salmon flies to Catskill-style wet flies—requires the use of the "soft-loop" technique. You should practice this technique until it becomes second nature.

Also, many tiers prefer to remove hackle fibers from the top portion of the fly, allowing a clear path for mounting the wings. Use a sharp pair of needle-nose scissors for performing this task—the fibers must be cropped tight against the feather stem. Another common practice is to bend fibers from the top side of the shank down to the bottom side using your fingers and two or three loops of thread angled backward.

## THE SOFT-LOOP TECHNIQUE

Paramount to successfully mounting the wings on salmon flies and many other flies, the soft-loop technique is easily learned. This technique allows for evenly distributed thread tension at the critical point when the thread is cinched down against the wing components. Mastery of this one technique often proves the impetus in learning to tie truly masterful salmon flies. I've provided here an outline of the soft-loop technique. Regardless of the feathers chosen or the type of wing, the basic technique remains consistent. If you are trying this technique for the first time, please read through the instructions in their entirety *before* beginning.

---

ABOVE: BLACK RIACH (TOP) AND EAGLE ROCK RIACH BY JOHN SHEWEY.

FACING PAGE: GREEN KING (TOP), SILVER-GREEN REEACH AND SILVER-GREEN FLY, THREE CLASSIC SPEY FLIES, EACH SHOWING SLIGHT VARIATIONS ON THE CHARACTERISTIC BRONZE MALLARD WINGS. DRESSED BY JOHN SHEWEY.

1. Grip the wings between your left thumb and middle finger. The pre-determined "thread point" (that part of the feathers that will receive the initial thread wraps) must be positioned between the pads of your thumb and finger, as you will need to grip this part of the wing.

2. Maintaining your grasp on the slips, guide the wing into position from above and slightly in front. If necessary you can use the underside of your thumb and finger to push hackle fibers down and back out of the way.

3. Set the bottom edge of the wing slips onto the hook shank so that your thumb and finger now grip the hook shank as well as the wing slips.

4. Maintaining this hand position, take the bobbin in your right hand and draw the thread straight up between your thumb and the wing slip underneath. Pinch the thread firmly against the hook shank and wing slip.

5. Leaving a small loop of thread above your fingers, draw the thread down in between your middle finger and the far wing slip so the bobbin once again arrives on the underside of the fly.

6. Now repeat Step 4, but this time draw the thread tight by pulling straight up with the bobbin. As you do so, maintain your grip on the wings and hook shank. Repeat the entire procedure a second time and then loosen your grip enough to check on the wings (some tiers make three soft loops before releasing their grip). If the mounting technique was properly executed, the wings should be set evenly atop the shank. If not, carefully remove the thread wraps and try again.

7. *Note:* Ideally, the thread wraps should line up evenly on both sides of the wing. The more perfectly you align the thread wraps, the more evenly distributed is the tension from drawing the thread tight allowing for perfect wing mounts. These instructions are written as if you were mounting a built wing on a full-dress salmon fly. For Spey and Dee flies you will find slight variations. In many cases, you may be mounting one wing at a time. Regardless, the idea of creating a soft-loop and then drawing tight a complete loop of thread remains a consistent technique in tying these flies. Otherwise, variations to the technique are described where appropriate in this chapter.

## CLEARING A PATH FOR THE WING

Most wing styles mount more easily when unobstructed at and immediately behind the tie-in point. Therefore, once the hackle and collar have been dressed, you can remove excess fibers with the aid of needle-nose scissors and tweezers. While not necessarily a functional requirement, clearing a path for the wing often aids in creating evenly mounted wings. Moreover, the judicious removal of un-needed fibers allows you to obtain a particular look to your flies—certainly a valid concern for display models.

A second and equally significant method is to fold fibers down and out of the way. After finishing the collar, simply use your left hand to stroke the top fibers down and back and then catch them with two or three wraps of thread, these being angled backward atop the hook.

Likewise, the actual tie-in point deserves ample attention. In short, the more clean and symmetric the tie-in point, the more easily the wings fall in line, so to speak. Yet the tie-in space allotted for the wings is often overlooked. This tie-in point should be slightly tapered, beginning at the base of the last turn of collar hackle or the last thread wraps securing a throat. A smooth taper is key—any sort of bump or sudden drop to the hook shank causes difficulties in mounting the wing strips.

Generally speaking, the tie-in space benefits from the removal of un-needed hackle fibers coupled with judicious application of tying thread. Also, maintaining the typically thin body characteristic of the Spey style allows for a smooth transition from the front of the body into the throat and then the wings.

Generally, most materials are secured on the underside of the hook, allowing the top side to remain free of the slight bumps that accompany those tie-down locations. One optional exception to this rule lies in the use of the collar-hackle stem to improve the shape of the wing-mounting area on a return-loop eye. To do this, make the turns of collar hackle and then secure the stem on the top side of the fly. As you do so, bend the stem in line with the eye of the hook, using it to fill in the gap between the two sides of the return loop. The resulting shape of the wing-mounting area is somewhat triangular when viewed from the front. The slight upward slopes on each side thus serve as platforms for each wing strip.

## BRONZE MALLARD WINGS

Over the years I have seen and tried numerous techniques for mounting wings of bronze mallard. After much experimenting and frustration, I eventually settled on several good techniques, all of which are detailed here and each of which obtains slightly different results. For display flies, where perfection or its proximity counts for something, I mount the wings simultaneously (for vertically arranged wings) or one at a time (for low-set horizontally arranged wings). Other tiers prefer to mount bronze mallard wings one side at a time, with or without a thread reversal.

For fishing flies, I often rely on a single or doubled-layer slip for the wing—an arrangement that proves quite durable. This method resembles the mounting of the roof on a full-dress salmon fly: Separate out a single slip of bronze mallard, slightly less than twice as wide as one wing slip. Before cutting, gently straighten the fibers as much as possible. Now cut the slip from the stem and fold in half, holding the butt end of the slip in your right fingers. "Hump" the slip by applying upward pressure with your left fingers. Then mount the wing in the same manner as shown for the simultaneous-mounting method.

For the double-layer version, cut a left and right slip and layer one wide slip atop the other. Shape the wing, and mount with a soft loop. Dave McNeese first introduced me to this technique for dressing durable bronze mallard wings on fishing flies. These methods are generally contrary to the typical techniques used to mount bronze mallard wings, which are described in detail herein.

Regardless of the method employed to mount bronze mallard wings, success hinges first on selecting proper feathers and then on proper technique. In this latter regard, practice is key and has no substitute.

# PREPARING THE BRONZE MALLARD FEATHERS

Bronze mallard wings begin with the matching and preparation of the feathers themselves. Begin by matching a left and right feather. Next, strip away all the fibers from the "off" side of the feathers. Then strip away all the fibers below the "sweet" spot on each feather. Hold the feathers by their bases, with the fibers on each facing away from one another and with the shiny side facing you: The feather on the left is now considered the "left-hand" feather; the feather on the right, the "right-hand" feather.

Some debate exists as to which slip (left or right) goes on which side of the fly—a debate that I think simply underscores the fact that there exists no rigid standard by which all Spey flies are dressed. The traditional Spey fly asks for low-set, drooping wings. Such an arrangement can be accomplished with either the "horizontal" or "vertical" set. In the former, a slip cut from the "right-hand" feather mounts on the near side of the fly, automatically producing the proper shape.

However, the reverse arrangement produces the desired low-set, drooping wings when the slips are properly aligned and then slightly "humped" so the tips droop down rather than pointing upward. In either case, the characteristic Spey-fly wing should resemble, as Pryce-Tannatt so accurately wrote, "a keelless racing-boat placed upside down."

Some Spey-fly enthusiasts embrace the "horizontal" arrangement in mounting the bronze mallard as it allows the wing tips to droop down nicely thus contributing to the slightly humped appearance of the finished fly. Other tiers appreciate the elegant curvature of the "vertical" style, in which the tips rise slightly to meet one another at the rear of the wings. Either style is appropriate and neither incorrect.

Bear in mind, however, that with bronze mallard the vertical wing arrangement is not the same as that used on built-wing salmon flies, where the wing assembly is mounted atop the hook. Instead, the vertical-style bronze mallard wing is mounted tent-like, with the roots of the wing fibers being compressed along the upper half of each side of the shank.

In any event, the "vertical-wing" method finds a slip cut from the "right-hand" feather mounted on the far side of the fly (for a right-handed tier). Then the slip cut from the "left-hand" feather goes on the near side of the fly. If you choose this vertical method of mounting the wings, you must "hump" the wings slightly to ensure that the slips meet along their top edges and also droop down along the body of the fly. To do this, simply apply a bit of forward pressure to the root of the wings after they are aligned edge to edge.

"Sprung" wings—wherein the tips of the left and right slips spring free at the top of the fly and end up crossing over one another—comprise a common problem with the vertical arrangement. Sprung wings result from using overly stiff bronze

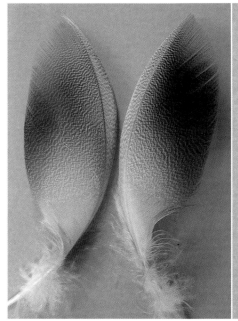

PAIRED BRONZE MALLARD QUILLS.

THE "SWEET SPOTS."

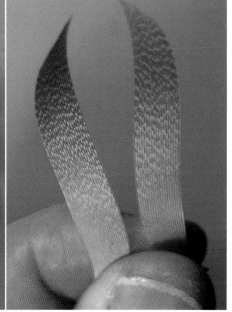

MATCHED MALLARD SECTIONS.

mallard slips, cut from too close to the tip of the plumes and/or from mounting highly curved strips too vertically.

In using the horizontal-wing arrangement, be sure that the upper edges of the slips meet one another along the crest of the wing and that the tips of the slips align with one another at the rear. Some tiers, when mounting bronze mallard in this "horizontal" arrangement, prefer a slight overlap along the crest of the wing, where the two slips meet. From a functional standpoint, the overlap makes sense as it allows the wing to hold its shape better in the water.

Should the curvature of a pair of bronze mallard plumes prove too radical, the feathers can be ironed. Place each plume between layers of soft cloth with the stem at the edge of the ironing board. Then gently press the cloth with a hot iron without ironing over the stem of the feather.

Regardless of style, the success of your endeavor rests largely in your choice of bronze mallard feathers and your ability to identify the aforementioned "sweet spot" in these plumes. Even a large pair of feathers yields but a few really good wing slips, these being located about mid-way up the shaft. Also, size your feathers to the size fly you are dressing: Small bronze mallard plumes are actually better suited to small flies with short wings than are the large plumes with the long fibers. Regardless of fiber length, the best tie-in point on the slips is that portion close to the stem where the fibers are somewhat "softer" and more flexible than farther out towards their tips. So save your extra-large bronze mallard pairs for large, long-shank hooks.

As for proportions, the wing should extend no farther than the end of the body and often somewhat short of that. Having said as much, I am reminded that there exist few hard-and-fast rules in the realm of the Spey-style dressing, especially as it relates to the modern steelhead tier. The shorter-than-body wing

derives from classic Spey flies. Likewise, the width of the wing slips deserves some comment.

Extra-wide slips, such as those perfectly dressed by the accomplished William Chin, Jr., actually encompass nearly the entire circumference of the hook shank at the tie-in point. This arrangement, which produces wondrous results for the practiced tier, does not represent the typical bronze mallard wing. Normally, only the upper half of the hook shank is reserved for the wing roots and any fibers that slip below the centerline do so at the potential cost of weakening or even separating the wing slip.

Many tiers prefer to cut the wing slips at the stem of the feather, leaving the fibers attached as shown below. Doing so allows for excellent control of the fibers on wing slips of normal width.

A word about cleaning and processing bronze mallard is in order: If you hunt ducks or have friends who do so, you can easily obtain matched pairs from the same drake mallard, these being the ideal acquisition for the dresser of Spey flies. Also, feathers from a fresh kill, if unsoiled by blood or mud, need no further cleaning as Mother Nature endows the feathers with a protective natural oil and because ducks are fanatical about preening and grooming their plumage.

Should the feathers come from any other source or if they are soiled after collection from fresh kills, they should be washed in a dish-detergent solution. Just soak them in warm, sudsy water for an hour, agitating frequently. Then rinse the feathers clean of soap. Now place them in a zippered linen pillowcase and toss them in the dryer on the heat setting for a few minutes until they fluff back to shape. Keep careful watch on the feathers during the drying process—you want them completely dry, but no so dry that the tips begin to curl. Finally, re-steam the individual feathers over a teakettle. Store them loose in a small, air-tight plastic tub.

## MOUNTING THE WINGS SIMULTANEOUSLY: VERTICAL ARRANGEMENT

**Step 1:** Cut the wing slips from the "sweet spot" on each quill.

**Step 2:** Match the slips as shown, so each has the same width.

**Step 3:** Align the two slips inside edge to inside edge, with these edges touching as shown. Hold these between the thumb and forefinger on your right hand and, using your left hand, push slightly forward to produce the slight hump in the wings.

**Step 4:** Position the two wings simultaneously, approaching from above and in front of the fly.

**Step 5:** Now reach in from the other direction with your left hand. Using your left thumb and left middle or index finger, grasp the wings and the hook simultaneously, bracing the wings in place atop the fly.

**Step 6:** Grasp the bobbin in your right hand and form a soft loop. Tighten the loop by pulling the thread upward on your side of the hook. Repeat once more and then relax your grip on the wings. If the wings are properly mounted, bind them in place with the thread, taking care not to roll them to the far side of the hook. If necessary, the wing slips can be manipulated by hand prior to tightening the thread. This top view shows the wings slips properly aligned atop the fly.

**Step 7:** When properly mounted as shown, the wings exhibit a slightly "humped" appearance. Carefully cut away the butt ends of the fibers.

# MOUNTING THE WINGS ONE AT A TIME: VERTICAL ARRANGEMENT

For those tiers who prefer to work with one slip at a time, I will offer brief instructions: Begin with the far slip and then place it at a slight angle across the top of the hook so that the butt ends extend slightly to your side of the shank. Add two loose wraps of thread while pinching the wing slip against the top of the hook. Slowly tighten the wraps by pulling the thread away from you across the top-side of the fly.

Once these two wraps are tightened, carefully grasp the butt end of the wing slip in your right fingers and the tip's end in your left hand. Very gently slide the bottom edge of the wing upward, helping to compress the fibers under the thread. Add a third wrap to continue the wing compression and then a fourth and fifth to secure the slip.

Now shape the second wing in your fingers and, with your *right hand* lay it along the near side of the fly, somewhat higher on the shank than its final position. Brace your right forefinger against the thread wraps on the far side of the hook while using your right thumb to hold the second wing slip in place.

With *your left hand*, gently loop the thread over the near wing slip and make two or three turns, tightening them by pulling the bobbin upward on your side of the hook. Check that the lower fibers do not fold upward and then switch hands so that your left fingers hold the wing in place and your right hand grips the bobbin. Before securing the wing, make sure its top edge braces against the top edge of the far wing. Tighten the thread wraps by pulling straight up with the bobbin so that the fibers compress upwards. Add several additional wraps of thread to secure the wings and then trim away the butt ends a fiber or two at a time.

Another procedure for mounting the wings individually involves reversing the thread such as you might do in mounting a Dee-style wing. To do this, first mount the near wing by pressing the slip against the side of the hook, just below the actual position it will occupy. Use a soft loop to compact the butt of the slip against the hook. As you do so, the wing slip will slide slightly upward into the correct position. Make sure that the top edge of the wing aligns perfectly with the centerline of the hook. If necessary, after adding a second wrap of thread, use your thumb and finger to manipulate the wing into the correct position. Likewise, you can use your free hand to manipulate the wing by its roots. Add a few more thread wraps to secure the wing.

Now reverse the thread and attach the far wing in the same manner using upward pressure from the thread to draw the slip up against the inner edge of the near-side wing along the centerline of the fly. Again, use your fingers to manipulate the precise position of the wing.

Carefully cut away the butt ends a few fibers at a time. Lastly, either teach yourself to finish the fly and tie off with the thread in reverse, or reverse the thread again to finish the head. (The other option, equally acceptable, is to reverse the thread initially and attach the far wing first before reversing the thread back to normal to mount the near wing and then finish the head).

Pryce-Tannatt offers a neat little technique that is worth mastering if you prefer to mount wings with a thread reversal. The trick is described in *How to Dress Salmon Flies*, one of the great works on the subject:

*The next manipulation requires a little nicety and some*

*practice to acquire proficiency in. It reverses the silk and secures the wing with the same movement. It is worth mastering, as it achieves simultaneously neatness, firmness, and a good 'set.'*

*Release the silk from "catch," taking in a loop round the tip of the middle finger of the left hand, and bring it round over the hook and towards you. Careful pressure downwards with the left middle finger, steadied by a controlling pull with the forefinger and thumb of the right hand holding the silk, will, with practice, secure the left wing in the correct position. Swing the loop under the hook to the left by flexing the middle finger of the left hand, and take three or four close tight turns of silk to the left. This will, or should, bring it to the point where the first turn of silk secured the right wing. Release the left middle finger from the loop, and bring the latter to lie on the top of the shank and exactly coinciding with the line of junction of the upper edges of both wings, where, after being twisted and pulled tight, it may be cut off close.*

## MOUNTING WINGS ONE AT A TIME: VERTICAL ARRANGEMENT

**Step 1:** First attach the far wing as described on page 77.

**Step 2:** Make sure the far wing is secured so its upper edge is aligned with the center of the body along the top of the fly.

**Step 3:** Now mount the near wing, drawing it up against the far wing. You may wish to cut away the butt ends from the far wing first so they do not hinder your efforts to position the near wing.

**Step 4:** The wing slips should meet along their upper edges.

# MOUNTING WINGS ONE AT A TIME: HORIZONTAL ARRANGEMENT

**Step 1:** Mount the far wing first, setting the slip atop the fly.

**Step 2:** Grip the wing slip and the fly with your left thumb and forefinger. With your right hand, bring the bobbin up and over the root of the wing. Make two such turns, tightening the thread gradually by pulling the bobbin toward you.

**Step 3:** Viewed from above, the wing slip is positioned with its inside edge aligned with the top of the body.

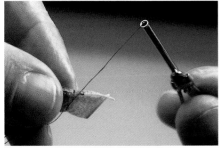

**Step 4:** Now mount the near wing by positioning the slip low on your side of the body and then using the thread to draw it up against the top edge of the far wing.

**Step 5:** With both slips mounted in this "horizontal" position, the wing exhibits the pronounced, low-set drooping arrangement.

**Step 6:** View from head-on, the wing is closed atop the fly, forming what Pryce-Tannatt termed "a keelless racing-boat placed upside down."

# DEE WINGS

The unique wings of the Dee fly are comprised of two matched slips of turkey tail and are set flat atop the fly, compressed at the head and opening over the back of the fly like scissors. Many contemporary tiers mount the Dee wings in a more vertical style and certainly the fly appears more elegant and beautiful in a frame when the wings are mounted in this manner. However, the advantage of the classic scissors-style wings becomes apparent when the Dee fly is quartered down and across on a favorite river. Upon close observation, the strip wings shimmy under force from the current while simultaneously exerting a downward planing action against the flow, helping to keep the fly upright during the swing. In short, the classic Dee fishes beautifully.

Still, I readily admit that wings mounted tent-style fish just fine and look better in a frame. But the wings should not be tied this way simply to avoid the sometimes-tedious task of mounting them flat—a job that causes many a fly dresser undue stress at the vise. Among the several methods of securing the strip wings, I have settled on two that the tier should master. The first of these is the traditional method described best by T.E. Pryce-Tannatt in his classic 1914 book titled *How to Dress Salmon Flies* (available in reprint). The wings are mounted one at a time, with the thread being reversed to mount the far wing so that it can be drawn up against the near wing.

Certainly one can mount the wings without reversing the thread. Just make sure to compress the far wing first by looping the thread completely around the slip and tightening by pulling the bobbin over and away or around once more and pulling back toward yourself. The near wing is then easily compressed against the far wing. Another technique for doing so was described by Kelson in *Salmon Flies* (1895) and involves mounting each wing separately by turning the hook in the vise and securing each wing with a soft-loop as if mounting the wing on a full-dress salmon fly.

THE KIMMEL KING BY JOHN SHEWEY.

The third technique, which is often my method of choice, especially when I'm in a hurry to produce fishing flies, involves compressing the wings in your left hand before attaching them to the hook. This method is sometimes termed "pre-compression" and dates well back into the 19th century.

THE TWO VARIATIONS ON DEE WINGS:
VERTICAL (LEFT) AND HORIZONTAL (RIGHT).

The first step in mounting Dee wings, regardless of method, is to choose and cut the wing slips. Ideally, the wings should be tied down quite close to their roots (the point at which they are cut from the feather stem) and the tips should extend out to or just past the bend of the hook. The reason for cutting the slips close to the feather stem becomes apparent when the fly is observed in the water and under tension from a taut line: The rigid fibers at the base of the wings allow the slips to plane against the current and thus help keep the fly upright.

In any event, the slip from the right-hand side of the quill generally goes on the left (near) side of the fly, this placement being opposite that used for full-dress salmon flies. The idea is to position the wing slips so their longest fibers are on the outer edges. While historically accurate, this need not be a hard-and-fast rule and the reverse arrangement often produces as nice a fly—it depends upon the wing feathers and on the tier's desire to attain a particular look or inherent fishing action. In addition, although you may impress your tying friends by mounting overly wide wings on Dee flies, such wide slips hinder the action of the wings. Keep them rather narrow.

# MOUNTING DEE STRIP WINGS, METHOD I:
## REVERSING THE THREAD AND TYING THE WINGS ONE AT A TIME

**Step 1:** Mount the near-side wing first using a soft loop arranged laterally so that you pass the thread over and around the far side, under and back to your side and then over to the far side. Now draw the thread tight by pulling directly away from you across the top of the fly (or by pulling toward yourself with the thread passing under the fly).

**Step 2:** Now reverse the thread: Catch the thread in a bodkin to maintain tension, double the thread back to the fly in the opposite direction and make several turns to secure. Cut away the loop left in the bodkin.

**Step 3:** Mount the far wing, holding it flat between your thumb and finger and forcing it to draw up against the wing already in place.

**Step 4:** As with bronze mallard, you may of course choose to reverse the thread initially and mount the far wing first, then reverse the thread again to mount the near wing.

# MOUNTING DEE STRIP WINGS, METHOD II: COMPRESSING THE WINGS IN HAND

STRIP WINGS COMPRESSED IN-HAND ARE EASILY MOUNTED ATOP THE FLY.

**Step 1.** Load a bobbin with waxed 6/0 thread. Align the wings inside edge to inside edge and pinch them flat in your left hand between the thumb and middle finger. Run the tag end of the thread up under your thumb and across the top surface of the wings.

**Step 2.** Double the thread back and run it down across the bottom surface of the wings, pinching it under your middle finger and forming a soft loop of thread around the wings. Once again run the thread up and under your thumb across the top surface of the wings and then slowly tighten the thread loops. Without removing your fingers, add several more tight turns of thread.

**Step 3.** Remove your fingers, maintaining some tension on the bobbin and examine your results. The wings should be neatly compressed against one another with the thread wraps forming a tight, narrow waist near the butt ends of the slips.

**Step 4.** Transfer the wings to the top of the fly and simply wrap them on with the same bobbin used to compress them. *Note:* Even upon removing the thread, most turkey tail slips will retain the set from the tight thread wraps used to compress them; thus you can remove the thread wraps after compressing the wings in hand and then carefully transfer the wings to the fly, mounting them simultaneously by soft looping over the compressed area. This technique helps reduce bulk at the head of the fly.

# SIMPLE STRIP WINGS

Simple strip wings refer to wings made from slips of goose shoulder, turkey, swan or similar quills. These differ from Dee-style wings in that they are mounted tent-style or in some way approaching tent-style rather than flat and scissors-like atop the

THE AUTHOR'S PURPLE PRISM FEATURES SIMPLE STRIP WINGS OF DYED TURKEY OR GOOSE SHOULDER.

fly, which is the defining wing position of the classic Dee fly. Simple strip wings adorn many contemporary Spey-style salmon and steelhead patterns. The tier can mount these in the tent-style by following the same procedures as outlined herein for bronze mallard or the strip wings can be mounted more upright, in the style of a built-wing salmon fly. In some instances, wings are mixed by adding a few fibers from different color feathers.

## MARRYING COLOR INTO THE STRIP WING

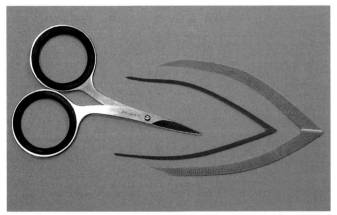

**Step 1:** Select matching left and right slips from each color of quill. In this case, the fibers are attached to the stems.

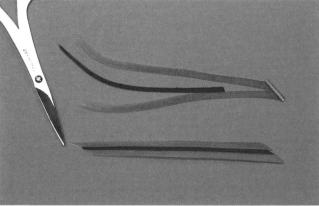

**Step 2:** Using a bodkin, separate the wing slip into two halves. Take one or more fibers from the second color quill and marry these to one edge of the separated slip. To do this, simply lay the fibers along the edge of the wing slip and with your fingers gently stroke from the roots to the tips.

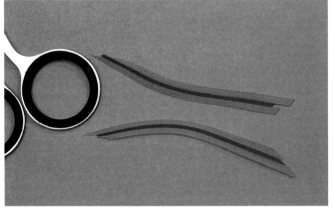

**Step 3:** Now re-marry the wing slip by placing the other half atop the newly added fibers. Again stroke with your fingers to secure the marriage of the fibers. Repeat for the other wing.

**Step 4.** To mount the wings, use a soft-loop technique, bracing the slips against the hook with your left thumb and middle finger.

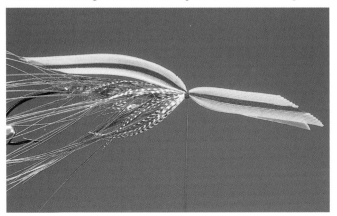

**Step 5.** Properly mounted, these married-fiber wings stand upright along the top of the fly in the manner of a full-dress salmon fly.

THE AUTHOR'S AUTUMN SKIES FEATURES A MARRIED-STRIP WING OF DYED TURKEY.

# HACKLE-TIP WINGS

Syd Glasso popularized the use of hackle tips for wings on Pacific Coast steelhead flies. Dyed rooster capes and saddles provide the necessary feathers. Look for hackles with high fiber density. If you can find hackles—saddle or neck hackles—with natural curves to the left and right, try to match these up as they will prove ideally suited to creating the low-slung wings typical of the Glasso flies. Otherwise you can force a curve into the stem quite easily by first soaking the feathers in water (with a little soap added) and then blow drying them, with the dryer aimed down the center of the hackles as you hold the feathers by their roots in one hand.

These wings are easily mounted atop the fly with a soft loop, just as if you were mounting a married wing on a salmon fly. You can add a slight tent-shape to the wings (especially on blind-eye hooks) by first flattening the stems at the tie-in area (with small pliers) and then pulling the stems forward and slightly downward, pulling a few fibers under the thread wraps.

In any event, mounting hackle-tip wings is a straightforward procedure: Align the four feathers so their tips are even and measure them against the fly to determine the proper length, which will vary from hook to hook and from tier to tier. I prefer that the wings reach only as far back as the top of the hook bend. Grasp the hackles together in your left hand. With your right hand, strip away all the fibers below the tie-in point. However, be sure to leave a width of about six fibers for the actual tie-in point. Leave intact about an inch of the stripped stems. Now re-grip the hackles between your left thumb and middle finger and guide the stems forward through the eye of the hook. (Obviously you will ignore this step for blind-eye hooks).

Grasp the ends of the hackle stems with your right hand. Push the wing down into place atop the fly with your left hand, pinching them to the hook. Now secure the wings with two or three soft loops before removing your left hand. Check the position and alignment of the wing and then pull forward ever so slightly with your right hand to help seat the wings under the thread wraps. Now secure the wings with additional thread wraps. See Chapter 10 for additional details.

1. Duck flank feathers mounted slightly off to each side of the hook.

2. Top view showing the proper position of the wings.

3. The matched duck flanks form a tent-shaped wing as seen from above.

## FULL-FEATHER WINGS

Some modern Spey-style flies employ matched flank feathers for wings. Duck flank plumes and golden-pheasant flank plumes are most commonly used on such flies. Full-feather wings are generally "tented" over the body. To achieve the desired affect, mount each feather just off to its side of the fly rather than directly on top of the hook. Position each wing slightly too long and after making a few thread wraps, pull the wing forward by its butt, trapping a few fibers under the thread and forcing the wing to be set at a slight angle over the top of the fly.

FLIES USING DUCK FLANK FEATHERS FOR WINGS.
DRESSED BY JOHN ALEVRAS.

## REVERSE-WING TECHNIQUES

Various 19th century authors, at least as far back as 1800, advocated the use of the "reverse-wing method" in mounting everything from simple strip wings to married wings. Many decades later, the reverse-wing method would find a receptive audience among tiers of hairwing steelhead flies on the West Coast of North America. As clearly stated by Kelson, the primary advantage of the reverse-wing method lies in its ability to allow the fly dresser to control the angle of the wing. A secondary consideration is the added durability facilitated by this method. Certainly durability is a primary consideration in designing flies intended for fishing, so the angler might well decide on reverse-mounting arrangements on certain fishing flies, although in virtually all cases, satisfactory durability is easily attainable with the more typical arrangements.

The reverse-wing technique is perhaps most easily applied to the hackle-tip wings used on Glasso-style flies. Terribly difficult to master is the "Kelson" method of reversing the bronze mallard slips to dress the Spey fly. I offer his method only as a "curiosity" and suggest that the technique has little practical value, especially considering the difficulties involved. His instructions are as follows:

*But it is in respect of the wings that some knowledge and much practice is needed. Take two strips, say, of Mallard, both from the same side of the feather; place one over and upon the other, so as to form one strip. Hold the fly in the left fingers by its loop. Place the strips so arranged on their backs, that the roots reach the throat hackle, with their points extending beyond the loop. Bind them down, headwards, from the throat hackle to half way along the space left for the wings. Now turn the fly round, and holding it the usual way, bend the strips back over the work and body, pass the silk to the end of the shank, and with it make close coils, tailwards, up to and just on upon the bent part of the wings. The object is to make the wings "sit up" in use. Put silk in CATCH; divide the strips into two equal parts, and work the silk first between them, and then round, in and out, in a figure of eight fashion, and finish off with a double half-hitch on the body side of them. Varnish.*

# Chapter 8

# Tying The Traditional Spey Flies

*"Spey flies, properly so-called, are simple and unassuming both
in composition and appearance, yet they are tied with as much skill
and care by the best native artists as is exhibited in the fabrication of
the most complicated, gaudy lures, formerly imported from Ireland. . ."*

—A. E. Knox

As shown herein, the first recorded "Spey flies" include those from Stoddart and Francis Francis, those two works presenting for us a total of seven patterns: the two un-named flies from Stoddart, the Spey Dog and Green Dog, Purple King, Purpy and Green King.

But in 1872, London publisher John Van Vorst published a wonderful collection of ramblings by one Arther Edward Knox. Titled *Autumns on the Spey*, the book is a collection of stories and observations about everything from salmon fishing on the Spey and deer hunting near Castle Grant to fossilized fishes and local fauna. Knox was especially fond of birds and also wrote *Ornithological Rambles In Sussex* and *Gamebirds and Wildfowl*.

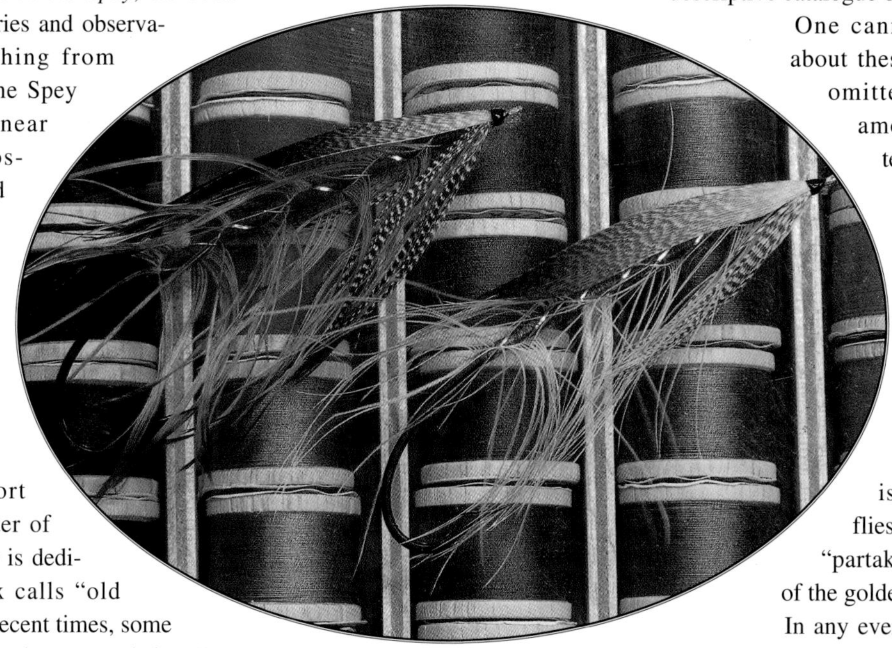

Only one short section of one chapter of *Autumns on the Spey* is dedicated to what Knox calls "old Spey flies." In more recent times, some writers have erroneously assumed that Knox originated these flies, but he himself simply states that they are old Spey flies and that the examples from which he translates the dressings were "tied by that accomplished artist, Shanks, of Craigellachie." What we wouldn't give for a few first-hand examples of Spey flies tied by the famed George Shanks, head fisherman at Gordon Castle for more than 50 years.

In any case, Knox lists 16 "old Spey flies" and then explains that "several varieties have of late years been added which, though modest and unassuming compared with the gaudy exotics to which I have already alluded, must still be considered innovations, partaking as they do, more or less, of the plumage of the golden pheasant; they are consequently omitted from the above list, which professes to be nothing but a brief descriptive catalogue of old Spey flies."

One cannot help but wonder about these dressings that were omitted by Knox; perhaps amongst them were patterns such as the beautiful Lady Caroline and her sister flies or the un-described Secretary; perhaps the vibrant creations of Major James Grant. These flies do indeed retain the essential characteristics of the "old Spey flies" while simultaneously "partaking. . .of the plumage of the golden pheasant."

In any event, a perusal of Knox's "catalogue" leads to several obvious conclusions about Spey flies. Generally they do not have tags or tails. Most have wings of mallard. The body hackle is characteristic: 13 of these dressings call for cock hackle, typically from the tail coverts, but from the neck on two occasions (Gold-green Reeach and probably the Silver-green Reeach). Only three of the 16 dressings call for heron hackle. Interestingly, Knox suggests that

**ABOVE:** PURPLE KING AND GREEN KING AS DRESSED BY DAVID BURNS.

**FACING PAGE:** THE LADY CAROLINE, NAMED AFTER LADY CAROLINE ELIZABETH GORDON-LENNOX, RANKS AS THE MOST POPULAR OF ALL THE CLASSIC SPEY FLIES. DRESSED BY JOHN SHEWEY.

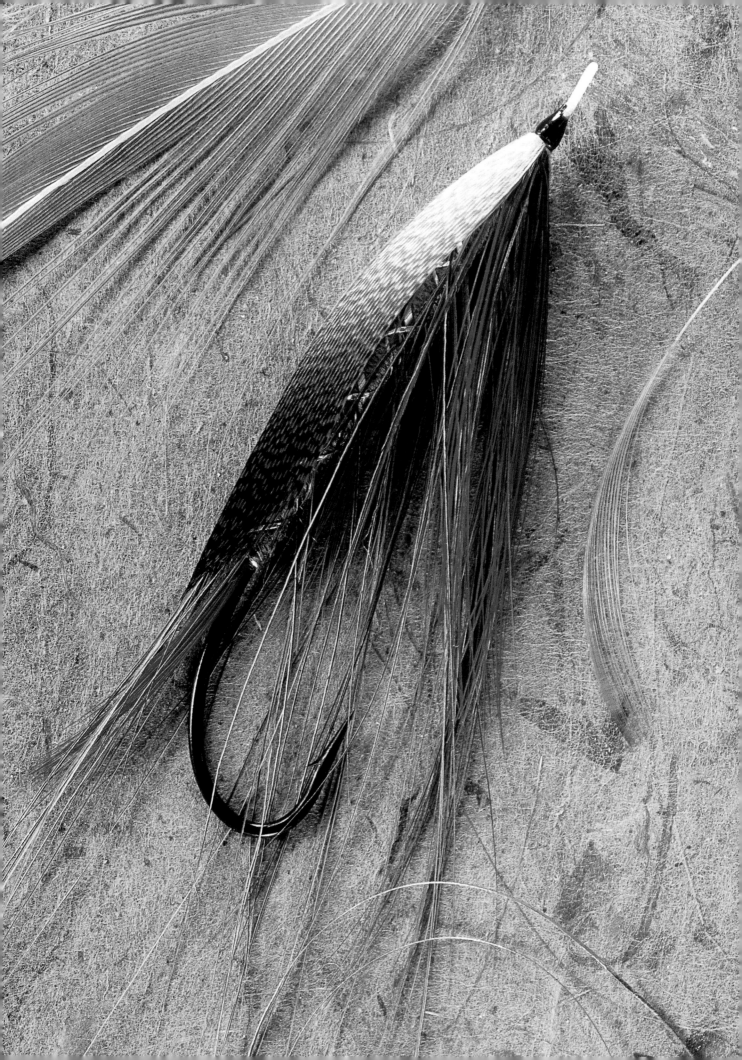

GOLD-GREEN REEACH (TOP) AND SILVER-GREEN REEACH AS DRESSED BY JOHN SHEWEY.

traditional Spey flies were often fitted with a scant three or four turns of wide tinsel as the main rib; five or six turns for the rib is the accepted form among today's tiers.

Likewise, there remain some conclusions from Knox that are certainly less obvious. For one, we must remember that in *Autumns on the Spey*, Knox simply translated the dressings by looking at the flies given him by George Shanks. Knox himself apparently did not dress salmon flies and therefore his descriptions might lack the precision that would be inherent to pattern descriptions penned by a devoted fly dresser. "Beading," for example, simply refers to oval tinsel or lace. Certainly we can ascertain the basic elements of the patterns—their color and general design—but to suppose anything relating to actual methods of construction would be presumptuous. On the other hand, Knox's reputation as an ornithologist and his familiarity with salmon flies and their use suggests that we can trust his descriptions of the plumage used in the 16 patterns given him by Shanks.

Among the dressings recorded by Knox are several distinct styles, including the "Heron flies," the "Kings" and the "Reeach's" (my quotes). Of the latter designation, James Leighton Hardy writes that the "Scottish word 'Riach' which Knox's flies carry, means "dun", or drab. . .Knox spelt the Riach flies 'Reeach.'"(1). Hardy's explanation regarding the term "Riach" disregards the evidence found in Kelson's book that these flies

took their name from their originator. Indeed there lived Speyside, during the 18th, 19th and 20th centuries, members of perhaps several families named Riach. Sir Thomas Dick Lauder, for example, in his fascinating account titled *The Moray Floods,* relates the daring rescue of an old lady whose house was inundated by the great flood of 1829: "'I will go!'—And I,' cried two lads of the name of Riach, though, I believe, not connected with her of the same name who they were thus volunteering to risk their lives to rescue."

One George Riach, as a young man, served as a caddy during the inaugural years of Spey Bay Golf Course. And a number of old Speyside gravestones bear the name "Riach" and at least one bears the name spelled "Reach." Kelson and others spelled it "Riach" while Knox used "Reeach." Knox may simply have chosen a phonetic version, for under the heading "Reach" in her cumulative index of names, compiler Alison Mitchell directs the reader to the heading for "Riach." In any case, almost assuredly there lived Speyside a 19th century fly dresser named Riach who contributed his name to the flies so called. Kelson, without offering any details, indeed credits "Riach" under his listing for the Gold Riach. (2)

Of the name "Speal," I can report only what is found in any thorough Scottish dictionary, namely that the term can be used as a noun to denote any game, match or play. In its verb form, "to speal" means to partake in any sport or game. Such does not rule

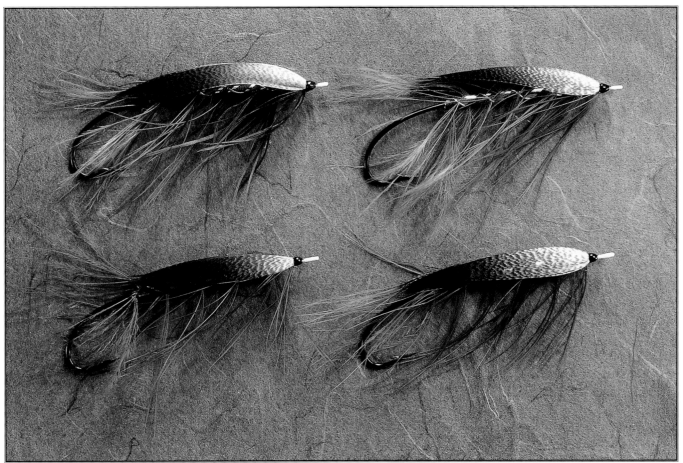

CLASSIC SPEY FLIES, CLOCKWISE FROM UPPER LEFT: GREEN KING, GOLD PURPY, SILVER SPEAL, GOLD SPEAL. DRESSED BY JOHN SHEWEY.

out the possibility of these flies also deriving their names from their inventor.(3)

While most of these flies have, unfortunately, fallen into antiquity, a few remain in use today. Here on the West Coast of North America, the Carron Fly and the Black Heron rank among the perennial favorites of a handful of Spey-fly aficionados, although in fairness it must be said that the Black Heron finds itself subjected to so many variations that its similarities to the original of the same name seems in some cases only circumstantial. The Purple King, lesser known and lesser used, has nonetheless enjoyed a slight resurrection on the Steelhead Coast.

A few notes on construction are in order. The wool bodies were comprised of both strands and loose dubbing. Early flies used pig's wool and mohair. At some point in history, however, Speyside tiers increasingly relied on crewel wools to make the bodies on their flies. The thin individual strands were mixed to arrive at the appropriate shade. Kelson provides us the details of a conversation once held with John Cruickshanks: "And with Berlin wools would 'Cruiky' select and mix two or three shades so as to get the exact colour of the body before he would rest and be satisfied."

Modern craft stores offer all manner of yarns satisfactory to the Spey-fly dresser's craft. Those of a soft and supple nature are superior in all regards to the harder, stouter varieties, though both will perform the work. In either event, bear in mind that you will be mixing multiple strands together to arrive at a particular shade, so thin yarns with a "combed-out" appearance blend better. The goal is to blend the individual strands into a reasonably cohesive color rather than slap them on so the finished fly looks like a barber's pole. Naturally, these same craft yarns are available in so many shades that such blending of strands is largely unnecessary today.

Speyside tiers also created bodies of loose dubbing materials, using the same techniques employed today. Dubbing techniques were covered in Chapter 5.

Wide tinsels often adorn the classic Spey flies, alongside narrow tinsels, oval tinsels, twist and even silk strands. On large hooks the best results are generally obtained by beginning the main tinsels at different starting points. In other words, bring the first tinsel around from the rear of the body, but allow for a turn or two of wool between the first tinsel and the initial wrap of the second tinsel as shown in Chapter 5.

These wide metal tinsels prove more manageable when the tie-in section is trimmed to reduce its width. Significantly, an angled cut at the tie-in point allows for a smooth, even initial turn at the rear of the fly. Also, trimming the tinsels allows for less bulk under the body and reduces the chance of the thread being cut by the edge of the metal.

GOLD-GREEN FLY AND SILVER-GREEN FLY AS DRESSED BY JOHN SHEWEY.

Finally, I defer to the words of Pryce-Tannatt to summarize the construction of the classic Spey fly:

*"They are out of the ordinary in every respect. The bodies are short, and have no adornment in the shape of tag, tail, or butt; and are usually composed of crewels or Berlin wools of various and varying colours, put on as sparingly as possible. The ribbing tinsel is individually broad and collectively plentiful, and, as often as not, besides thread and twist, gold and silver tinsel are used on one and the same body. The hackles are long and very mobile. Both grey and black Heron hackles are used, but the hackle of the typical Spey fly is obtained from the lateral tail feathers of a certain breed of domestic fowl, known as the 'Speycock.' These are not easy to procure. The method of putting them on is contrary to the general rule, as they are tied in base first instead of tip first. . .and they are sometimes wound round the body in the reverse way to the tinsel, a piece of twist or fine oval tinsel being wound on last over the hackle, to prevent it from getting torn by the fishes' teeth. . .The wings are almost invariably plain brown Mallard strips. . ."*

The dressings listed by Knox provide the fly dresser a challenging assemblage of patterns that do indeed conform to Pryce-Tannatt's summary. Most are rather similar, varying only by slight alterations in body tone, hackle color and tinsels used; a few offer further departure. The following is an excerpt from pages 67-70 of *Autumns on the Spey*:

***N.B.:*** *The dubbing—or bodies—of all these flies is composed of Berlin wool.*

***Gold Speal:*** *Is generally on a large hook. Body black, with only two or three turns of very broad gold flat tinsel and with a single turn of fine silver beading between the bars of tinsel. Red cock hackle, very soft, taken from the tail coverts of the bird. Wing, mallard.*

***Silver Speal:*** *Same as above, but the flat tinsel is of silver and the beading between the bars of gold.*

***Gold Reach:*** *Body black with three bars of flat gold tinsel, between which are three rows of very fine gold beading. Tip of the tail sometimes finished with orange silk. Red cock hackles from the tail coverts—soft and fine—along the body of the fly. Shoulder hackle of teal or guinea-fowl. Wing, mallard.*

***Silver Reach:*** *Same as above, except that silver tinsel and beading are used instead of gold, and grey cock hackle along the body of the fly instead of red cock hackle.*

***Gold-Green Reach:*** *Body olive, composed of a mixture of red, green and purple fine Berlin wool. Red cock hackle from the neck. Tinsel and beading same as in Gold Reach. Shoulder hackle and wing ditto.*

***Silver-Green Reach:*** *Same as above, but with silver tinsel and beading instead of gold.*

***Gold-Green Fly:*** *Dubbing the same as in green Reach. Three or four turns of gold tinsel, according to its width, and between each of these a single turn of orange silk. Red cock hackle. Wing, teal or grey mallard.*

CLASSIC HERON-STYLE FLIES DRESSED BY GARY GRANT.

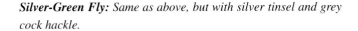

TINY CLASSIC SPEY FLIES (PURPLE KING AND GREEN KING)
DRESSED BY CAL MOHNEY.

BLACK KING (LEFT) AND CULDRAIN FLY AS DRESSED BY JOHN SHEWEY.

*Silver-Green Fly: Same as above, but with silver tinsel and grey cock hackle.*

*The flies known as "Kings" are characterized by having alternate bars of gold and silver tinsel. No beading of any kind.*

*Green King: Body same as green Reeach. Alternate bars of gold and silver tinsel. Red cock hackle. Shoulder hackle, teal feather. Wing, mallard.*

*Purple King: Body lake colour, composed of scarlet and purple mixed. Alternate bars of gold and silver. Hackle, grey or red cock, according to fancy. Shoulder hackle, teal. Wing, mallard.*

*Black King: Body black. Alternate bars of gold and silver tinsel. Hackle, black cock. Shoulder hackle, guinea fowl. Wing, mallard.*

*Gold Purple Fly, commonly called Gold Purpy: Body purple. Red cock hackle, with bars of gold tinsel. Wing, mallard.*

*Culdrain Fly: This is generally tied on a large hook. Body black. Bars of silver tinsel, rather far apart, and between each bar two threads of silk, one orange, and one yellow. Hackle, jet-black cock. Wing, grey mallard.*

*Gold Heron: Body black, with bars of gold tinsel. Between the bars two threads of gold and silver beading. Hackle very long, of the slate-coloured back hackles of the heron. Wing, mallard.*

*Black Heron: Same as the last, but instead of the slate-coloured back hackles of the heron, use the tips of the black feathers from the breast of that bird.*

*Carron Fly: Body orange, bars of silver tinsel. Hackle, black feather from the breast of the heron. Wing, mallard.*

# DRESSING A PURPLE KING

The Purple King seems to have been so popular that it was subjected to endless variations, such as those flies that came to be called the "Purpys." Knox listed the Gold Purpy and given the rich tradition of minor variations amongst their flies, I would imagine that Speyside anglers likewise had a Silver Purpy as well. My dressing

PURPLE KING VARIATIONS BY PAUL PTALIS (TOP),
G.S. SCOVILLE AND ROGER PLOURDE.

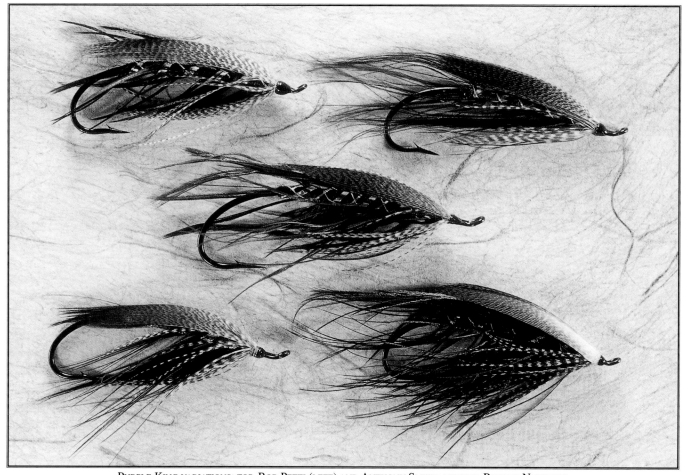

PURPLE KING VARIATIONS: TOP, BOB PETTI (LEFT) AND ANTHONY SMITH; MIDDLE, ROBERT NEWMAN;
BOTTOM, SCOTT PETERS (LEFT) AND JON HARRANG.

for this example is straightforward, but other variations are common. I suspect that during the 19th century, Speyside anglers devised just about every possible variation on the Purple King and its "thirty-second cousin" (to use Charles Grant's description to Francis), the Purpy. One of my favorite variations on the Purpy is as follows and is based on Grant's notes to Francis:

PURPLE KING VARIATIONS, DRESSED BY (CLOCKWISE FROM UPPER LEFT): BRAD BURDEN, CHUCK MOXLEY, STEVE SCHWEITZER, DAVE TUCKER.

| | |
|---|---|
| ***Body:*** | A mix of purple and deep red wool yarns, well blended |
| ***Ribs:*** | Wide flat gold tinsel and purple silk, with small oval gold tinsel, locking down the hackle |
| ***Hackle:*** | Coque (rooster side tail) or schlappen, natural red or dyed to approximate |
| ***Throat:*** | Teal flank |
| ***Wing:*** | Bronze mallard |

In this example, however, I've chosen a dressing more akin to the Purple King itself and as such the rib of purple silk is omitted. The body material is UNI-Yarn, a fine, spooled wool yarn commonly available in fly shops. In this case, two strands of purple and one of deep red comprise the body and they are brushed out with a small bore-cleaner to blend the two shades of yarn.

| | |
|---|---|
| ***Body:*** | Purple and claret wool yarn |
| ***Ribs:*** | Wide flat silver and small flat gold; small silver oval as a counter |
| ***Hackle:*** | Black or gray coque or schlappen |
| ***Throat:*** | Teal or similar |
| ***Wing:*** | Bronze mallard |

# DRESSING A PURPLE KING

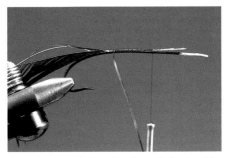

**Step 1:** Attach the tinsels and the hackle (one side stripped). Attach the small flat gold slightly ahead of the flat silver, leaving room behind the flat gold for two or three turns of the body material.

**Step 2:** Run the thread forward again to attach the wool yarn, wrapping rearward to bind them down. Return the tying thread to the front.

**Step 3:** Hold the wool yarns taut in your left hand and tease them with the bore-cleaner or similar brush to blend the colors.

**Step 4:** Wrap the wool yarn forward and secure at front.

**Step 5:** Now spiral the flat tinsels forward, beginning with the large flat silver.

**Step 6:** Wrap the hackle forward, following along the rear edge of the flat silver tinsel. Follow with the counter-rib.

**Step 7:** Add a collar of teal or similar (Eurasian widgeon is used in this example).

**Step 8:** Mount the wings of bronze mallard.

# DRESSING A BLACK KING

This pattern is the variation listed by Kelson and probably submitted to him from one of the Speyside anglers. Obviously it varies from the simpler version listed years earlier by Knox. In this example, the body material is embroidery floss, a fine multi-strand cotton yarn available in craft stores. Marketed by DMC of Paris (and other companies), this embroidery floss comes in myriad shades. It does not blend like wool yarns, so single colors make better bodies than do mixed strands. The floss is comprised of six two-thread strands. The six strands are easily separated to produce the desired thickness for any given size hook. The main ribs are dressed in reverse and then the hackle is wrapped in the normal direction, producing a different effect than the more usual arrangement of dressing the hackle in the reverse direction.

| | |
|---|---|
| **Body:** | A butt of orange yarn and then black yarn |
| **Ribs:** | Flat silver and flat gold tinsel; small oval as a counter-rib |
| **Hackle:** | Black coque or schlappen |
| **Throat:** | Teal flank |
| **Wings:** | Bronze mallard |

**Step 1:** Attach the ribs, orange yarn (3 strands) and the hackle. Again, be sure to leave a space between the starting points of the two main ribs.

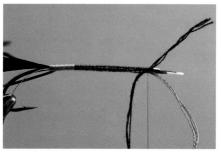

**Step 2:** Form a butt of orange yarn, comprising about 1/5 the total body length. Bind the tag ends down along the length of the shank and then attach the black yarn at front (3 strands).

**Step 3:** Wrap rearward, binding down the black yarn and then return the thread to the front.

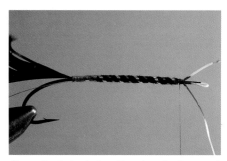

**Step 4:** Spiral the flat tinsels forward (when reverse-wrapping the ribs, you may wish to reverse the thread to more easily secure the tinsels).

**Step 5:** Now wrap the hackle forward in the normal direction, crossing over the ribs.

**Step 6:** Wrap the counter-rib forward in the opposite direction, following along the trailing edge of the flat tinsel and binding down the hackle stem.

**Step 7:** Add two turns of teal at the collar. If desired, create a clearing for the wing by removing and folding fibers on the top side of the fly.

**Step 8:** Mount the bronze mallard wings.

**Step 9:** The finished fly shows the typical low-set, slightly humped wing.

# DRESSING A CARRON FLY

In this example, I have chosen the later version of the Carron, which features an additional rib of scarlet silk as listed by Pryce-Tannatt. However, the version presented here is dressed on an eyed hook, with only two ribs and can be assembled quite rapidly, making it a pragmatic choice for fishing. It can be dressed even more rapidly than many hairwing patterns. The hackle, in this example, is black-dyed blue eared pheasant, reverse-wrapped without stripping either side.

| | |
|---:|:---|
| ***Hook:*** | Alec Jackson Spey Hook, No. 1.5-3 or Partridge CS10/1, No. 1-2 |
| ***Body:*** | Orange yarn strands |
| ***Ribs:*** | Scarlet silk and silver oval as a counter rib |
| ***Hackle:*** | Black-dyed blue eared pheasant or similar |
| ***Collar:*** | Teal flank |
| ***Wing:*** | Bronze mallard |

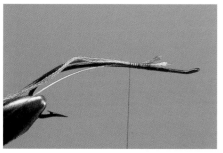

**Step 1:** At the front of the hook, attach the ribs and body materials.

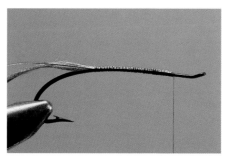

**Step 2:** Wrap rearward with the thread, binding down the materials along the shank. Return the thread to the front.

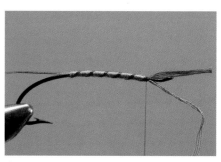

**Step 3:** Wrap the body materials forward and then rib with the scarlet silk.

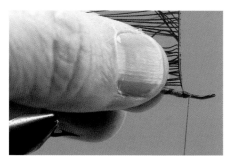

**Step 4:** Attach the hackle by its root at the front of the fly, then hand-fold the fibers as shown.

**Step 5:** Wrap the hackle rearward, using your left hand to free any fibers that get trapped forward. Then bring the oval tinsel forward, locking down the hackle stem.

**Step 6:** Attach the teal feather by its tip and fold the upper fibers as shown.

**Step 7:** Wrap a collar of just one or two turns of the teal flank.

**Step 8:** Add slender wings of bronze mallard.

# ADDITIONAL CLASSICS

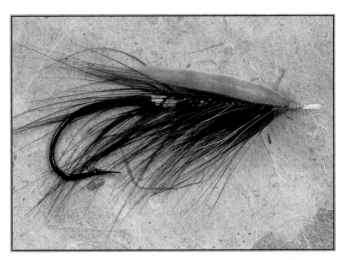

## LADY CAROLINE (dressed by Mark Waslick)

| | |
|---|---|
| *Tail:* | A few fibers from a golden-pheasant flank feather |
| *Body:* | An olive-brown mix of wool or dubbing |
| *Ribs:* | Medium or narrow gold flat tinsel; gold and silver twist (or oval) |
| *Hackle:* | Gray heron or substitute |
| *Throat:* | Two turns of golden-pheasant flank |
| *Wing:* | Bronze mallard |
| *Head:* | Black |

## SPEY DOG

| | |
|---|---|
| *Body:* | Black |
| *Rib:* | Wide silver and gold oval |
| *Hackle:* | Black rooster (coque or schlappen) reversed over tinsel by its roots |
| *Throat:* | Teal |
| *Wing:* | "A good wad of golden pheasant tail" and bronze mallard |

## NO. 1 FROM STODDART

| | |
|---|---|
| *Tail:* | A tuft of yellow or orange mohair, or similar |
| *Body:* | Black or brown mohair; or mixed black and brown pig's wool or similar dubbing |
| *Hackle:* | "Pendant breast feather of the male heron" (substitute blue eared pheasant or similar) |
| *Rib:* | Broad silver or gold lace |
| *Wing:* | Bronze mallard |

## NO. 2 FROM STODDART

| | |
|---|---|
| *Tail:* | A tuft of yellow or orange mohair, or similar |
| *Body:* | Black or brown mohair; or mixed black and brown pig's wool or similar dubbing |
| *Hackle:* | "Pendant breast feather of the male heron" (substitute blue eared pheasant or similar) |
| *Rib:* | Broad silver or gold lace |
| *Wing:* | A pair of crest feathers from the golden pheasant |

## THE DALLAS FLY (dressed by David Barlow)

(as per Kelson)

| | |
|---|---|
| *Body:* | Three turns of yellow wool, followed by black wool |
| *Ribs:* | Silver tinsel, gold tinsel (oval, narrow), red thread and blue thread, all running at equal distances apart |
| *Hackle:* | A black Spey cock's hackle (coque or schlappen) from end of body, but wound the reverse way, and so crossing over the ribs |
| *Throat:* | A red hackle from the golden pheasant |
| *Wings:* | Two strips of plain cinnamon turkey |
| *Head:* | Orange wool, picked out |

**Note:** Kelson writes: "This capital fly on the Spey was christened by Mr. Little Gilmore. Like other local patterns, the body is short and begins a full 1/8 of an inch in front of the point of the hook. The description given is from a pattern forwarded by Mr. C.M. Burn's Fisherman at Pitcroy; and proved to be correct by one being sent to me by Dallas himself."

## THE RED KING

(as per Kelson)

| | |
|---|---|
| *Body:* | Red Berlin wool (brick colour) |
| *Ribs:* | Gold from far side, silver tinsel (narrow) from near side, wound the reverse way and equal distances apart |
| *Hackle:* | A red Spey-cock hackle from the end of the body, but wound in the usual direction from the root instead of from the point, thus crossing over the ribs at each turn |
| *Throat:* | Teal, one turn only |
| *Wing:* | Two strips of mallard |

## GRAY HERON

(as per Pryce-Tannatt)

| | |
|---|---|
| **Body:** | First third, lemon Berlin wool; remainder, black Berlin wool |
| **Ribs:** | Flat silver tinsel; silver and gold oval tinsels |
| **Hackle:** | Gray heron or similar (substitute blue eared pheasant) |
| **Throat:** | Guinea |
| **Wings:** | Bronze mallard |

# THE BLENDING OF FLY STYLES

The purist in me resists the urge to mix elements of Dee flies with characteristics unique to Spey flies and to mix with either the fanciful elements of the full-dress salmon fly. Yet such resistance is at once both futile and misguided, for this inevitable blending of styles has driven fly evolution since the earliest times. Indeed, the Spey and Dee flies found themselves subjected to such evolution, if you will, even during their heyday.

As noted by 19th century authors, the Irish flies had invaded Scotland in the early decades of the 1800s. The newcomers brought with them new materials and new ideas about fly design. That the imports would affect local fly dressers was certainly inevitable and indeed soon local styles exhibited characteristics formerly associated with flies from other regions.

Fine examples of the blending of styles include the works of Major Grant, namely the Glen Grant, Mrs. Grant and Glen Grant Special.

Kelson says of the Glen Grant that it is an "old standard on the Spey." Perhaps it was a standard, but judging by its conspicuous use of jungle cock in the wing, it seems the fly could date no further than the 1860s and likely it is substantially more modern even than that. For starters, Kelson himself claims that jungle-cock plumage was first introduced to the Spey during the 1850s. Even more telling, however, is the fact that Major James Grant— the fly's inventor— was born in the year 1849.

Thus, in the case of the Glen Grant, "old" becomes rather relative when compared to the Reeach's and Speal's and Kings. Yet this single fly also serves nicely to illustrate the blending of styles, for it was devised by Major Grant for his river and features the typical cock's hackle wound through the body while simultaneously displaying quite prominently a hint of the exotic in the jungle-cock wings.

The prolific Grant also produced the Allan's Fancy and the Glen Grant Fancy. Kelson terms the former a "general standard" and the latter a "modern standard on the Spey." With their complex wings, both flies depart rather abruptly from the traditional Spey flies. If these flies by Major Grant were indeed standards on the river, then certainly the blending of styles had begun in earnest almost as soon as the Irish exotics arrived Speyside. Indeed, other 19th century Spey flies to survive the ravages of time include the beautiful Rough Grouse, recorded by Kelson

and deriving from the talented hands of John Cruickshanks, along with the Pitcroy Fancy, apparently devised by Turnbull and named for the Pitcroy Beat at Ballindalloch.

Contemporary tiers mix their media unabashedly and the resulting Spey-style and Dee-style dressings include many creations exhibiting both artistic and functional design. Included are Spey-style flies dressed with Victorian-style built wings, whose inherent beauty and complexity offer radical departure from the idea of "simple elegance."

In private correspondence, Dave Burns, the talented fly dresser from McCall, Idaho, summarizes the blending of styles rather well when he relates, ". . .I won't reiterate the stories of the Oxbow Spey and South Fork Salmon River Spey; except to remind you that the former is more Dee-like & the latter is more Spey-like, but neither is really either!"

Indeed, who can fault the fly dresser who, in designing such flies, is fully cognizant and intentional in abandoning more traditional tenets? If such flies achieve grace and flow and fish as they are intended then certainly their designers deserve credit for furthering the art of the Spey and Dee flies.

## THE GLEN GRANT (dressed by Gary Grant)

(Major Grant, as per Kelson)

| | |
|---|---|
| **Tail:** | Golden pheasant yellow rump (point) |
| **Body:** | Yellow wool three turns, and black wool |
| **Ribs:** | Silver lace and silver tinsel (usual way) |
| **Hackle:** | A black Spey cock hackle from the end of the body, but wound from root the reverse way crossing over ribs |
| **Throat:** | Teal |
| **Wings:** | Two long jungle cock (back to back), two reaching halfway, and two still shorter, and teal |
| **Head:** | Yellow wool |

"An old standard on the Spey."

**Note:** Just to avoid any confusion, the word "Glen" refers not to a person but to what we might term a ravine or narrow valley. Major Grant's whiskey distillery was (and is) named Glen Grant. The word derives from Gaelic and Welsh.

## THE MISS GRANT (dressed by John Shewey)

(as per Kelson)

| | |
|---|---|
| **Tag:** | Silver twist |
| **Body:** | Two turns of orange silk followed by olive-green Berlin wool |
| **Ribs:** | Silver tinsel |
| **Hackle:** | Grey Heron, from second turn (substitute blue eared pheasant) |
| **Wings:** | Two strips of Golden Pheasant tail |

"A modern Spey pattern."

## GLEN GRANT FANCY

(Major Grant, as per Kelson)

| | |
|---|---|
| **Tag:** | Silver twist and red-claret silk |
| **Tail:** | A topping |
| **Butt:** | Black herl |
| **Body:** | Light olive-green Seal's fur |
| **Rib:** | Silver tinsel |
| **Throat:** | Jay and teal |
| **Wings:** | Tippet strands, Gallina, light mottled turkey, Golden Pheasant tail, Mallard, and a topping |
| **Head:** | Black herl |

"A modern standard on the Spey."

Major James Grant, in 1872, inherited Glen Grant Distillery from his father, the distillery has enjoyed continual operation since its founding by the two Grant brothers John and James, in 1840. Years previous, the elder James Grant had participated in "The Raid on Elgin," the last of the Scottish clan risings, during which "hundreds of the men of the Clan Grant marched on the city from Strathspey to release their chief from the clutches of the lowland mob."

The Major married three times. His first marriage produced four sons and three daughters (Christina, Rose and Hilda). Presumably, Shanks named his Miss Grant pattern after one of the daughters. Iain Russell quotes the March 22, 1893 issue of *The National Guardian* as saying of the Major, "On the river he throws a line yards farther out than anyone else can do, and knows exactly where and how to lay it down for alluring the wily fish to his fly."

Russell also relates that, "The Major visited India and southern Africa during the 1890s, on hunting expeditions. We don't have any information about any fishing trips he may have made, although his recollection of visiting water holes in Africa in 1898 suggests he had other things than fishing on his mind: 'We had to take great care when we came to water holes that we were not caught by crocodiles, and we could only bathe in water a few feet deep, keeping a good look with a rifle beside us. When we came to a hole where there were crocodiles, we used to put in three or four dynamite cartridges and blow them up. This rather astonished them!' "

"According to family tradition," continues Russell, "when the Major was confined to his bed during what proved to be a fatal illness he was distraught at the prospect of missing his time on the river. He sent his grandson Douglas Mackessack and his youngest daughter Mary (from his third marriage) off with the gillie to fish the beat every day – although the gillie insisted there were few fish worth catching.

"An obituarist wrote in the *Moray and Nairn Express*, 9 May 1931, 'His greatest sport and pastime, however, was with rod and line on the Spey, and he soon became one of the finest anglers in the North. For many years he enjoyed a great reputation in this respect.' "

THE GLEN GRANT, A FANCIFUL SPEY FLY DESIGNED BY MAJOR JAMES GRANT DURING THE LATTER HALF OF THE 19TH CENTURY. DRESSED BY RICHARD YOUNGERS.

**THE ROUGH GROUSE** (dressed by John Shewey)
(John Cruickshanks)

| | |
|---|---|
| *Tail:* | Yellow macaw fibers or similar |
| *Body:* | Black wool yarn, thin and short |
| *Ribs:* | Silver and small silver oval over the hackle stem |
| *Hackle:* | Gray heron or similar from third turn of tinsel |
| *Throat:* | Speckled turkey or similar |
| *Wings:* | Strips of speckled white turkey |

Without question John Cruickshanks ranked amongst the most highly regarded salmon anglers in Speyside history. His father Charles had established Speyview Cottage at Aberlour and served as innkeeper until his tragic drowning in the massive flood of 1829, an event graphically and dramatically told by Sir Thomas Dick Lauder in *The Moray Floods*. Residing Speyside at Aberlour all his 70 years, John Cruickshanks gained a reputation as "the best living adept at the 'Spey cast,' throwing the line with a lightness and success almost unapproachable."(4). At the time of his death, a few days after Christmas in 1897, Cruickshanks had enjoyed 50-odd years' tenure as ghillie at Carron House, first employed there around mid-century as fisherman and keeper to William Grant. Subsequently he enjoyed continual employment by the Grants of Elchies until the time of his death.

Augustus Grimble, in *The Salmon Rivers of Scotland* relates that from the "celebrated Dalmonach Pool. . .the late J. Cruickshanks killed a fish of 42 lb., the heaviest ever got above Craigellachie Bridge." In fact, despite the fact that "to his own rod in one year there fell over one ton of fish," Cruickshanks had never killed a fish over 30 pounds until the year of his death. In

that season, fishing the Carron water, Cruickshanks killed two such brutes within eight days: The fish mentioned by Grimble may have weighed as much as 45 pounds and the other either 30 or 39 pounds, depending upon which source is accurate. (5).

Grimble reports further that, "Perhaps the most extensive collection of flies ever owned by one man was formed by the late Mr. H. Grant of Wester Elchies; they were tied by himself, Mr. Charles Grant, and Cruickshanks, and many hundreds were kept in a large box made from the timber of the Old Gean Tree of Elchies, the trunk of which had a diameter of four feet."

Certainly Cruickshanks was as talented a fly dresser as he was a salmon angler. Unfortunately, his precise contribution to the Spey-fly dresser's craft remains elusive. Kelson credits to him the Rough Grouse as listed at left, an elegantly designed fly that, when reasonably well dressed, no doubt represents the deft skill of its originator, a "famous fisherman, and considered by some as, perhaps, the best angler on the Spey."(6).

**THE GREEN QUEEN** (dressed by David Barlow)
(Kelson)

| | |
|---|---|
| *Tag:* | Gold tinsel (narrow) |
| *Tail:* | Yellow rump, Golden Pheasant (point) |
| *Body:* | Same mixture of Berlin wools as for "Green King" |
| *Ribs:* | Gold tinsel |
| *Hackle:* | Crown Pigeon or Grey Heron—one side of the feather stripped—from second turn |
| *Throat:* | Bittern dyed yellow—the white speckled feather |
| *Wings:* | Dark cinnamon Turkey with lightish points; or, better still, the "Gled." |

## End Notes

1. From Appendix II to the 1999 reprint of *Autumns on the Spey*.
2. From Alison Mitchell's *Speyside Gravestones*.
3. From *Chambers's Scot's Dictionary*, 1965.
4. From the Banffshire Herald, January 1, 1898.
5. In their respective editions for January 1, 1898, the *Banffshire Herald* and the

*Banffshire Journal* both published obituaries for John Cruickshanks, each story offering different weights for the two huge salmon landed by Cruickshanks in his final season.
6. From the *Banffshire Journal*, January 1, 1898.

# Chapter 9

# Tying The Classic Dee Flies

*". . .In truth there are two occasions on which they are
used—when fish are taking and when they are not."*

—*George M. Kelson*

---

Francis Francis offers the first detailed description of the so-called Dee flies and in doing so he gives dressings for the Gled Wing, Tartan and the Eagles. "Most of these flies" reports Francis, "are from Mr. Brown's patterns, the well-known tackle maker of Aberdeen, the inventor of the phantom minnow. He dresses them as few others can.

"*The Gled Wing* or *Red Wing*, as it is termed, is perhaps the most useful of the local flies. Tag, silver tinsel; tail, gold pheasant saddle; body, one-third orange-yellow, and two-thirds claret, or light purple claret mohair, dressed very sparely; broadish silver tinsel laid on rather thinly and in long spirals; black heron's hackle of the largest size, or two if one will not go far enough, dressed down to the yellow mohair. They must be of the longest fibre, the longer the better; teal hackle on the shoulder, without which no Dee fly is thought complete; wings, two good strips of swallow-tailed gled of the largest fibre, or of red dun turkey of the like colour. Of course these feathers must be of thin substance and fine in the fibre, to give them play, and they are to be set apart—a rather nice operation to do neatly, the strips requiring to be carefully prepared first by tying in at the extreme butt; no head, as it is thought to cause a ripple, while the sharp head of a regular Dee fly cuts the water with a smooth even gliding motion, opening and shutting its large fibres with most life-like appearance."

"*The Tartan* is a strange-looking fly and is rather a troublesome fly to dress. Tag, gold tinsel; tail, gold pheasant rump; body, half orange and half scarlet-red mohair laid on sparely, of course; broadish gold tinsel also spare; hackle, first a stripped sandy-red cock's hackle. . . and on top of this, the large blue-grey hackle feather from the heron's back and rump; the larger the better, they cannot be too large, as when the hackle is laid on, the fibres are expected to extend from the very head to the farthest bend of the hook. It is an awkward feather to lay on, as are all heron's hackles, being very delicate. It should be tied in, to commence from as low down as it can be conveniently tied, so as to leave enough for a good thick brush from the head. . .at the shoulder, a teal hackle of course. Wings, two strips of silver-grey mottled turkey (the small mottled feather); these feathers are not easy to get. . ."

"*The Eagle.*—There are two Eagles, the grey and the yellow. . .The tail, body, etc., are precisely similar to those of the gled wing; a quantity of the down or fluffy part of the golden eagle's feather—the part on and above the thigh is, I fancy, the best—is then wound on like a hackle, till the fly looks like the butt end of a largish eagle's feather itself; on the shoulder is of course the invariable teal hackle;

---

**ABOVE:** The Gardener (top) and Akroyd, classic Dee flies expertly dressed by Philip Glendinning of Aberdeen, Scotland.

**FACING PAGE:** Classic Dee flies by Philip Glendinning.

wings, two broadish strips of silver grey turkey; the large mottled or broad striped and banded feather being selected."

Later authors recorded many additional Dee dressings, although quite a substantial number have been more or less obscured by the passage of time. Aberdeen's Philip Glendinning has made a concerted effort to recover and record many of the forgotten patterns, including the Minister of Drumoak, whose photograph appears in Chapter 1. The aforementioned 19th century tackle dealers from Aberdeen—Garden and Brown as well as angler and sometimes-writer William Murdoch—are largely responsible for coining the majority of these old Dee flies.

Murdoch, in fact, compiled a list of dressings that appeared in a series of articles published in *The Fishing Gazette* during the 1880s. Interestingly, his dressings tend to vary from those later listed by Kelson, Pryce-Tannatt, Taverner and others. In fact, Murdoch's articles provide empirical evidence that—much like with the Spey flies—the well-known Dee patterns were subjected to many variations. He recorded three variations on the "Glentanar," labeling them as Glentanars I, II and III.

In any case, Deeside anglers reserved the classic flies primarily for spring fishing when the water ran high and cold. During the summer and fall they relied more on small hooks, ranging from complex, built-wing dressings to rather simple flies dressed on double irons. Because they were fished during spring, the Dee flies exhibited bodies dubbed thin and sparse, allowing them to sink more readily.

Dub the fur in small amounts and then pick it out afterwards using a bodkin or teaser. The ribs are generally pronounced and tightly wound so as to reinforce the fly's physical integrity. Ideally the Dee fly is tied on long-shank, light- or medium-weight hooks. Among contemporary hooks, good choices include the Partridge Long-shank Bartleet (available in sizes 1/0-3/0) and the Alec Jackson Blind Eye Hook. For fishing flies, I recommend a loop constructed of 30-pound Dacron backing material, treated with Sno-Seal (available at ski and outdoor stores). If you prefer an eyed hook, try the Alec Jackson Spey Hook or the Partridge Bartleet. Flies intended for winter steelhead fish well on the Partridge Code N, a medium-weight hook with a straight, relatively long shank.

CLOSE-UP OF THE EXACTING DETAIL OF A BRAD BURDEN AKROYD.

# DRESSINGS FOR CLASSIC DEE FLIES

I've taken the liberty of selecting dressings for these flies from various sources, including Kelson, Pryce-Tannatt, Maxwell and Francis. In addition, I have included dressings presented by the learned William Murdoch in his aforementioned articles, which appeared in *The Fishing Gazette* during the 1880s.

DAVID & GOLIATH: AKROYDS BY GEORGE "STACK" SCOVILLE.

## THE AKROYD
(as per Pryce-Tannatt)

| | |
|---|---|
| **Tag:** | Silver tinsel |
| **Tail:** | A topping and a tippet in strands |
| **Body:** | First half, light orange seal's fur (or Angora dubbing); second half, black floss (divide the halves with a joint of black ostrich herl) |
| **Rib:** | Oval silver tinsel over the orange seal's fur; a black heron's hackle over the black floss (substitute: dyed blue eared pheasant hackle) |
| **Throat:** | Teal |
| **Wing:** | A pair of cinnamon turkey tail strips |
| **Cheeks:** | Jungle cock, drooping |

**Note:** For the "White-winged Akroyd" substitute white turkey for the wing.

## THE BALMORAL
(as per Kelson)

| | |
|---|---|
| **Tag:** | Silver twist |
| **Tail:** | A topping and tippet strands |
| **Butt:** | Black herl |
| **Body:** | Green and dark blue seal's fur, equally divided (substitute: Angora dubbing) |
| **Ribs:** | Silver lace and silver tinsel (wide, flat silver tinsel) |
| **Hackle:** | Black heron through green fur (substitute: Angora dubbing) |
| **Throat:** | Widgeon (i.e. Eurasian widgeon; substitute: pintail flank) |
| **Wings:** | Two strips of plain cinnamon turkey |
| **Sides:** | Jungle cock, short and drooping |

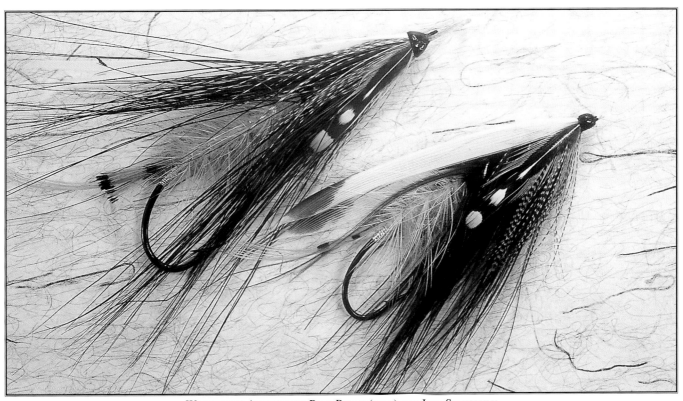

WHITE-WING AKROYDS BY PAUL PTALIS (LEFT) AND JOEL STANSBURY.

AKROYDS, BY G.S. SCOVILLE (TOP),
PAUL ROSSMAN AND ROBERT NEWMAN.

AKROYDS, BY ROGER PLOURDE (TOP),
STEVE SCHWEITZER AND SCOTT PETERS.

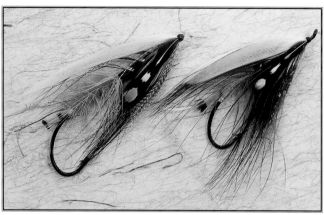

WHITE-WING AKROYDS BY BRAD BURDEN (LEFT) AND JON HARRANG.

## THE BALMORAL

(as per W. Murdoch)

| | |
|---|---|
| *Tag:* | Silver twist and orange silk |
| *Tail:* | A topping and tippet strands |
| *Body:* | 3/5 green and 2/5 black mohair (or similar) |
| *Ribs:* | Flat silver tinsel and gold twist |
| *Hackle:* | Black heron, "well down the body" |
| *Wings:* | Dark brown turkey with black tips |
| *Cheeks:* | Jungle cock |
| *Head:* | Black |

## THE DUNT

(W. Murdoch; as per Kelson)

| | |
|---|---|
| *Tag:* | Silver twist and light blue silk |
| *Tail:* | A topping and teal |
| *Body:* | Yellow, orange and red-claret seal fur in equal sections |
| *Ribs:* | Silver lace and silver tinsel |
| *Hackle:* | Black heron, from claret fur (substitute: dyed blue eared pheasant) |
| *Throat:* | Teal |
| *Wings:* | Two strips of plain brown turkey with black bars and white tips |
| *Sides:* | Jungle cock, short and drooping over throat hackle |

"Mr. Murdoch writes: 'There is not a better all-round of the plain sort than the Dunt put upon the Dee in Spring or Autumn.'"

## THE GARDENER

(W. Garden; as per Kelson)

| | |
|---|---|
| *Tag:* | Gold twist and crimson silk |
| *Tail:* | A topping and tippet strands |
| *Body:* | Yellow, green and dark blue seal's fur in equal divisions |
| *Ribs:* | Silver tinsel |
| *Hackle:* | A topping (as hackle) from yellow fur |
| *Throat:* | Black heron (or dyed blue eared pheasant) |
| *Wings:* | Two strips, plain cinnamon turkey |
| *Sides:* | Jungle cock (short and drooping) |

"One of Garden's best Dee patterns."

## THE GLED WING

(as per Francis Francis)

| | |
|---|---|
| *Tag:* | Silver tinsel |
| *Tail:* | Golden pheasant saddle |
| *Body:* | One-third orange-yellow, and two thirds claret or light purple-claret mohair |
| *Ribs:* | Broadish silver tinsel |
| *Hackle:* | A black heron's hackle of the largest size, or two if one will not go far enough, dressed down to the yellow mohair |
| *Shoulder:* | Teal |
| *Wings:* | Two good strips of the swallow-tailed gled or red dun turkey of the same color |

## THE GLENTANA

(W. Garden; as per Kelson)

| | |
|---|---|
| *Tag:* | Silver twist |
| *Tail:* | Red breast feather of golden pheasant |
| *Body:* | One-third light orange seal's fur and light claret seal's fur |
| *Ribs:* | Silver lace and silver tinsel |
| *Hackle:* | Black heron, from orange fur (or dyed blue eared pheasant) |
| *Throat:* | Widgeon |
| *Wings:* | Two strips of plain cinnamon turkey showing light points |

"An old Dee fly"

## THE GLENTANAR I

(as per W. Murdoch, March 1884)

| | |
|---|---|
| *Tag:* | Silver tinsel |
| *Tail:* | Golden pheasant rump |
| *Body:* | orange, and brown mohair |
| *Rib:* | Silver tinsel and gold twist |
| *Hackle:* | Black heron |
| *Throat:* | Teal |
| *Wings:* | Brown turkey |

**Notes:** Glentanar II is dressed the same except that the body is orange and claret instead of orange and brown.

## THE GLENTANAR III

(as per Murdoch, March 1884)

| | |
|---|---|
| *Tag:* | Silver tinsel |
| *Tail:* | Golden pheasant rump |
| *Body:* | Yellow, blue and orange mohair in equal portions |
| *Rib:* | Silver tinsel |
| *Hackle:* | Long black heron hackle |
| *Throat:* | Guinea |
| *Wings:* | Brown turkey showing light points |

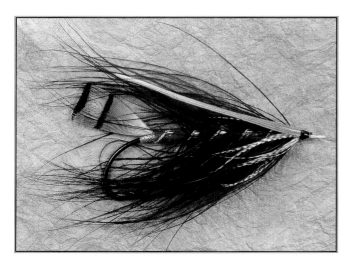

## THE GLENTANAR (dressed by Philip Glendinning)
(as per W. Murdoch, Feb. 1884)

| | |
|---|---|
| **Tag:** | Gold tinsel |
| **Tail:** | Golden pheasant tippet fibers |
| **Body:** | Orange, red and blue mohair in equal proportions |
| **Ribs:** | Gold tinsel and silver twist |
| **Hackle:** | Black heron |
| **Throat:** | Teal |
| **Wings:** | Natural red turkey |

## THE JOCK O'DEE
(as per Pryce-Tannatt)

| | |
|---|---|
| **Tag:** | Silver tinsel |
| **Tail:** | A topping and Indian crow |
| **Body:** | Two-fifths lemon-yellow floss, followed by black floss silk |
| **Ribs:** | Flat silver tinsel and silver twist |
| **Hackle:** | A gray heron hackle, wound from the third tinsel turn (or blue eared pheasant) |
| **Throat:** | Widgeon |
| **Wings:** | Two sections of cinnamon brown turkey |

## THE DEE TARTAN
(as per Sir Herbert Maxwell)

| | |
|---|---|
| **Tag:** | Gold tinsel |
| **Tail:** | A red rump feather of golden pheasant |
| **Body:** | Dressed thin, half orange, half scarlet pig's wool (or Angora dubbing) |
| **Ribs:** | Broad gold tinsel |
| **Hackle:** | Red cock's undyed over lower two-thirds of body. Above that a long-fibred blue-gray heron's rump feather, leaving a full mass at shoulder |
| **Throat:** | A pintail or teal hackle, tied above the wing |
| **Wings:** | Two long strips of silver-grey turkey |

## THE TARTAN
(as per W. Murdoch)

| | |
|---|---|
| **Tag:** | Silver tinsel |
| **Tail:** | Red cock hackle |

| | |
|---|---|
| **Body:** | 1/6 orange, 2/6, blue, 3/6 scarlet mohair (or similar) |
| **Ribs:** | Broad silver or gold tinsel |
| **Hackle:** | Gray heron, sparingly |
| **Throat:** | Teal |
| **Wing:** | Distinctly marked black-and-white turkey or brownish turkey |

## THE TRI-COLOUR
(as per Kelson)

| | |
|---|---|
| **Tag:** | Silver twist |
| **Tail:** | Red breast feather of golden pheasant |
| **Body:** | Yellow, light blue and scarlet seal's fur |
| **Ribs:** | Silver lace and silver tinsel |
| **Hackle:** | Natural gray heron, from blue fur (or blue eared pheasant) |
| **Throat:** | Widgeon (teal, large patterns) |
| **Wings:** | Two strips of plain, cinnamon turkey |

"A standard fly on the Dee, which, when dressed with a red breast hackle of the Golden Pheasant and with white (strips) wings, is known by the name of "The Killer."

## THE MOONLIGHT
(as per Pryce-Tannatt)

| | |
|---|---|
| **Tag:** | Silver tinsel |
| **Tail:** | Topping and a pair of jungle cock feathers |
| **Body:** | Front half, silver tinsel, veiled above and below with a pair (or two pairs) of Blue Chatterer feathers, back to back (substitute Asian Kingfisher); second half, black floss |
| **Ribs:** | Fine oval silver tinsel over flat silver tinsel; broader oval gold tinsel over black floss |
| **Hackle:** | A black heron's hackle over black silk |
| **Throat:** | Guinea |
| **Wings:** | White strips |

# THE EAGLE FLIES

## THE GREY EAGLE
(Jewhurst; as per Kelson)

| | |
|---|---|
| **Tag:** | Silver twist |
| **Tail:** | Red breast feather from the golden pheasant |
| **Body:** | Yellow, light blue, and scarlet seal's fur |
| **Ribs:** | Silver lace and silver tinsel |
| **Hackle:** | Gray eagle, from blue fur (substitute marabou) |
| **Throat:** | Widgeon (teal for large patterns) |
| **Wings:** | Two strips of brown mottled turkey, with black bars and white points |

"A well-known dark water fly on the Dee."

## THE YELLOW EAGLE

(as per Kelson)

| | |
|---|---|
| *Tag:* | Silver twist |
| *Tail:* | Red breast feather of the golden pheasant |
| *Body:* | Yellow, scarlet, and light blue seal's fur |
| *Ribs:* | Silver lace and silver tinsel |
| *Hackle:* | Eagle dyed yellow, from scarlet fur (substitute marabou) |
| *Throat:* | Widgeon (teal, large patterns) |
| *Wings:* | Two strips of gray mottled turkey having black bars and white points |

"A well-known dark water fly on the Dee."

## THE GOLDEN EAGLE

(Partridge; as per Kelson)

| | |
|---|---|
| *Tag:* | Gold twist and gold silk |
| *Tail:* | Tippet in strands |
| *Body:* | Gold and fiery brown pig's wool, equally divided |
| *Ribs:* | Gold tinsel |
| *Hackle:* | Eagle hackle dyed gold over one-third of body (substitute marabou) |
| *Throat:* | Teal |
| *Wings:* | Two strips of silver mottled turkey |

"An old standard at Ringwood."

## THE HALLIDALE EAGLE

(as dressed by Paul Rossman)

| | |
|---|---|
| *Tag:* | Silver tinsel and yellow silk floss |
| *Tail:* | Topping, red and green parrot, widgeon |
| *Butt:* | Black ostrich |
| *Body:* | 3/5 light yellow seal, 2/5 light orange seal |
| *Ribs:* | Two strands of silver oval |
| *Hackle:* | Golden eagle dyed yellow (substitute marabou) |
| *Wing:* | Two tippets, red and yellow swan, golden pheasant tail, golden mohair and a topping |
| *Sides:* | Double jungle cock |
| *Throat:* | Guinea |

## THE QUILLED EAGLE (dressed by Steve Gobin)

(as per Kelson)

| | |
|---|---|
| *Tag:* | Silver twist and quill dyed yellow |
| *Tail:* | Topping, and two strands of peacock herl (sword feather) of bustard and ibis |
| *Butt:* | Black herl |
| *Body:* | Quill dyed yellow, leaving space for four turns of orange seal's fur at the throat |
| *Ribs:* | Silver tinsel (oval) |
| *Hackle:* | A gray eagle feather, from centre (substitute marabou) |
| *Throat:* | Gallina (spotted feather) |
| *Wings:* | Two tippets (back to back) veiled with extending jungle cock, a strip of ibis and bustard, and a topping |
| *Sides:* | Jungle cock (to center of former pair) |

"I rarely use any other "Eagle" but this, though I sometimes dress it with a yellow instead of a grey hackle."

# DRESSING THE TRI-COLOUR

**Step 1:** Attach the tag and tail as described in Chapter 5.

**Step 2:** Next attach the two rib materials, both on the same side of the hook.

**Step 3:** Dress the rear third of the body with yellow seal and then attach the hackle by its tip.

**Step 4:** Now dress the rest of the body with blue and then scarlet dubbing.

**Step 5:** Spiral the ribs through the body and then follow with the hackle.

**Step 6:** Dress a collar of teal flank.

**Step 7:** Now mount the wings as described in Chapter 7.

**Step 8:** The completed fly, when viewed from above, exhibits the characteristic V-shaped wings.

# Chapter 10

# Northwest Classics: Syd Glasso, Dick Wentworth, Walt Johnson & Dave McNeese

*". . .if I did not crowd him on a riffle and approached him politely, there wasn't much he wouldn't share with me. . ."*

*—Bob Arnold speaking of Syd Glasso*

---

Syd Glasso's contribution to the Spey-tier's art is both monumental and well documented. Trey Combs recorded Glasso's steelhead patterns for the 1979 book *Steelhead Fly Fishing & Flies*. Some years later in his subsequent work titled *Steelhead Fly Fishing*, Combs added substantive additional details about Glasso. These references remain valuable recordings of the flies and contributions made by a man who can rightly be called the father of modern Spey flies.

Glasso inspired several of his contemporaries to delve into this style of fly tying, among them Dick Wentworth, Walt Johnson and Pat Crane. In private correspondence with me back in the early 1990s, Walt Johnson related the following:

"I had the good fortune to meet Syd Glasso in the early fifties while he visited Al Knudson at his camp next to mine on the North Fork of the Stillaguamish River. Syd invited me to come over to fish with him on the Olympic Peninsula streams for winter steelhead. I spent several years as his guest and at that time most of us were fishing bucktail or hair-winged patterns, but after seeing and using Syd's flies and [seeing] how effective they were, I wanted to learn more about this man and his beautiful creations.

"Syd was a perfectionist in both his tying ability as well as his angling prowess. Isolated more or less on the Peninsula, most of his talents were self taught. He took the Spey-style concept of the river in Scotland 100 or so years prior and created patterns particularly suited to the steelhead of his rivers, namely, Sol Duc, Calawah, Bogachiel, Hoh, Queets and Quillayute. His Orange Heron, Sol Duc, Sol Duc Spey, Black Heron and Courtesan are just a few which have attained legendary status.

"While the original Spey-fly design from Scotland had wings of bronze mallard flank or similar, Syd often substituted full-length hackle wings tied parallel on top of the body. I believe this concept was intended to obtain better action in the fly. The rivers of the Peninsula were short, swift and heavy with precipitous flow in the winter and the silk and nylon lines of the day were not noted for their sinking qualities. Syd told me that several years previous he had tried in vain to convince line manufacturers to develop [a fast-sinking line] to no avail. . .undaunted and working alone in his remote area, Syd set out to remedy his own problem.

---

ABOVE: GLASSO'S SOL DUC SPEY, BEAUTIFULLY DRESSED BY RICHARD YOUNGERS.

FACING PAGE: THE COURTESAN, A GLASSO PATTERN AS DRESSED BY JOHN SHEWEY.

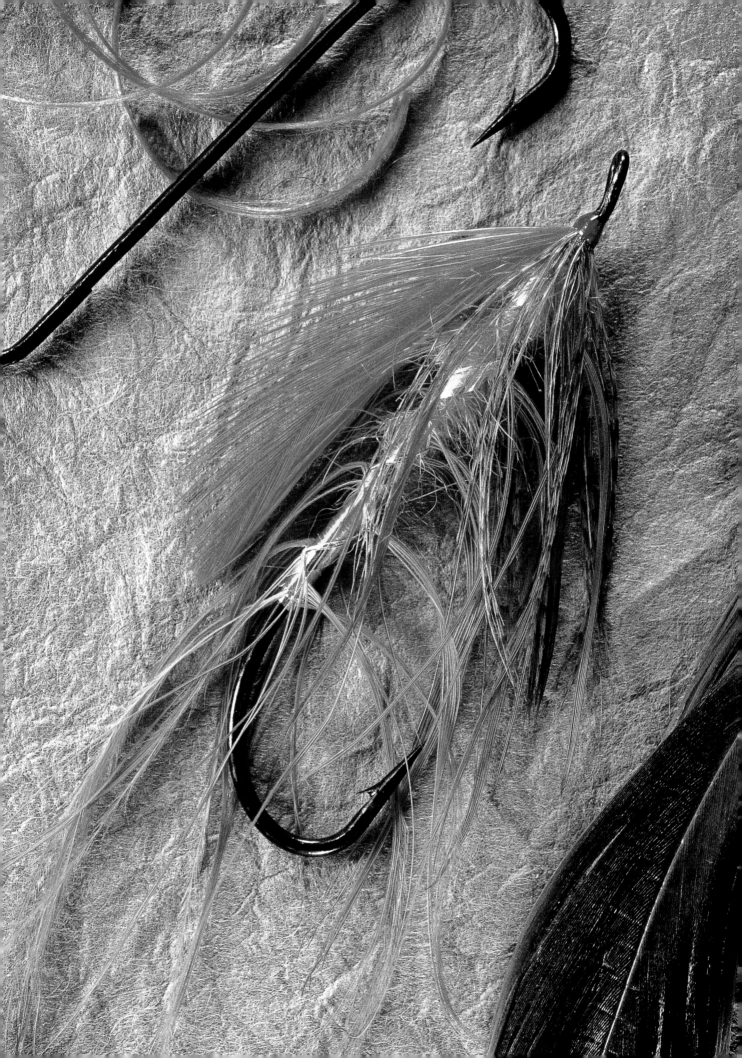

AN ORANGE HERON AS DRESSED BY JOHN SHEWEY.

By taking braided Dacron line and removing the finish, he would then rub on a coating of red lead with his fingers and then apply a subsequent coating of jap drier. He would hang this line horizontally in his basement, repeating the process until he had achieved the desired weight. This was determined by weighing on a grain scale. With this method, heads of varying weights were obtained for different water heights. He then added a loop on the back end and knotted on a monofilament running line. Although the line could not be mended or false cast, it certainly achieved the purpose of attaining immediate depth in the steelhead lies.

"Syd Glasso taught school in the small town of Forks, Washington on the Olympic Peninsula and had in his class at the time a young man named Dick Wentworth. With Syd as his mentor, Dick learned the art of tying from the master. Dick's gorgeous Spey flies today are a testimonial to the meticulous detail which evolved in his own creations. One of Dick's patterns was dedicated to Syd and named the "Mr. Glasso" in honor and respect for his dear friend. Dick became a very talented steelhead angler and is to this day admired by all his peers. He was also one of the best waders I have ever seen and I will always remember the day I witnessed him wade across the Quillayute directly below the confluence of the Sol Duc and Bogachiel Rivers. This is a feat I would not attempt and doubt many other anglers would either.

"As most of the anglers of my acquaintance during Syd Glasso's time used bucktail, hairwing and spider type patterns along with dry flies, I never had occasion to encounter many anglers fishing Spey flies, although no doubt there were a few. My long time fishing buddy Craig Shreeve was one but only after Syd moved to the Seattle area in his latter years did any great numbers [of fly dressers] succumb to fly's charms."

## TYING THE GLASSO FLIES

Syd Glasso and Dick Wentworth dressed their flies, such as the Orange Heron and Quillayute, in unique fashion, building the dubbing into the same floss used to build the butt section. This technique results in a gradual build-up of the body with no distinct segmentation between the silk portion and dubbed portion. This trick is accomplished by splitting the silk into two strands and then gently spinning the seal dubbing between those two strands.

Glasso's flies generally featured hackle-tip wings, although sometimes, even on his Orange Heron, he used quill segments. Included in Dave McNeese's collection is a badly moth-eaten specimen of an Orange Heron dressed by Glasso. Little remains, save the wings, which are dressed of hot orange goose shoulder slips, tied in the fashion of a salmon fly and set low over the body. Nonetheless, it is the hackle-tip wings that appear on most Glasso Spey flies. As Walt Johnson testifies, Glasso employed these wings because the hackle tips moved and breathed easily in the water.

Though quite unusual, hackle-tip wings enjoy some historical precedence; even some measure of fame. In 1897, on the Gordon Castle fishings, W.G. Craven killed the 53-pound record rod-caught salmon on the Spey. A.E. Gathorne-Hardy describes the event in *The Salmon* (1898), reporting in part that Craven ". . . was fishing the Dallachy Pool, not more than a mile from the sea, with a small No. 4 Carron fly, with lemon body, silver twist and black hackle wing, tied on a double hook. . ."

ORANGE HERON BY SCOTT O'DONNELL.

# DRESSINGS FOR SYD GLASSO AND DICK WENTWORTH FLIES

## GOLD HERON

(Glasso)

| | |
|---|---|
| *Body:* | Two thirds flat gold tinsel and one third hot orange dubbing |
| *Rib:* | Gold oval |
| *Hackle:* | Gray heron or substitute |
| *Throat:* | Widgeon or merganser |
| *Head:* | Orange |

## ORANGE HERON

(Glasso)

| | |
|---|---|
| *Body:* | Rear 2/3 orange silk, front 1/3 hot orange seal dubbing or substitute |
| *Rib:* | Medium flat silver and silver oval |
| *Hackle:* | Gray heron or blue eared pheasant |
| *Throat:* | Teal flank or hooded merganser flank |
| *Wing:* | Four hot orange hackle tips |
| *Head:* | Red |

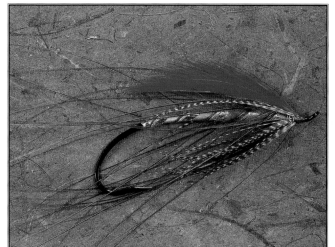

ORANGE HERON BY DEC HOGAN.

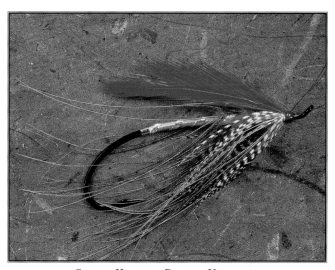

ORANGE HERON BY RICHARD YOUNGERS.

TWO VARIATIONS ON THE GLASSO BLACK HERON BY RICHARD YOUNGERS (LEFT) AND JOHN SHEWEY.

## BROWN HERON

(Glasso)

| | |
|---|---|
| ***Body:*** | Rear 2/3 orange silk, front 1/3 hot orange seal dubbing or substitute |
| ***Rib:*** | Medium flat silver and small silver oval |
| ***Hackle:*** | Gray heron or blue eared pheasant |
| ***Throat:*** | Teal, widgeon or hooded merganser flank |
| ***Wing:*** | Bronze mallard or widgeon |
| ***Head:*** | Red |
| ***Wing:*** | Bronze mallard, wigeon or merganzer |

## BLACK HERON

(Glasso)

| | |
|---|---|
| ***Body:*** | Silver flat tinsel overlaid at front third with black dubbing |
| ***Rib:*** | Silver oval |
| ***Hackle:*** | Gray heron (or substitute) |
| ***Throat:*** | Guinea |
| ***Wings:*** | Gray or black goose shoulder strips or hackle tips |

**Notes:** Obviously Glasso's version of the Black Heron differs substantially from the original.

## COURTESAN

(Glasso)

| | |
|---|---|
| ***Body:*** | Same as Orange Heron |
| ***Ribs:*** | Flat silver |
| ***Hackle:*** | Soft brown schlappen; long fibers |
| ***Throat:*** | Widgeon, merganser or none |
| ***Wing:*** | Four orange hackle tips |
| ***Head:*** | Red |

## SOL DUC SPEY

(Glasso)

| | |
|---|---|
| ***Tag:*** | Flat silver tinsel |
| ***Body:*** | Rear 2/3 orange silk; front, hot orange seal dubbing or substitute |
| ***Rib:*** | Flat silver tinsel |
| ***Hackle:*** | Yellow schlappen, from second turn of tinsel |
| ***Throat:*** | Black heron or substitute |
| ***Wing:*** | Four hot orange hackle tips |
| ***Head:*** | Red |

## QUILLAYUTE

(Dick Wentworth)

| | |
|---|---|
| ***Tag:*** | Silver |
| ***Tail:*** | Amherst topping |
| ***Body:*** | Orange floss and hot orange dubbing |
| ***Rib:*** | Medium flat silver |
| ***Hackle:*** | Teal flank, from second turn of tinsel |
| ***Throat:*** | Black heron substitute |
| ***Wing:*** | Four matching golden pheasant flank feathers |
| ***Topping:*** | Amherst pheasant topping |

## MR. GLASSO

(Dick Wentworth)

| | |
|---|---|
| ***Body:*** | Rear portion orange silk; front, hot orange seal dubbing or substitute |
| ***Rib:*** | Medium flat silver and silver oval |
| ***Hackle:*** | Blue eared pheasant, dyed black |
| ***Throat:*** | Guinea dyed hot orange |
| ***Wing:*** | Four hot orange hackle tips |
| ***Head:*** | Red |

## DRESSING THE ORANGE HERON

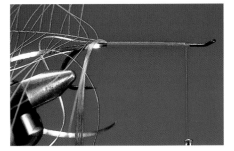

**Step 1:** Secure by its tip a gray hackle (blue eared pheasant, or similar). Then attach to the shank lengths of wide flat silver tinsel, small silver oval and hot orange silk (use two strands of silk on larger hooks).

**Step 2:** Form a butt of the orange silk, keeping the wraps even and smooth (using single-strand floss for the tying thread helps in building a smooth underbody).

**Step 3:** About 1/3 of the way forward, divide the silk into two strands as shown.

**Step 4:** Hold these strands close together in your left hand, maintaining tension on the strands.

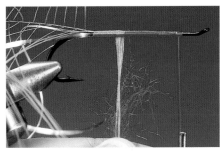

**Step 5:** With your right hand, insert sparse amounts of dubbing between the strands and then twist the silk strands with your fingers.

**Step 6:** Continue wrapping the silk forward, forming the remaining two-thirds of the body. The finished body should feature a gradual transition from silk butt to dubbed body.

**Step 7:** Now spiral forward with the tinsels, followed by the hackle. Form a collar of teal flank or similar.

**Step 8:** Mount the wings (four orange hackle tips). First align the hackles, then strip away the fibers below the tie-in point. Slip the bare stems into the eye of the hook as shown while you secure the wings.

**Step 9:** The finished Orange Heron.

# TYING THE WALT JOHNSON FLIES

Trey Combs wrote that, "Walt Johnson is best known in steel-head fly-fishing circles for developing some of the most beauti-ful—and most effective—wet flies in all of angling."

Indeed, I have often opened letters from Walt and found one of his beautifully crafted flies inside. Each of these treasures is designed and dressed in a manner that nearly begs the flies to be cast upon the river. Each time I've managed to resist the temptation, however, and my Walt Johnson steelhead flies remain the safe and cherished members of my fly collection.

Having never fished a Walt Johnson original, I decided the next best thing would be to learn how to dress them myself. In doing so, I discovered first-hand the creative toolings that pro-duce the signature look of a Walt Johnson Spey-style fly. His flies, at first glance, appear somewhat intricate and involved. Yet with a few tricks and a delicate touch, they are more easily con-structed than might be imagined. However, I've never quite cap-tured that Walt Johnson "look" unique to his flies—nor have I seen any other tier who can dress a Walt Johnson pattern the way Walt himself does.

Each of the Walt Johnson Spey flies is sparsely dressed and almost always they are tied on hooks no larger than size 2. The "Sasquatch of the Stilly" designed his flies for the gentle flows of his home river, Washington's North Fork Stillaguamish, near whose banks he still resides today.

Without question, Walt Johnson's contribution to steelhead tying and angling permeates every aspect of the sport that enam-ored him from before the second World War. He ranks among just a handful of men who, beginning in the 1930s and 40s, built the foundations for artistic steelhead flies. His patterns—Spey-style and otherwise—represent a rare combination of functional elegance, purposeful design and remarkable beauty. The beauty in Walt's patterns derives from their quiet simplicity and attention to detail. Each is a work of art.

I cherish my collection of Walt Johnson flies, each of them given to me by him over the years of our correspon-dence. Yet it is not their beauty and unique nature that causes me to treasure these flies among all the others in my collec-tion. Rather it is that Walt Johnson embodies my ideal steel-head fly-angler: He is generous almost to a fault—not just with his flies, but more significantly with his knowledge and his anecdotes. And despite his deserved reputation as one of the pioneering Washington steelheaders, Walt remains a study in humility. He at once deplores the "body count" mentality of many modern anglers yet when asked politely, he makes time for anyone wishing to benefit from his vast store of historical information.

TWO WALT JOHNSON ORIGINALS, THE RED SHRIMP SPEY (LEFT) AND AN UN-NAMED VARIATION, BOTH DRESSED BY WALT DURING THE EARLY 1990S.

# DRESSINGS FOR WALT JOHNSON FLIES

## DEEP PURPLE SPEY

| | |
|---|---|
| *Hook:* | Partridge Single Wilson |
| *Tag:* | Flat silver tinsel |
| *Body:* | Deep purple mohair |
| *Rib:* | Flat silver tinsel |
| *Hackle:* | Ring-necked pheasant rump hackle, brown |
| *Throat:* | Hen hackle dyed deep purple |
| *Wings:* | Two golden-pheasant flank feathers tented low over the body |

## RED SHRIMP SPEY

| | |
|---|---|
| *Hook:* | Partridge Single Wilson |
| *Tag:* | Flat silver tinsel |
| *Body:* | Fluorescent orange floss dubbed over with sparse red seal |
| *Rib:* | Flat silver tinsel |
| *Hackle:* | Ring-necked pheasant rump, dark brown |
| *Throat:* | Hen hackle dyed red |
| *Wing:* | Red hackles set low over the body |
| *Topping:* | Golden-pheasant crest |

## ROYAL SPEY

| | |
|---|---|
| *Hook:* | Partridge single Wilson |
| *Tag:* | Silver flat tinsel and cerise silk |
| *Body:* | Peacock herl with a band of fluorescent pink wool at center |
| *Hackle:* | Heron breast hackle (white center/black tips) dyed fluorescent pink* |
| *Throat:* | Hen hackle dyed fluorescent pink |
| *Wing:* | Two light-blue hackles set low over the body |
| *Cheeks:* | Lady Amherst pheasant tippet dyed kingfisher blue |

## GOLDEN SPEY

| | |
|---|---|
| *Hook:* | Partridge single Wilson |
| *Body:* | Fluorescent yellow floss dubbed over with sparse yellow seal |
| *Rib:* | Embossed gold tinsel |
| *Hackle:* | Heron breast hackle dyed golden-olive* |
| *Throat:* | Hen hackle dyed tangerine |
| *Wing:* | Two light brown hackles set low over the body |
| *Topping:* | Golden-pheasant crest |
| *\*Substitute:* | Tip-dyed marabou hackles in appropriate shade. |

WALT JOHNSON'S DEEP PURPLE SPEY AS DRESSED BY JOHN SHEWEY. PHOTO BY JIM SCHOLLMEYER.

## UN-NAMED

| | |
|---|---|
| **Hook:** | Alec Jackson gold, No. 1.5-5 |
| **Tag:** | Two turns fine embossed gold |
| **Body:** | Yellow dubbing |
| **Hackle:** | Golden-yellow dyed pheasant, heron or schlappen, from third turn |
| **Throat:** | Red orange and then light pink hackle, soft |
| **Wing:** | A matched pair of cerise-dyed hen hackles, tented over the body |
| **Sides:** | Matched tangerine-dyed hen hackles, extending about half-way along the wings |
| **Topping:** | Dyed-red golden-pheasant crest |
| **Head:** | White |

# DRESSING THE RED SHRIMP SPEY

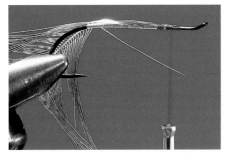

**Step 1:** Dress the tag by attaching flat tinsel at the front and wrapping rearward, reversing direction above the hook point. Then attach the hackle at front by its tip.

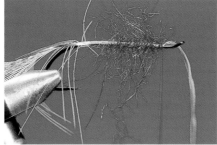

**Step 2:** Attach a length of orange silk and silver tinsel at front. Wrap the silk rearward, binding down the tinsel. At the rear, reverse direction, forming the butt. About a third of the way up the shank, split the silk and spin red dubbing into the strands. Wrap forward to the front (this is the same technique as outlined for the Orange Heron).

**Step 3:** Wrap the rib forward, followed by the hackle.

**Step 4:** Dress a collar of red hen neck.

**Step 5:** Mount the wings and add a topping.

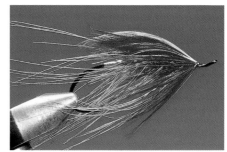

**Step 6:** Completed Red Shrimp Spey.

# THE DAVE MCNEESE FLIES

Dave McNeese's contribution to the Spey-tier's art has been largely understated in contemporary literature. Yet McNeese ranked among the very first "modern" enthusiasts to embrace this style of tying. His initial introduction to the Spey flies began with his meeting Syd Glasso in the early 1970s. At the time, steelhead Spey flies were little known outside of Glasso's immediate influence. It was McNeese who introduced a new generation of Oregon tiers to this style and by pure happenstance his audience included Deke Meyer and myself, both of us struggling as outdoor writers and both of us eager to sell articles derived from the gold mine of creative fly-tying that surrounded McNeese's Fly Shop during the 1980s.

McNeese Spey-style flies dating from 1975 through 1990 are rather hard to come by, yet I managed to save a few from the ravages of the fly shop. McNeese rarely stored collectible flies properly and hardly ever kept many of his own Spey flies for any length of time. His earliest flies are amongst the most intriguing, for they proclaim at once Dave's capacity for creative expression. He was and is a master at combining colors, materials and methods that produce flies with perfect flow and symmetry.

Without question, Dave McNeese and McNeese's Fly Shop propelled the art of steelhead and Spey-fly tying to new heights. His influence was felt throughout the region and many of today's top tiers reflect in their own work the innovative tying style and attention to artistic detail of Dave McNeese.

McNeese himself contributed several articles on the Spey-style flies. These appeared in Dick Surette's *Fly Tyer Magazine,* which became the popular *American Angler* published by Abenaki Publishers. A few years ago, Abenaki revived the old title and now publishes *Fly Tyer,* along with *American Angler.* In any event, Dave's articles appeared during the early days of the publication, whose circulation at the time was minimal. Yet Dave's articles intrigued a rather broad audience.

Among McNeese's various ingenious tying tricks are several methods of dubbing with coarse furs such as seal and Angora. Soon after meeting McNeese, I was fortunate in watching him dress a large hair-wing steelhead fly in which he spun the fur into the thread by hand, very loosely, and then used a coat of varnish to bind the hairs in place. The effect is a long-lasting body of shaggy, well-picked-out dubbing. He applied this same tactic to many of his Spey-style flies.

A HILTON SPEY VARIATION BY DAVE MCNEESE. THE FLY FEATURES A "BUNCHED" WING OF EURASIAN WIDGEON FLANK.

# RETURN OF THE SPEY FLY

By Dave McNeese (1983)

My affection for Spey patterns began in 1974 when I first met Syd Glasso, the reclusive tier from Washington. I gave Syd two hooded merganser skins in exchange for several Spey patterns he tied for me from the prized flank feathers. As I watched him tie his Brown Heron Spey fly and others, never had I seen such elegant, slender flies. These flies became examples I would duplicate in color and in materials, but not necessarily in the Glasso style, as I have my own. It is sad so little has been published about Syd as his 1982-83 salmon-fly patterns demand a price equal to that of the finest salmon tiers of all time, including Megan Boyd or George Kelson. He was a very private person and seemed to feel unworthy of the attention he received for his fly-tying skills.

In 1983 I obtained a very large collection of Atlantic salmon flies from Scotland dated from 1845 to 1910. Besides the magnificent fully-dressed salmon flies, there were several dozen Spey patterns, each labeled by date and name of pattern. These were all unfished and in excellent condition. The patterns were tied with a variety of material such as widgeon flank, barred land rail, kite flank, heron and spey cock hackles. Most any long hackle that the local Scottish tier could get went into simple patterns in the period from 1840 to 1880. Patterns were later more refined and bright body colors became prominent. Heron and Spey cock became the standard hackles. The Spey cock disappeared in the early 1900s, leaving heron as the main source of long hackle for Spey flies.

Feathers for Spey flies have lately become a problem since England no longer sells heron hackles and the only supply now comes from old stock or road kills, which are rare. Having examples of the old Spey patterns, I can suggest many good alternatives: brown (American) widgeon flank, coot rump, ring-necked pheasant rump, and pheasant tails of the ring-neck, silver, Amherst, and golden. My favorite of these would be the pheasant tails.

I have found the best method of making long hackles for Spey flies is by stripping the pheasant tails with chlorine bleach. I cut the tail section into 4" to 6" pieces, then submerge them into 1 gallon of hot water mixed with one cup of bleach. Within a few minutes the fibers will slowly start to separate as the hurl burns away. Caution must be taken here so as not to leave the feathers in the bleach bath too long or they

SPAWNING SPEY VARIATION BY DAVE MCNEESE.

**Purple Spey** 2,1/0

Bronze MALLARD
Purple Hackle tips, showing
Silver Tinsel
Fine S. oval
Black Heron
Guinea Throat

**Brown Heron**

Hooded Merganser 1/0
Gold Tinsel Flat – Fine Oval
Lt Orange Seal
Hot Orange up front
Brown Heron
Teal Throat

**Orange Heron** 2,4/0

Topping Golden Ph.
Orange Hackle tip
Silver Tinsel Flat
Fine oval
Grey Heron – Butt. Fluor. Orange Floss
Orange Seal
Teal or Grizzly Hackle

**Grey Heron** 4,1/0

Silver tinsel. Butt, Fine Oval
Black Seal
Black Heron
Spotted Guinea
Iron Dun Hackle tips

**Orange Heron** 4,2

3 Toppings. Golden Ph. Dyed Orange
Silver Tinsel – Fine oval
Black Heron – Fluor Orange Floss – Lt Orange Seal
Throat – Widgeon

**Hilton Spey** 4-4/0

Silver Tinsel. Butt. Forward
Fine Oval
Black Seal
Grey Heron
Teal Throat
Grizzly Hackle tips

**Spawning Spey** 1/0 – 4/0

Orange Golden Ph. Tail
Flour. Orange Floss 1/3
Hot Orange Seal
Silver tinsel, Fine Oval
Orange Heron, Two Turn Purple Heron Throat
Long Teal Throat
Golden Pheasant Tippet. Bundle
Hot Orange Hackle tips Set on top

Forming Solid Hackle tip Wing
Larger, Set on Sides!
Slender Hackle tip Set First

DAVE MCNEESE OFTEN PLANS OUT HIS FLY DESIGNS ON PAPER BEFORE CRAFTING THEM AT THE VICE,
LEAVING A VALUABLE REFERENCE ABOUT CONSTRUCTION.

will become thin and brittle. After bleaching, you can dye the tail. Silver pheasant, which becomes white after bleaching, is easily dyed any color.

Following are directions for tying the pheasant-tail fibers around the hook shank for the Glasso Brown Heron:

1. Usually I have fluorescent orange floss on a bobbin and use this like thread tying down both flat and oval tinsel. Starting behind the eye, run the shank with floss and tinsel to above the hook point. Then start forward, with floss only, to 1/3 of the shank length.
2. At this point I tie in small amounts of orange seal or other dubbing. Spin this on to the floss and wrap two turns forward.
3. Next tie down a dozen pheasant-tail fibers on top of the hook shank. Rotate the fibers evenly around the hook shank with your fingers. Add more dubbing to the floss and wrap forward. Repeat the same step with the pheasant fibers, continuing forward to the throat area. Here I add another pinch of fibers, but keep them on the under side of the hook shank. This helps keep the wing very low.
4. Bring flat and oval tinsel forward, and tie off under the throat area. Tie in teal and make two tight turns, tying off.
5. Tie in sections of bronze mallard for the wings, extending to the end of the floss.

## UN-NAMED, CIRCA 1977

| | |
|---|---|
| *Butt:* | Yellow silk |
| *Body:* | Brick red dubbing |
| *Ribs:* | Medium flat silver |
| *Hackle:* | Brick red cock hackle from second turn and gray heron from rear |
| *Throat:* | Hooded merganser |
| *Wings:* | Sections of golden-pheasant tail |
| *Head:* | Claret |

**Notes:** This is one of McNeese's very early Spey-styles, designed and tied the same year that Dave opened his fly shop in Salem, Oregon. Among the McNeese flies in my collection, it remains a favorite.

AN UN-NAMED DAVE MCNEESE ORIGINAL.

LIGHT UMPQUA SPEY VARIATION BY DAVE MCNEESE. NOTE THE BODY COMPRISED OF LAYERED VEILINGS OF ASIAN KINGFISHER RUMP FEATHERS.

## LIGHT UMPQUA SPEY

| | |
|---|---|
| *Tag:* | Silver tinsel |
| *Rib:* | Wide gold oval and counter of fine gold oval |
| *Body:* | 2/5 kingfisher blue and 3/5 black seal or similar |
| *Hackle:* | Gray heron or blue eared pheasant |
| *Collar:* | A turn of blue marabou or pheasant then blue-dyed mallard |
| *Wing:* | White goose shoulder, each topped with a small kingfisher rump feather |
| *Cheeks:* | Jungle cock |
| *Head:* | Bright red |

## BROWN HERON

(a.k.a. River Spey), circa 1984

| | |
|---|---|
| *Body:* | Rear 2/5 orange floss, then hot orange seal |
| *Ribs:* | Medium flat gold |
| *Hackle:* | Black heron shoulder or similar |
| *Throat:* | A turn of pintail or mallard |
| *Wings:* | Hooded merganser flanks, paired and tented over body |
| *Head:* | Black |

**Notes:** In my collection I have the proto-type of this Glasso-inspired pattern by McNeese and at the time (around 1984 if my memory serves faithfully), Dave referred to this pattern simply as the "River Spey." Later, in Trey Combs' 1991 work *Steelhead Fly Fishing*, the same fly appears with the title "Brown Heron." This latter version differs only in the use of gray hackle for the body, though I prefer the original version, listed here. Often McNeese would add jungle cock and a dyed-orange topping.

## KNOUSE

| | |
|---|---|
| *Tag:* | Fine flat silver tinsel |
| *Tail:* | A topping, dyed purple and fruit crow or substitute |
| *Body:* | A butt of fluorescent red floss, then hot pink seal followed by purple seal |
| *Rib:* | Medium silver oval |
| *Hackle:* | Hot pink Spey hackle (schlappen, coque, etc), through purple seal |
| *Throat:* | Long purple-dyed pintail flank |
| *Wing:* | Purple-dyed pintail flank topped with purple-dyed topping |
| *Cheeks:* | Jungle cock |

# Chapter 11

# Tying Contemporary Spey & Dee Flies

*"I enjoy flies so much that I rarely stick with one pattern for very long.
That is I like taking advantage of the steelhead's aggressive nature,
by hooking them on a steady diet of new patterns and colors."*

—Dec Hogan

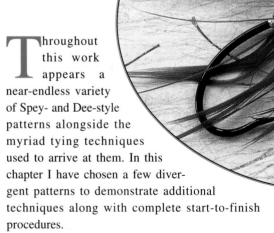

Throughout this work appears a near-endless variety of Spey- and Dee-style patterns alongside the myriad tying techniques used to arrive at them. In this chapter I have chosen a few divergent patterns to demonstrate additional techniques along with complete start-to-finish procedures.

Essentially, a broader selection of materials available to today's tier differentiates the contemporary Spey- and Dee-style flies from those of decades long past. Along with these new materials arrive a few new tying techniques peculiar to them. For the most part, however, today's fly dressers rely on the same diverse array of tying methods dreamt up by creative minds long ago.

Given the many effective methods of arriving at the same end product, it goes almost without saying that there exist any number of "right" ways to tie these flies or to dress the various parts therein. The patterns that follow continue the theme presented throughout this work: Namely that beautiful, durable and functional flies arrive by way of a wide number of different tying procedures and applications of materials.

**ABOVE:** MIKE KINNEY'S DRAGON'S TOOTH AS DRESSED BY JOHN SHEWEY.

**FACING PAGE:** CREAMSICKLE SPEY AND PURPLE PLUS, FANCIFUL SPEY-STYLES DESIGNED AND DRESSED BY JOE HOWELL.

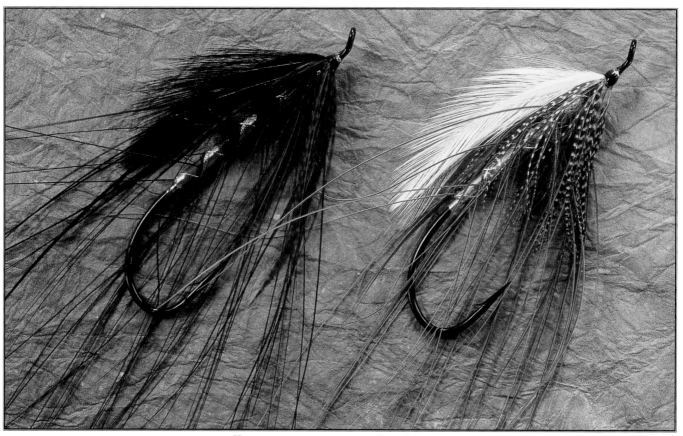

HERON VARIATIONS DRESSED BY JOHN SHEWEY.

STEVE GOBIN'S SKYKOMISH DARK AS DRESSED BY JOHN SHEWEY.

SKAGIT MIST AND SKAGIT STORM BY DEC HOGAN.

SPEY DESIGNS BY RICHARD YOUNGERS.

D.C. CUTTHROAT SPEY BY RICHARD YOUNGERS.

MIDNIGHT MADNESS BY JOE HOWELL.

STEELHEAD AKROYD BY DAVID BARLOW.

HARLEQUIN SPEY, A HAIR-WING DESIGN BY STEVE BROCO.

# DRESSING THE SANTIAM SPECTRUM

| | |
|---|---|
| *Tag:* | Flat silver tinsel |
| *Body:* | Fluorescent red single-strand floss, then purple wool yarn or dubbing |
| *Ribs:* | Silver oval and fine silver oval counter-rib |
| *Hackle:* | Bleach-burned goose shoulder, dyed purple |
| *Collar:* | Teal flank |
| *Wings:* | Strips of purple goose shoulder |

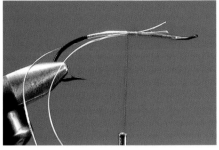

**Step 1:** Using the single-strand floss as tying thread, dress the tag (beginning the tinsel near the front of the shank) and attach the two rib materials.

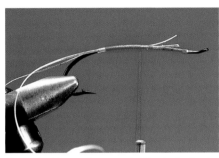

**Step 2:** Form the rear half of the body with the single-strand floss, wrapping rearward and then forward to form a double layer.

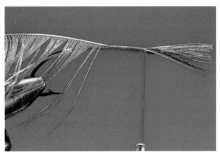

**Step 3:** At the front of the hook, attach the hackle by its tip and then wrap rearward so the first turn of hackle will begin at mid-shank.

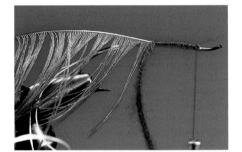

**Step 4:** Switch to a small red thread and then attach a length of purple wool yarn.

**Step 5:** Wrap the wool yarn forward to form the front half of the body.

**Step 6:** Spiral the rib forward, working around the hackle.

**Step 7:** Wrap the hackle forward and then bring the counter-rib forward in the opposite direction.

**Step 8:** Make two turns of teal as a collar.

**Step 9:** Mount a pair of purple goose shoulder strips for the wing.

# DRESSING THE PURPLE BEDSPRINGS

| | |
|---|---|
| *Tag:* | Gold tinsel and orange silk |
| *Tail:* | Golden-pheasant crest, dyed hot orange |
| *Body:* | 2/5 hot orange, 3/5 deep purple dubbing |
| *Rib:* | Gold oval and fine gold oval counter |
| *Hackle:* | Purple marabou or purple-dyed blue eared pheasant through front 3/5 of body |
| *Collar:* | Natural gadwall flank or purple-dyed teal |
| *Wing:* | Bronze mallard or purple-dyed bronze mallard |

**Step 1:** Wrap a tag of flat gold tinsel. Then attach a strand of fine orange silk.

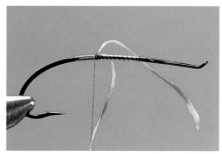

**Step 2:** Wrap the silk rear-ward, covering all but two turns of the gold tinsel. Reverse directions with the silk and wrap back to starting point.

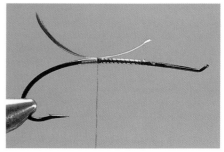

**Step 3:** Mount a tail of dyed golden-pheasant crest feathers. Secure the tail with three turns of thread, purposefully tying it slightly too long. Then pull forward into the correct position, trapping a few of the long fibers under the thread wraps before securing.

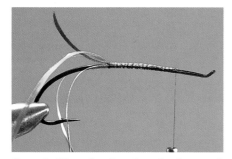

**Step 4:** Wrap the thread to the front and attach the tinsels along with another length of orange silk. The medium oval runs along the far side of the hook shank and the fine oval, along the near side. Maintaining this positioning, run the thread rearward to secure the ribs and silk and then return the thread to the front.

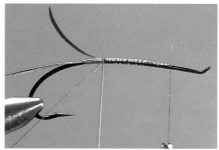

**Step 5:** Now split the silk into two strands as shown, holding them apart with your fingers.

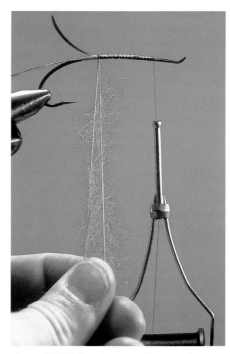

**Step 6:** Holding the two silk strands close together in your left hand as shown, insert sparse amounts of dubbing between the strands.

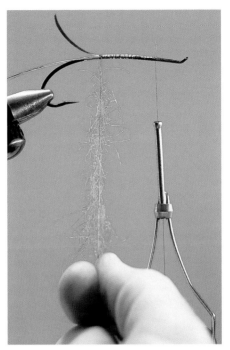

**Step 7:** Now spin the two strands together with your fingers, locking in the dubbing.

**Step 8:** Wrap the silk forward, creating the rear portion of the body. Do not cut away the remaining silk as this will be used to create the front portion of the body.

**Step 9:** As shown, select a prime marabou feather featuring a thin stem and fibers with minimal fuzz, especially on their outer half.

**Step 10:** Leaving about an inch or so of the "sweet spot," attach this marabou plume by its tip as shown, binding it down along the hook shank.

**Step 11:** Again split the silk into two strands, insert the purple dubbing, twist, and wrap the forward portion of the body in the same manner as the rear portion. Spiral the medium oval through the body forming the rib.

**Step 12:** Using the blade of your scissors, fold the top fibers on the marabou plume. (See Chapter 6 for folding instructions).

**Step 13:** Wrap the hackle forward, following behind the rib and then bring the counter-rib through the hackle in the opposite direction.

**Step 14:** Dress the collar, using two turns of gadwall flank or similar.

**Step 15:** Mount the wings to envelop the upper portion of the body and hackle fibers.

# DRESSING THE SUNBURST SPEY

| | |
|---:|:---|
| *Tag:* | Fine silver oval and yellow silk |
| *Tail:* | A topping |
| *Body:* | Silk in three parts: orange, red-orange, purple |
| *Ribs:* | Small flat gold and fine oval gold as a counter |
| *Hackle:* | Orange hackle (bleached and dyed blue eared pheasant or marabou) |
| *Collar:* | Ring-necked or blue eared pheasant, dyed black |
| *Wings:* | Turkey tail, married: orange and red, purple in between and at edges; a topping |
| *Cheeks:* | Jungle cock, optional |
| *Head:* | Bright red |

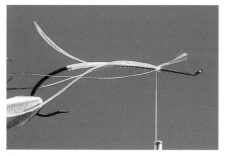

**Step 1:** Dress the tag and tail as shown (see Chapter 5). Then return the thread to the front and attach the tinsels and the yellow silk.

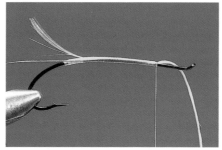

**Step 2:** Wrap the orange silk rearward, binding down the tinsels; at the rear, reverse direction and form the first third of the body. Continue wrapping the orange silk back to the front and tie off.

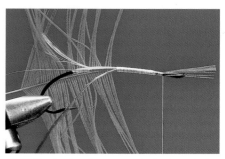

**Step 3:** At the front, attach the hackle by its tip along with the red-orange silk. Wrap the thread rearward binding down both materials. At the 1/3 mark, reverse direction and return the thread to the front.

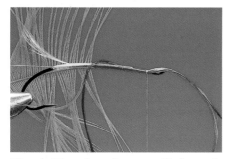

**Step 4:** Wrap the red-orange silk forward. At the 2/3 mark, slip a length of purple silk under the last turn or two of the red-orange silk (for weight, you may wish to attach hackle pliers to the red-orange silk while doing this).

**Step 5:** Wrap forward with the purple silk, binding down the tag ends. Wrap the flat tinsel forward.

**Step 6:** Fold and wrap the hackle and the counter-rib.

**Step 7:** Dress the collar with a turn or two of the black hackle.

**Step 8:** Mount the wings and topping and add the jungle cock sides.

LA PATRIOTE (LEFT) AND LA TOUQUE, ARTISTICALLY DESIGNED DEE-STYLE FLIES BY JEAN PAUL DESSAIGNE.

# Chapter 12

# Fishing Spey & Dee Flies

*A birr! A whirr! the salmon's out,*
*Far on the rushing river;*
*Onward he holds with sudden leap,*
*Or plunges through the whirlpool deep,*
*A desperate endeavour!*
*Hark to the music of the reel!*
*The fitful and the grating:*
*It pants along the breathless wheel,*
*Now hurried—now abating.*

*—Thomas Tod Stoddart*

Few avenues in fly-angling offer the satisfaction of hooking and beaching a fine fish on a well-dressed fly deriving from one's own hands. Nowhere is this satisfaction more profoundly felt than when fishing elegant and artfully dressed flies for steelhead or salmon. Hence my own fascination with these flies and with the Spey and Dee styles in particular.

Like so many other Spey-fly enthusiasts, my first introduction to the style came in the pages of Trey Comb's first book. At the time I simply admired the Glasso flies appearing in that single tantalizing black-and-white photo. When Trey's second book arrived I was hooked and shortly thereafter I began my long-time association with Dave McNeese. It was he who inspired me to lend more of my fly-dressing attentions to the style. By the time my first book arrived, I was a thoroughly dedicated Spey-fly enthusiast whose work often bore the mark of McNeese's strong influence. Many of the flies I tied and fished during the 1980s combined elements of both Spey and Dee flies and it wasn't until the latter part of that decade that I developed my interest in the classic Spey flies.

While working on this text, I consulted the little notebook I first began keeping in the mid-1980s. In reviewing its pages I found many patterns that once adorned the clips in my Wheatley but which have since fallen into the realm of little used and oft-forgotten flies. Nonetheless, I habitually fished all of my designs, for I've always cherished that moment when a newly devised pattern connects with its first steelhead. In this regard, I find a kindred spirit in the aforementioned Dec Hogan, whose dressings I always admire.

A current review of my battle-scarred Wheatley finds a dozen Spey-style flies. Several variations of the Orange Heron stand bright and tall amidst a collection of more somber offerings. Of the latter, I find a Cummings Special Spey, two Black Riachs, an Eagle Rock Riach and a Bogus Creek Riach. Slightly chewed, this latter fly accounted for back-to-back steelhead on the first morning of a September stay on the upper waters of the North Umpqua. The oldest fly in the box is a service-worn Bedsprings Spey and next to it a Carron, also bearing the scars of swimming many pools.

ABOVE: HALLOWEEN HERON, A VARIATION BY JOHN SHEWEY.
FACING PAGE: READY FOR THE RIVER: AN ORANGE HERON DRESSED BY JOHN SHEWEY.

In turning the leaf on this old Wheatley, I find my collection of Spawning Purples, Purple Matukas and a variety of hairwings; but here too I find two additional Spey-styles. One is a nameless fly, made up on the hoof a few years back and whose purple silk body and gray hackle were brutalized by a late-season buck of about 12 pounds. The other is a tiny rendition of the Carron, tied on a No. 4 hook, and dressed sleek and small.

Missing from the box are many flies that, at one time or another over the past two decades, I would have listed among my standards. Some have been superceded by newer designs; others have fallen victim to my habit of reserving but minimal tying time for filling my own boxes. In all cases, however, I fish the flies I design and those examples not intended for fishing are dressed as if they were meant for nothing else. My only exception is reserved for those flies specifically dressed for framing, in which case I allow myself the leniency of securing only the shortest length of gut on blind-eye hooks.

I've yet to find a Spey or Dee that won't fish, the steelhead in my home rivers apparently being substantially less particular about flies than the anglers pursuing them. Therein lies the inherent beauty of these anadromous fish: For reasons completely unknown to even the most accomplished of anglers, steelhead and Atlantic salmon are prone to grab hold of just about anything at one time or another. Far from concerning myself with their unpredictable natures, I take the peculiarities of these fish to heart and treat their inexplicable behaviors as an invitation to dress my flies for reasons other than what I think might attract their attention. Instead, I dress the flies that appeal to me. Then I fish with purpose, striving always to improve in the areas that matter far more than fly choice, these being the conjoined arts of presenting the fly the right way and in the right place.

## DOES THE FLY MATTER?

Much conflicting and confusing information surrounds the issue of fishing Spey and Dee flies. Some say they fish best in fast flows; others insist they fish better in slow flows. Heated arguments have ensued over whether the Spey fly fishes better with one side of the hackle stripped or with the hackle left full. Other debates rage over the best hooks and best wing-styles.

Before tackling any of these questions, I must first insist that the angler doing the fishing exerts substantially more influence over the fly's success than does the fly itself. This I firmly believe, for it is the angler adept at first reading and then covering the water (in a productive manner) whom enjoys the most consistent success, regardless of fly pattern. Evidence to this effect arrives in two forms, the first being simple empiricism: Countless steelhead and salmon dressings have proven their effectiveness over the years and yet no single dressing, color, scheme or style can claim supremacy. Given the centuries-old evolution of the many hundreds of different salmon and steelhead patterns, I should think if one particular style or color or pattern were indeed more effective than all others, we would all be using that fly by now.

Second, a salmon or steelhead's selectivity to pattern or color or style cannot hope to be tested under the scrutiny of scientific method—too many variables are left unaccountable no matter what test we might dream up.

No less an authority than the venerable Sir Herbert Maxwell relates, "I have killed salmon with the fly in thirty-one different rivers in England, Scotland, Ireland, and Norway, and have never been able to detect preference on the part of the fish for any particular colour or shade of light and dark.

"Fishing just above high tide mark in the Water of Luce," continues Maxwell, "I raised a small fish five times without touching him, changed the fly every time and killed him, seven pounds, at the sixth rise. I cannot think that the result would have been any different had I made no change, which is the course I should follow now in the unromantic light of experience."[1]

Indeed, for many decades, the old quiet-toned salmon flies proved entirely adequate on the salmon rivers of Scotland. When the guadily-hued, fancifully-designed Irish patterns arrived, they were met with ridicule on many waters. But the locals soon realized, often by sheer force of evidence, that the intricately dressed, bright-colored newcomers killed as well as the indigenous flies. In many instances, to quote Eric Taverner, "The old sombre local patterns have been driven out and the invading gaudy flies, to use a time-honored epithet, are taken quite as well. The salmon, the supreme arbiter, is evidently not at all particular."

Even the accomplished Stoddart, early in the 19th century, remarked:

"...It is erroneously supposed, both Tweedside and in the north, that the Irish and other gaudy flies are all hum; accordingly, such as use them are not a little ridiculed by the prejudiced claudhoppers of those districts, who insist upon their own sagacity and experience. Now, we inform all who wish to angle successfully, that there is no dependence to be placed upon stubborn prejudice; and we further advise them to be shy of being advised by downright ignoramus. Truly, as for ourselves, we can say without boast, that, in the matter of Irish flies, we have upset before their eyes the doctrines of such as pertinaciously held them to be useless on our Scottish waters. Nay, we feel assured that salmon will rise at **them**..." (2)

Stoddart would likely feel compelled to make the same argument today, for the same debates still rage over the issue of what qualities render a salmon or steelhead fly either effective or useless. Myself and many other anglers would argue that effectiveness lies not so much in the fly as it does in the persistence, experience and insight of the angler.

Indeed, there exist so many theories on fly choice that I think the sheer quantity in itself of such theories testifies to the assertion that pattern choice generally doesn't matter much to the fish. Certainly there are those times when a particular *style* of fly might prove more effective, say for example, when skittish fish bolt at the sight of anything larger than a trout fly. But even those considerations are prone to frequent exceptions—so much so that I've abandoned any pretense that I should ever again need a hook smaller than a No. 4 for my summer steelhead angling.

In any case, anglers who preach particular theories about the supremacy of one fly or style of fly over all others tend to abandon those beliefs over the course of many seasons spent chasing salmon or steelhead. Along the way, however, do their carefully crafted theories, if well publicized, do more harm than good to the newcomer? I think not. Conversely, in the case of fly anglers accustomed to trout-angling wherein fly choice often proves the critical variable in determining success, some sort of reasoning about fly choice often proves the critical ingredient to initial success in steelhead angling.

I've watched this scenario play itself out on people in my own circle of acquaintances: As the casting hours mount in their quest for that first steelhead, they quite logically begin to question their choice in tactics and flies. Along comes some sage who says this fly or that proves predominantly effective under some particular set of circumstances. The novice grabs hold of this new theory, ties or acquires the recommended flies and then begins angling again with renewed confidence.

Therein lies the key. The *confident* angler pays attention to detail. She fishes each cast from top to bottom; each pool from head to lip. Somewhere in that process, her fly dances past a willing combatant and that first magnificent steelhead is hooked. Along the way, the newcomer learns to enjoy the wading, to appreciate the river and its surrounds, to revel in each well-executed cast. When Jennifer hooked her first steelhead—on a dry line and a No. 2 Max Canyon—she later explained that she had made what seemed a perfect cast and thought to herself, "that cast deserves a fish." The steelhead Gods agreed that evening.

Certainly where flies are concerned the angler must learn to reverse his or her thinking with regards to salmon and steelhead. We know why trout eat artificial flies. We have no idea why salmon and steelhead eat these contrivances of fur and feather. The trout-fisher learns that pattern choice ranks high on the list of critical variables that will ultimately determine success. The steelhead angler must, at some point, decide that reading water, covering water and spending lots of time on the water are factors ranking high above pattern choice.

This idea that fly choice just doesn't make much difference to the fish is a concept that proves rather unpalatable to many novice steelhead anglers, and even to many veterans, so they look for magic bullets, if you will—some fly pattern, fly design or theory that will give them an edge when in fact such energies would be better spent learning where and when to find fish and how best to present the fly.

Should any steelhead angler decide they know why steelhead grab flies and wish to convince me of their findings, then perhaps they can likewise explain why steelhead rise for leaves, bark, bugs, bobbers, birds and just about any other object. They seem, after all, equally prone to rising for a somber little hairwing as for a bejeweled Jock Scott. Some years back I hooked a spectacular buck on the Grand Ronde River using a 3/0 Jock Scott dressed for me by David Burns. Fifteen minutes later a second wild fish felt compelled to inhale a No. 4 Black Max, about as somber-colored a hairwing as one could imagine these days.

Moreover, I am reminded of an episode that perfectly illustrates my point with regard to theories about flies. Some time ago I enjoyed a visit from a friend hailing from the trout-rich waters of the American Rockies. Not only is this fellow a superb trout-angler, but he is also a salmon-fly dresser of the highest order. Steelhead, however, were still somewhat perplexing to him and on this visit he arrived armed with a new borrowed theory. He had recently read about and then dressed a litany of "optically blended" flies, each one so beautifully dressed that I would have fished them with a sense of pride borne simply of my acquaintance with their creator.

But after two fish-less days, I insisted that he change to my own favorite steelhead fly (which he dresses more expertly than I do). I made him change only because, after two days of fishing him through superb water, I more than him, needed to embrace utter confidence in his choice of flies. That morning he hooked a fish. Then in the span of a day he took four more steelhead, all on the same fly. He enjoyed a red-letter day during a time when one or two hook-ups per day was about average.

I imagine any other fly would have done as well. He had simply enjoyed the fruits of first fishing long and hard and second of employing supreme confidence in his choice of flies. Jokingly, I told him later, "Well, it's too bad you didn't stick to the 'optically blended' fly because if you had you might have hooked eight or ten fish instead of only five!"

Ultimately, I believe each angler must arrive at his or her "confidence flies"—those patterns he or she will fish without questioning the choice. In that sense, pattern choice becomes paramount, for the angler who trusts completely in his or her choice of flies immediately abandons all concerns over whether this or that fly is the better option. Having abandoned such concerns, the confident angler is then free to concentrate on the important elements of fishing the right water in the correct manner.

In that regard, those anglers who devise theories about fly choice and fly design—whether it be the supremacy of "marabou Speys" or "optically blended" flies or classic Spey or Dee styles—had better stick to their theories because doing so makes them better anglers. They are better anglers because they are confident anglers. Most of the truly experienced anglers in my circle of acquaintances would agree with that statement.

This is an old debate, this question of whether the salmon or steelhead show a decided preference for one fly over another. Some anglers espouse theories that a single component renders a fly somehow more effective than a fly left wanting for that attribute. Such ideas stirred debate in the 19th century and they continue to do so today. I suspect Thomas Stoddart would be bemused to find his words as applicable today as they were more than 150 years ago:

*"Seriously speaking, are the tastes and habits of salmon, as some assert, of a revolving nature? Is the fish, too, so capricious, that a single fibre wanting in the lure, a mis-placed wing, a wrongly asserted hue, will discompose and annoy it? . . .From this dark, insoluble, and thoroughly speculative subject, it is high time to retire. My apology for introducing it at all, rests on the*

*desire I have to discover, to those who make of it a matter of argument, the absurdities they are liable to run into. There is, I cannot help thinking, a great deal of prejudice, self-conceit, and humbug exhibited by salmon-fishers generally, with respect to their flies—a monstrous mass of nonsense hoarded up by the best of them, and opinions held, quite at variance with reason and common sense."*

## A VIEW FROM THE RIVER

For many anglers, fly choice is contingent upon the belief that the way in which we hook a steelhead counts for more than the final tally. My closest steelheading friends, for example, prefer to say, "I fished the pool well," rather than relate our body count. We all enjoy the thrill of the hook-up and we fish beautiful flies because doing so heightens our sense of what is right about our chosen sport. Our best efforts at the vise and on the river pay homage to a game fish whose remarkable life story demands a deep reverence and continual wonderment.

Of course the veteran of many years of steelheading more easily embraces such opinions than those new to the sport. Certainly, however, veteran and novice alike can appreciate and enjoy the art of tying and fishing Spey flies, for many of these flies are as easily dressed as a simple hairwing fly.

Having shared that, allow me now to discuss this idea of how the fly should fish. We tie and design our Spey and Dee flies with a certain idea of how they will act in the water. The fly "fishes well" if, once in the water, it performs as intended. Here's the problem: How do we know? Hooking a fish is no indication of how the fly performs in the water. Hooking a fish only tells us that the fly hooked a fish.

However, steelhead and salmon will hit just about anything at one time or another, so to say your fly hooked a fish is really not remarkable, no matter how the fly fishes. I once read an article about marabou Spey flies in which the author stated that the reason marabou Spey flies are so effective is because of the way the marabou breathes and undulates in the water. Really? If breathing and undulating are so important, how do we explain the super-success of Corkies—colored foam balls—used by drift fishermen? Again, where is the scientific method?

If we want our flies to fish in the manner we intend, we better go have a good look at that fly while it is actually fishing. That, of course, is no easy task. But it is one in which I have participated for the sole purpose of debunking the ideas spread so diligently by those who *think* they know how a fly fishes. My methodology involved nothing more than good old-fashioned, get-your-feet-wet observation. Only I got a lot more than my feet wet and I'm lucky not to have caught pneumonia.

Here's how it worked. I first tied several styles of Spey flies on several styles of hooks in various sizes. I then conned a couple fishing partners into helping me, though they certainly got the easy job. Naturally, we had to choose a clear-water river. I positioned my partner somewhere in the pool and then I walked a cast's length downstream. We then measured out enough line

so the fly passed as near my position as possible. Next came the fun part. I carried an anchor tied to a short rope and wore a mask and snorkel.

When properly positioned, I would signal my accomplice to deliver the cast exactly as if fishing. Having already measured out the line, I would first watch the cast and then at the appropriate time I'd pull myself under water via the anchor rope. Soon the fly would come into view where I could scrutinize its behavior. We carried these "tests" to various water types and proceeded with various presentations. My observations are as follows:

1. Flies with hackles tied in by the butt and wrapped forward tend to retain their shape in the water. This method of tying allows the fibers at the rear (where the hackle stem is thickest) to spread out and "open up" around the rear of the fly. The thickness of the hackle stem and the way in which it lays upon the fly's body forces the fibers to stand out rather rigidly and the fly retains this shape even in fast water—in fact, the force of comparatively violent currents seemed to enliven the hackles once

AN ANGLER CASTS A STEELHEAD RUN DURING THE SUMMER SEASON IN OREGON.

the fly began to swing across the flow. Whether the hackle was doubled appeared to have little influence over the performance characteristics of the hackle. Flies dressed with "split" hackles of pheasant tail or goose shoulder generally resisted the force of current better than all others.

2. When hackled tip-first, the flies exhibited a different behavior, the hackle fibers being more prone to "collapse" around the body of the fly. Such flies dressed with heron or blue eared pheasant hackles appeared lively and full on the drift, but collapsed to varying degrees when swinging across the flow. However, these flies also exhibited a unique vibration to the hackle fibers: Under tension from the current, the collapsed fibers, laying streamlined along the body and trailing behind, "shimmied" violently, not at all unlike the workings of a marabou tail on a Woolly Bugger. The effect was especially pronounced with long heron hackles and blue eared pheasant hackles. Naturally, the shorter fibers found on cock hackles, including schlappen, lacked this feature (although they were more difficult to observe in detail).

3. Marabou flies seemed likewise to vary their behavior depending on the method of construction. All the marabou patterns tested exhibited some movement on the dead-drift or anything approximating such. On the swing, however, all of the flies collapsed to varying degrees in the manner of the flies aforementioned. Least prone to severe collapse were marabou flies tied with a bracing hackle of duck flank. Again, however, when the force of the currents caused the marabou fibers to collapse around the body, the fly shimmered violently, acting like a minnow imitation or some such contrivance.

4. Many of the flies tended to sag, hook-bend riding lower than the eye of the hook, during the dead drift; but most righted themselves during the swing. Interestingly, the pull of a hard current caused many, if not most, flies to turn sideways on the swing. All of the flies dressed on single hooks tended to flip sideways on the swing, seemingly quite at random.

As one might expect, I soon grew tired of conducting these "tests," which might better be termed very general observations. Certainly one could spend a great deal more effort observing the underwater action of Spey flies and perhaps arrive at more precise conclusions. I'm not about to suggest that the fish themselves have any preference, but the angler gains a boost in confidence by knowing his or her fly is performing as intended. Confidence is critical and far more significant, in my opinion, than any single characteristic of a given fly. In other words, if you believe your fly should play fully in the current and you believe movement is paramount, then you should design your flies to achieve those behaviors. It matters not whether your idea of movement is the breathing, vibrating effect of a traditionally hackled fly or the "shimmyings" of long-fibered hackle as the fly swings across the flow.

With all of that in mind, allow me to revert to the argument of whether the Spey fly is better suited to fast or slow flows. Certainly everyone has a slightly different idea of what constitutes a fast or slow current, but I'll not abandon the argument on those grounds. Most of us, when comparing two or more flows, could certainly agree on which are fast and which are slow. My observations lead me to conclude that Spey flies and Spey-style flies behave equally well in virtually any current speed assuming the angler designs his or her flies with a particular behavior in mind and then fishes them in the manner consistent with those expectations. In other words, if you design a marabou-style Spey fly with the expectation that it will offer maximum movement in slow to moderate flows then you must fish the fly in those waters and use your angling skills to control the fly's behavior.

These skills include the ability to control the speed and depth at which the fly swims as well as the angle at which the fly is presented to the fish. In fact, those three variables constitute the only worthwhile concerns over the fly's behavior once it enters the water.

# FISHING THE FLY

Writers have penned volumes on the subject of fly angling for salmon and steelhead. I won't venture into the realm of offering detailed instruction in the art but will instead insist that the classic methods of angling for these fish are not nearly so complicated as modern literature might leave one to believe. The basic idea is simple: cast the fly down and across and allow it to swing back to your side of the river. Take two steps downstream and repeat. Such is the inherent simplicity of the so-called "wet-fly swing."

This easily learned method of angling ranks as perhaps the most efficient method of thoroughly covering the water on the average salmon or steelhead stream. As for the particulars, I defer to the learned John Ashley-Cooper, whose book *The Salmon Rivers of Scotland* says:

*"In big pools, and in these rivers the majority of them are big, you should normally fish quickly, especially when fish are scarce. On no account pause to do two or three casts in the same place (this is almost an endemic fault in nervous waders). This leads to a deplorable waste of time. Keep moving on steadily at a rate of two or three yards between each cast and so get the water covered. Only if you locate a spot where likely takers are lying, or if you rise fish that do not take hold, should you slow up. It is much better to fish a big pool twice, fairly fast, in a given period of time than once, slowly."*

The wet-fly swing has its variations. Some anglers cast and swing the fly, but strip line as they do so. Others prefer to "swim" the fly using the "grease-line" tactics. As David Burns says, "The trick is to stay in control of the fly. Dead drifting Spey & Dee flies is a waste of the style. Their hackles only work under proper tension. Down and across works. Greased line works. Drift, swing and pull works. The only thing I'd add is that if you want to dead drift flies you should choose something that takes less time to tie. Breaking off a Spey or Dee fly on a rock during a dead drift seems like a terrible waste to me."

Controlling the fly means you concern yourself with its depth and speed. Those are the only two variables of any significance unless you count yourself among those who place some significance on the fly's attitude in the water. On this latter count, I contend that on large, complex rivers, any attempt to control the fly's actual orientation in the flow—whether the fly points upstream or cross-stream—is wasted energy. The fish seem unconcerned about such trivialities and on long-line presentations, proponents of the "swimming" fly exert substantially less influence over the fly's attitude than they might believe.

This so-called wet-fly swing, the basic technique employed by steelhead anglers, derives from a centuries-old method of fly angling for Atlantic salmon. The basic idea is to cast down and across, mend upstream to straighten the line and leader (not always necessary) and then allow the fly—under tension from the current—to swing back to your side of the flow. In short, you make the fly drag. We spend most of our trout-fishing days learning to eliminate that evil thing called drag. No wonder steelheading is so easy: We *want* the fly to drag. Throw the fly down and across, mend once, allow the fly to drag back to your side of the river. Take two steps downstream and repeat. Pretty simple.

Specific current structures dictate the angle of the downstream cast, but generally speaking, the steeper the angle, the easier it becomes to control the fly's speed as it swings across the flow. In fact, the speed of the fly and its depth in the water column comprise the two critical elements in steelhead presentation. When fishing floating lines and wet flies during the summer, fly depth more or less takes care of itself, especially when you control the more important element of fly speed. Steep angles of presentation and some timely mending control the speed of the fly.

Controlling depth and speed becomes a more critical issue with winter steelhead, which won't chase down a fly so aggressively as a summer-run fish. Thus, you must present the fly closer to the steelhead's level. You needn't dredge the bottom, but you must swing the fly deeper in the water column, often just a foot or two above the streambed.

High-density sinking fly lines help achieve depth. Most anglers carry several different densities of sinking lines or "heads" to confront different water types. In this regard, the new multi-tip fly lines are ideally suited to steelheading. These sinking lines carry the fly to depth, but the angle of presentation is paramount in maintaining that depth. In short, the steeper the angle of presentation, the more control you have over the fly.

On wide, cobblestone rivers where steelhead might hold anywhere from bank to bank, the best tactic is to cover as wide a swath of water as possible during each swing. So you follow the classic approach of quartering downstream and allowing the fly to swing all the way across the current. On more defined water, however, where you can expect the steelhead to hold in specific, narrow lies, you can make the cast more downstream than across and thus gain increased control over the speed and depth of the fly.

A couple tricks help with fly control: First, you can hold a large loop of line in your hand during the swing and steadily release this slack line to slow the fly's speed and thus increase its depth. Second, try stepping downstream *after* the cast rather than before. During the summer, the typical pattern is to fish out one swing, take a step or two downstream and then cast again. During the winter, however, try fishing out one swing and then making the next cast from the same position. After making the cast, take those two steps downstream, allowing the line a few more feet of drag-free drift to gain depth.

An angler's choice in casting station often dictates the methods used to control fly speed and the degree to which these methods prove effective. An oft-overlooked pool on one of our local rivers exemplifies the importance of the angler's position: Located at the lip current, deep in the tailout of a much larger pool, a narrow pocket in the bedrock allows migrating steelhead a respite after negotiating the falls immediately below.

We can fish this slot from either side of the river, but only if we position ourselves above and within a rod's length laterally of the pool. In other words, we stand almost directly upstream from the holding area. Try to fish the slot from a steeper angle and the fly and line either latch onto ledge-rock or dash across the pocket so quickly as to render the presentation ineffective.

I could cite countless similar examples. In short, the steeper your angle of presentation, the easier it becomes to control fly speed without mending. This idea of fishing steep angles may be the best justification for casting a long line on large western rivers. Basically, it's a matter of geometry. When thrown at identical down-and-across angles from the same position, the longer cast covers a wider swath of water *at the appropriate speed* than does a shorter cast.

Initial positioning in the pool allows you to fish the best possible angle of presentation, but rod position and rod movement also play a critical role in fly control. You can either "follow" the fly or "lead" the fly with the rod, depending again on particular current structures in relation to the path of the line and fly. "Following" the fly means that once the line straightens, you keep the rod tip pointed out over the river. Doing so allows you direct contact throughout the presentation and allows you the opportunity to hang the fly in particular places, at least towards the end of the crosscurrent swing.

Leading the fly helps to slow the fly's speed appreciably as you allow the rod tip to drift downstream slightly faster than the fly. Doing so causes the fly to swing cross stream in a more angled arc—a valuable ploy when you can't get a steep enough angle on a narrow slot well out in the flow.

Regardless of the particulars of your presentation, success ultimately hinges on your ability to fish the fly in the proper place. In other words, reading a river and then identifying the likely holding water ranks as the most significant factor in determining your ability to consistently hook fish. In some rivers, the good pools are so well known that you need only watch for other anglers. Still, learning such pools yourself allows you to find the "sweet spots" in any given stretch of water.

My experience lies in steelhead angling in the Pacific Northwest. Steelhead occupy a wide variety of places in any given river. When asked precisely where to cast a fly, I answer as follows: "Look for water between your hips and your eyebrows in depth, sometimes a little deeper, that flows at about the pace you can walk."

In other words, steelhead prefer water of moderate depth and moderate speed. Of course it's never that simple, right? But it's almost that simple. You must also add a basic understanding of the nature of rivers and how river characteristics influence the migratory habits of steelhead.

For starters, steelhead—especially summer-run fish—generally stick to the main current structure of the river. You won't find them in the frog water up near the banks. Also, the current structure and configuration of the river dictates where steelhead stop and where they don't. In short, they look for something comfortable. Forget about rapids. The water is too fast. Sometimes steelhead hold in pocket-water chutes and seams within a large rapids, but they are more prone to hold in the pools dividing the rapids, whether these pools take the form of broad, classic affairs or just narrow slots called "runs."

Any given pool can be divided into its parts: The head of the pool is that portion at the upstream end where the faster water above settles and slows. The body of the pool is the wide expanse at the middle and the tailout is the lower end, where the water often reaches its slowest speeds and shallowest depths, immediately above the next rapids or riffle.

Steelhead are creatures of habit. Barring any major changes in the river's structure and flow, these fish utilize the same holding lies over and over, not only from day to day but from year to year. Therefore, steelhead anglers fish the same water religiously. If you hook a fish in a particular spot, remember that place—the exact place—and fish it in the future.

Because our large western steelhead rivers rarely allow the angler to see his quarry, it makes strategic sense to fish each pool from top to bottom even if you know, for example, the best holding lay—the place that most often produces a fish—awaits way down in the tailout. If you don't know how many steelhead occupy the pool, we better start at the top and fish over all the suspected or known lays. After all, the "garden spot" down in the tailout isn't going anywhere and you just might hook a fish from a place not typically as productive.

Armed with the knowledge that steelhead tend to follow the main current structure of the river and knowing they stop and hold, for varying time periods, in particular places, you must now begin to dissect the river. Steelhead orient to structure of various kinds, ranging from single small rocks to ledges to gravel birms. If you can locate such structural elements within a pool or run, fish them carefully. On large rivers, learn to intimate the nature of the bottom by reading the water's surface. Large rocks leave telltale bulges and wakes; chutes leave slicks; ledges often create current seams and so on.

The river's course can help you read for steelhead water. Look for "inside bends" in the river—those places where the streambed curves to the left or right, creating a soft-water pocket along the inside of the bend. Steelhead find comfortable holding water where the river wraps around a corner. Add a few boulders or depressions and so much the better. Don't ignore the outside bends, however, as they too can offer good holding water, often close to the bank.

Study the river's surface, looking for smooth glides and choppy runs. Classic pools are easy to recognize, but smaller runs often prove equally productive and in many places escape notice from most anglers. Even on familiar rivers, look for new runs and chutes and single-fish lays that may have escaped your attention in the past. When you recognize potential steelhead water, whether a large pool or tiny slot, make at least a few casts each time you visit the spot. Eventually you'll either hook a fish there or you'll decide fish don't hold in that place. Regardless, the best way to learn new water is to wade and fish your way through.

Steelhead anglers must persist in fishing new runs and pools, for experience is the best teacher: The more fish you hook from numerous pools and runs, the more you understand about steelhead water. As your experience mounts, you learn what to look for and soon begin to recognize certain patterns that help you ferret out steelhead on many different rivers. For the observant angler, each hook-up offers a chance to learn something new—something about reading a river for steelhead and something that can be filed away and applied to new rivers in the future.

Meanwhile, each day spent fishing adds to your arsenal of skills. As I have said, the basic technique for steelhead fly angling is decidedly easy to learn and execute. Yet there remains ample room for skill to prevail over a common flogging of the water by the inexperienced angler. Take for example that perfect October day when chance allowed me the privilege of introducing some friends from Wisconsin to the famed North Umpqua River.

Late that afternoon I found myself perched atop a riverside rock, above a complex and challenging little steelhead run. I was pointing out the sweet spot where the fish was likely to take if indeed a steelhead occupied the run. One of the fellows, Dave, accepted the challenge. The cast alone covered 80 feet, but Dave was equal to the task. He wasn't quite mending the line right, however, so the fly, even when it landed in the right place, darted away too quickly. I continued to yell instructions from atop my perch: "Put it in the same place again, Dave. . .perfect, okay, now mend upstream, quick, and hold your rod tip out toward the slot."

Soon the light went on. Dave saw how incorrect presentation caused the fly to dart out of the soft water that offered the only haven for a steelhead. No steelhead would chase a fly into the rushing white water immediately adjacent to the little slot, so the angler had to hang the fly in the slow water long enough to

draw a reaction. Quite suddenly my Midwestern friend, who had honed his skills on streams of a different nature, understood why I had admonished him all day to swing the fly slowly through the pools.

Dave finally got one just right: perfect cast, perfect mend, perfect rod position. Just as the fly straightened into the slot, I yelled, "Now that cast deserves a fish."

Wham! Fish on. Dave landed a beautiful native buck and of course I was worshiped as some kind of divine fish god. My partners failed to realize, of course, that I mutter that phrase, at least to myself, every time I make a decent cast. Save some knowledge of the pool on my part, it was Dave's ability to depart from his normal thought process and make the perfect cast and presentation that earned him that fish.

Later, as we ate dinner, Dave and I talked about the nature of that presentation. The configuration of the river dictated his choice in line control: A fast current ran a path straight through the middle of the river, which was bound on both sides by ledge-rock. The far bank offered a narrow slot, where a seam in the current offered ideal holding water against a rock ledge. This slot—just a bathtub-sized mini-pool—was un-fishable unless an angler stood on a narrow gravel birm way up at the head of the fast water.

The long cast dropped the fly atop the slot. An upstream flip and loft positioned all of the fly line above the fly and well to the left of the current. The angler's position left him at the steepest possible angle to the pool and he held his rod out to the left and kept it there as the line came taut. Combined with his initial positioning, Dave's cast, mend and rod position allowed him to dance the fly slowly through the narrow slot. No written labels describe the presentation that earned Dave his fish—it was an instinctive reaction to the structure of the pool. Once Dave understood why the fly had to swing slowly through the little pool, he simply flew by the seat of his pants and did what needed doing. I was yelling instructions, sure, but Dave's fishing instincts translated my simple instructions ("okay, now mend") into the perfect presentation.

# A STEELHEADER'S INSTINCTS

The bad news first: you can't develop a steelheader's instincts overnight. Instead, you have to fish and fish a lot. That's the good news. This is a learn-on-the-job game. Steelheading teaches you to cast and control line; to wade and read water. The more you fish for steelhead, the better you get at fishing for steelhead. Each hook-up teaches you something about reading water and presenting a fly.

Like most steelheaders, I fish my favorite rivers so regularly that I have learned many of the most likely places to expect a hook-up. I'm not surprised when I hook a fish from certain specific holding areas in my favorite pools. Likewise, when I fish rivers and pools new to me, I expect to find fish in certain places. Some places just look too perfect not to hold fish, although the steelhead don't always agree. That's one reason I learn from each hook-up: Some fish confirm that I read the water correctly and fished the pool effectively.

Other steelhead, meanwhile, come as more of a surprise, teaching me that I must tirelessly study the nature of the rivers and the steelhead living therein. Instincts tell me to stop and throw a cast or two over a run or slot I may have overlooked in seasons past. Sometimes I'm pleasantly surprised; other times I'll fish that place a dozen times in a season before I'm convinced of the futility in persisting further. Either way, my steelheading instincts derive from time spent on the water.

Naturally, I take satisfaction in knowing my instincts were correct and that I read the water well and earned a fish through proper presentation. Still, perfect presentation does not assure success in this game, for steelhead must first occupy the pool and then be willing to bite. On the big western rivers, anglers must simply assume that steelhead occupy each pool. Then we simply cover as much water as possible in search of a willing fish. Indeed, the veteran steelhead angler, accomplished at the art of instinctive presentation, measures his success not by the number of hook-ups but instead by how well he fished.

When a steelhead does chase and take the fly, the confident, accomplished angler never reacts with surprise. Quite the opposite: The angler thinks, "Well, it's about time—I can't believe it took this long to hook the morning's first fish."

Having tempted the fish with graceful cast and elegant fly, the angler feels rewarded for playing the game right. Rather than deliver the fly to the fish, the angler has in that moment mastered the far more reverent task of delivering a fish to the fly—the defining gesture of fly-angling for steelhead in the classic manner.

# THE CONFIDENCE FACTOR

Steelhead fly-anglers are a decidedly twisted lot. We have little choice in the matter because our chosen pastime assures that we spend far more time fishing than actually catching. We operate on faith; on the assumption that if we just keep fishing, sooner or later we'll hook a steelhead.

Here in the Northwest, most of us fish big water—the Deschutes, Skykomish, North Umpqua, Rogue, Clearwater, Skagit and many more. For some of these rivers you can watch the fish counts at the dams and at least garner some rough guess as to how many steelhead have migrated to your favorite reaches. Even so, you simply assume that each pool holds fish because rarely on these rivers can one actually spot fish in the water.

Your faith must never falter. You must always believe that fish are in the river, in your favorite pools, and in a mood to chase your flies. In fact, confidence may well constitute the single most important attribute of the successful steelhead angler.

Confidence transcends technique and strategy. More than that, confidence elevates your angling skills because it instills in the belief that there exists no doubt about the fact that you will hook a steelhead. Not burdened by doubt, you come to decide that casting, wading and reading water are skills at which you will tirelessly try to better yourself.

Any doubts about hooking steelhead are pushed far out of your mind. As you deliver a cast there exists not a shred of doubt that a steelhead will grab the fly on that presentation. When this fails to happen, you are at the very least mildly surprised. Your confidence doubles on the ensuing cast; after all, if the last cast failed to tempt a fish, there is simply no question that the next one is sure to score. When this next presentation goes fishless, you find yourself flabbergasted and when you fish out the pool without touching a fish you are entirely astounded.

Your astonishment only re-doubles your confidence. No question about it, you will certainly hook a fish in the next pool. Should the day pass without a hook-up, you find yourself brimming with confidence about your chances the following day. Should a week pass without a hook-up, your confidence has reached epic proportions: It builds in direct correlation with your astonishment at not catching fish.

Never does your confidence wane; rather it follows this inverse relationship, mounting appreciably with the passage of fishless casts, pools and days. Your reasoning is simple; fundamental. How can there exist any doubt that the next cast will hook a steelhead since the last 500 have failed to do so?

Indeed, doubt never enters the confident steelheader's mind. In this way you become a better angler, concentrating fully on your efforts. When your fly hangs in the current directly downstream at the end of the swing, you stand there entirely befuddled that a steelhead did not give chase. Then you can't wait to deliver the next presentation because you are more certain than ever that the forthcoming cast will hook a fish.

The confident steelheader, unencumbered by doubt, appreciates the fact that reading water and effectively covering water rank as the two most significant factors in hooking fish. The confident angler never worries over pattern choice. He or she chooses a favorite, ties it on and forgets about the fly. The confident angler believes in every pool and fishes each one from top to bottom, knowing full well that giving up even one cast short of the lip current might be the difference.

Unburdened by worries, the steelhead angler now begins to appreciate the fact that few angling pursuits place her in more intimate quarters with a favorite river. As the seasons mount and the wading and casting miles add up; as those ever-cherished hook-ups become many; as life-long angling friendships are forged; as new rivers become old stomping grounds; the steelhead angler learns that he persists in this game simply because he loves to fish and because these noble game fish and the rivers in which they live deserve a special reverence.

**End Notes**

1. From Sir Herbert Maxwell's introduction to the 2nd edition of Francis Francis.

2. Thomas Tod Stoddart, *Art of Angling in Scotland*, 1836.

# A Gallery of Dressings

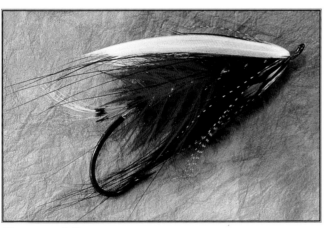

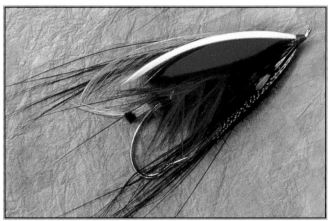

## SKAGIT MIST
(Dec Hogan)

| | |
|---|---|
| **Hook:** | Jackson Spey, black 1 1/2 - 3/0 |
| **Tag:** | Flat silver tinsel |
| **Tail:** | GP crest and tippet |
| **Butt:** | Purple ostrich herl |
| **Body:** | First half claret seal fur; second half black seal fur |
| **Rib:** | Oval silver tinsel over first half; oval silver tinsel and flat blue tinsel over second half |
| **Hackle:** | Hot red saddle over first half; black Spey hackle over second half |
| **Throat:** | Teal flank |
| **Wings:** | White turkey tail |
| **Cheeks:** | Jungle cock eyes |
| **Head:** | Red |

## SKAGIT STORM
(Dec Hogan)

| | |
|---|---|
| **Hook:** | Jackson Spey, nickel 1 1/2 - 3/0 |
| **Tag:** | Flat silver tinsel |
| **Tail:** | GP crest and tippet |
| **Butt:** | Purple ostrich herl |
| **Body:** | First half claret seal fur; second half purple seal fur |
| **Rib:** | Oval silver tinsel over first half; oval silver tinsel and flat blue tinsel over second half |
| **Hackle:** | Hot red saddle over first half; purple Spey hackle over second half |
| **Throat:** | Teal flank |
| **Wing:** | White black-edged hen neck dyed cerise veiled by thin strips of white turkey tail |
| **Topping:** | Golden pheasant crest |
| **Cheeks:** | Jungle cock eyes |
| **Head:** | Claret |

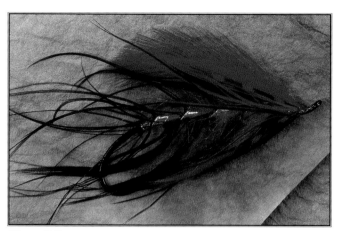

## THE MAHONEY
(Dec Hogan)

| | |
|---|---|
| *Hook:* | Alec Jackson Spey, sizes 8 - 3/0 |
| *Thread:* | 6/0 burgundy |
| *Body:* | Rear third red floss; balance hot red seal fur or substitute |
| *Rib:* | Flat pearl Mylar followed by medium oval silver tinsel |
| *Hackle:* | Black rooster schlappen: one side stripped |
| *Collar:* | Hot red schlappen followed by red guinea |
| *Wing:* | Four matching hackle tips from a hot red rooster neck |

## UN-NAMED
(Fred Vargas)

| | |
|---|---|
| *Tag:* | Fine silver tinsel |
| *Butt:* | Blue silk |
| *Body:* | blue dubbing |
| *Ribs:* | Silver oval |
| *Hackle:* | Blue eared pheasant |
| *Collar:* | Blue Flashabou or similar, blue hackle, and blue guinea |
| *Wing:* | White goose shoulder |
| *Head:* | Red |

## O'DONNELL #3
(Scott O'Donnell)

| | |
|---|---|
| *Tag:* | Green tinsel reinforced with fine red wire |
| *Body:* | Fluorescent red floss and then red sparkle dubbing |
| *Rib:* | Flat gold trailed by silver oval |
| *Hackle:* | Black, from second turn of tinsel |
| *Collar:* | Amherst pheasant tail, dyed red |
| *Wing:* | Bright red hackle tips |

## O'DONNELL #4
(Scott O'Donnell)

| | |
|---|---|
| *Tag:* | Silver tinsel reinforced with fine silver wire |
| *Body:* | Orange silk and then orange dubbing |
| *Rib:* | Flat silver trailed by silver oval |
| *Hackle:* | Black, from second turn of tinsel |
| *Collar:* | Amherst pheasant tail, dyed orange |
| *Wing:* | Bright orange hackle tips |

## SKYKOMISH DARK

(pattern by Steve Gobin; dressed by the author)

| | |
|---|---|
| *Body:* | 1/3 orange silk, 2/3 red dubbing or wool yarn |
| *Rib:* | Medium or wide oval silver and a counter-rib of fine silver oval |
| *Hackle:* | Yellow schlappen or coque |
| *Collar:* | Black heron shoulder (substitute) (dyed blue eared pheasant or marabou) |
| *Wing:* | Bronze mallard |

## DRAGON'S TOOTH

(pattern by Mike Kinney; dressed by the author)

| | |
|---|---|
| *Tag:* | A few turns of fine silver oval |
| *Body:* | Purple wool yarn or similar |
| *Ribs:* | Flat silver and oval silver |
| *Hackle:* | Purple schlappen or coque |
| *Throat:* | Teal or gadwall flank |
| *Wing:* | 4 red golden-pheasant flank feathers, tented, with a single golden-pheasant rump feather alongside each and tied slightly shorter |

## D.C. CUTTHROAT SPEY

(Rich Youngers)

| | |
|---|---|
| *Tag:* | Flat silver tinsel |
| *Body:* | Rear 2/3 orange silk; front 1/3 orange dubbing |
| *Rib:* | Small flat silver and fine oval silver |
| *Hackle:* | Dyed-orange blue eared pheasant from 4th turn of tinsel |
| *Wing:* | Whiting American hen cape, black-laced white (dyed orange) |
| *Collar:* | Orange-dyed gadwall |
| *Cheek:* | Tragopan |

## PURPLE PLUS

(Joe Howell)

| | |
|---|---|
| *Tag:* | Silver tinsel |
| *Tail:* | Golden-pheasant crest, dyed orange |
| *Butt:* | Red-dyed ostrich herl |
| *Body:* | Purple silk |
| *Rib:* | Gold oval |
| *Hackle:* | Purple-dyed blue eared pheasant or similar from third turn of tinsel |
| *Collar:* | Red-dyed guinea |
| *Wings:* | Slips of white swan or goose |
| *Cheeks:* | Jungle cock |
| *Head:* | Red |

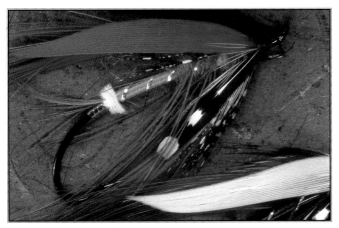

## CREAMSICLE SPEY
(Joe Howell)

| | |
|---|---|
| *Tag:* | Silver tinsel |
| *Tail:* | Golden-pheasant crest dyed orange |
| *Butt:* | White ostrich herl |
| *Body:* | Hot orange floss, then hot orange dubbing |
| *Rib:* | Silver oval |
| *Hackle:* | Orange-dyed blue eared pheasant or similar from third turn of tinsel |
| *Collar:* | Guinea |
| *Wings:* | Slips of hot orange swan or goose |
| *Cheeks:* | Jungle cock |
| *Head:* | Red |

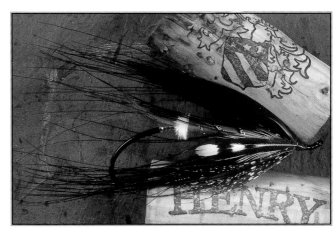

## MIDNIGHT MADNESS
(Joe Howell)

| | |
|---|---|
| *Tag:* | Silver tinsel |
| *Tail:* | Golden-pheasant crest dyed hot orange |
| *Butt:* | White ostrich herl |
| *Body:* | Fluorescent flame orange floss |
| *Rib:* | Silver oval |
| *Hackle:* | Black-dyed blue eared pheasant or similar from third turn of tinsel |
| *Throat:* | Natural guinea |
| *Wings:* | Slips of black swan or goose |
| *Cheeks:* | Jungle cock |
| *Head:* | Claret |

## UN-NAMED
(Dave Tucker)

| | |
|---|---|
| *Tag:* | Two turns of fine silver oval |
| *Body:* | 1/3 magenta silk; 2/3 deep purple seal |
| *Ribs:* | Medium flat silver and small oval silver; counter of fine silver oval |
| *Hackle:* | Blue eared pheasant or similar |
| *Throat:* | Guinea, dyed royal blue |
| *Wing:* | Strips of cerise goose shoulder with bronze mallard as a roof |
| *Head:* | Red |

## UN-NAMED
(Dave Tucker)

| | |
|---|---|
| *Body:* | In three equal parts: scarlet red silk, red dubbing, magenta dubbing |
| *Ribs:* | Wide flat silver trailed by small oval silver |
| *Hackle:* | Red-dyed rooster neck hackle with long, soft fibers, from red dubbing |
| *Throat:* | Hooded merganser flank |
| *Wing:* | Bronze mallard |
| *Head:* | Red |

## UN-NAMED
(John Olschewsky)

| | |
|---|---|
| *Tag:* | Flat gold tinsel |
| *Body:* | Chartreuse silk; chartreuse dubbing |
| *Ribs:* | Small gold oval |
| *Hackle:* | Tip-dyed marabou, chartreuse with black tips, or similar, from second turn |
| *Throat:* | Silver pheasant dyed chartreuse |
| *Wing:* | Strips of natural dark gray goose shoulder or secondary |
| *Cheeks:* | Jungle cock |
| *Head:* | Black |

## SOUTH FORK SALMON RIVER SPEY, 1994 VERSION
(David Burns)

| | |
|---|---|
| *Tag:* | Three turns fine silver oval |
| *Body:* | Purple silk; black wool yarn |
| *Ribs:* | Pink prismatic rib material trailed by fine silver oval; fine wire as a counter |
| *Hackle:* | Purple bleach-burned goose or similar |
| *Throat:* | Mallard flank |
| *Wing:* | Bronze mallard |
| *Head:* | Black |

**Notes:** A 1997 version of this fly (in my collection) differs by having fine silver oval as a counter-rib, dyed-purple blue eared pheasant (long) as a hackle, and Coch-y-bondu hackle at the throat. Burn's Salmon River Red is similar, but features a body of purple wool yarn tipped with magenta-purple silk; the throat is red-dyed guinea.

## JEAN'S IRIS SPEY
(Dave Burns)

| | |
|---|---|
| *Tag:* | Three turns fine silver oval |
| *Body:* | A butt of electric purple silk and then olive-green wool yarn |
| *Ribs:* | Chartreuse prismatic tinsel trailed by small silver oval; fine silver oval as a counter |
| *Hackle:* | Blue eared pheasant dyed purple |
| *Throat:* | Guinea dyed highlander green |
| *Wing:* | Mallard dyed purple |
| *Head:* | Black |

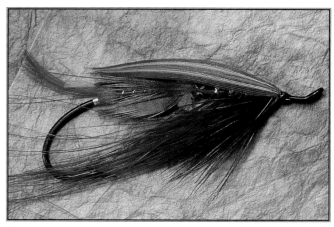

## SUNSET SPEY
(Dave Burns)

| | |
|---|---|
| *Tag:* | Five turns fine silver oval and hot pink silk |
| *Tail:* | Fluorescent red-dyed topping, topped with kingfisher rump |
| *Body:* | Rear half: a joint of pink-dyed ostrich herl, magenta silk ribbed with fine gold oval and veiled top and bottom with a pair of kingfisher body feathers (mounted vertically) |
| *Front half:* | Another joint of pink ostrich, then purple silk ribbed with small flat silver |
| *Hackle:* | Blue eared pheasant, dyed magenta-purple, through front half and countered with fine silver oval |
| *Throat:* | Blue peacock |
| *Wing:* | Goose shoulder, married as follows: (top to bottom) 4 purple, 3 kingfisher blue, 1 purple, 2 fluorescent red, 1 purple, 3 kingfisher blue, 4 purple; mounted vertically |
| *Head:* | Black |

## UN-NAMED
(Dave Burns)

| | |
|---|---|
| **Tag:** | 5 turns fine gold oval |
| **Body:** | A butt of orange silk, then golden-yellow dubbing |
| **Ribs:** | Small gold oval, reversed over hackle |
| **Hackle:** | Blue eared pheasant or similar |
| **Throat:** | Shell-pink saddle hackle |
| **Wing:** | Bronze mallard |
| **Head:** | Black |

## UN-NAMED
(Dave Burns)

| | |
|---|---|
| **Body:** | Golden-tan dubbing |
| **Ribs:** | Fluorescent orange prismatic rib material and small silver oval as a counter |
| **Hackle:** | Black-dyed blue eared pheasant |
| **Throat:** | Teal |
| **Wing:** | Slips of orange goose shoulder or swan |
| **Head:** | Black |

## BLACK DRAGON DEE WING
(Gary Grant)

| | |
|---|---|
| **Tip:** | Silver oval |
| **Tag:** | Royal blue silk |
| **Tail:** | Golden-pheasant crest and jungle cock |
| **Butt:** | Ostrich herl |
| **Body:** | Rear half: flat silver tinsel ribbed with fine gold oval, veiled top and bottom with three red-dyed toppings, each slightly longer than the preceding topping. Joint, heron or similar dyed orange. Front half: black silk ribbed with medium silver oval and black heron hackle from second turn; countered with medium gold oval |
| **Throat:** | Teal and golden-pheasant crest top and bottom, the top crest extending to the tail and the bottom crest extending to the butt |
| **Wing:** | White-tipped turkey slips, tied Dee-style flat and V-shaped atop the fly |
| **Sides:** | Jungle cock |

## PURPLE KING (MARABOU)
(Thomas Duncan)

| | |
|---|---|
| **Tag:** | Four turns fine gold oval |
| **Body:** | Purple silk |
| **Ribs:** | Flat gold tinsel, lavender silk and fine gold oval, respectively; the gold oval being brought over the hackle stem |
| **Hackle:** | Purple marabou, from rear |
| **Throat:** | Teal flank |
| **Wing:** | Bronze mallard slips, thin |
| **Head:** | Black |

## HARLEQUIN SPEY
(Steve Broco)

| | |
|---|---|
| *Tag:* | Six turns of fine gold oval |
| *Body:* | In equal portions, hot orange, red and blue dubbing |
| *Ribs:* | Fine gold oval |
| *Hackle:* | Blue eared pheasant, then golden pheasant flank, both tied in at the front and wrapped so that the pheasant hackles are dense enough that they appear to palmer through the front half of the body |
| *Wing:* | White polar bear hair |
| *Collar:* | Mallard showing brown points, two turns |
| *Head:* | Red |

## GOLD-DIGGER SPEY
(Mike Yarnot)

| | |
|---|---|
| *Tag:* | Six turns fine gold oval |
| *Body:* | Flat gold tinsel; golden-yellow dubbing |
| *Ribs:* | Fine gold oval |
| *Hackle:* | Blue eared pheasant, through front half |
| *Throat:* | Rump hackles (yellow) from the golden pheasant |
| *Wing:* | Matched pair of yellow rump feathers from the golden pheasant |
| *Topping:* | Three golden-pheasant toppings showing red points |
| *Head:* | Lemon yellow |

## AMETHYST
(John Schaper)

| | |
|---|---|
| *Tag:* | One turn each of the rib materials |
| *Body:* | A tip of hot pink silk followed by an equal portion of fuscia silk and then bright claret dubbing for the balance |
| *Ribs:* | Flat silver trailed by fine oval silver |
| *Hackle:* | Deep claret rooster neck hackle through dubbing |
| *Throat:* | Two turns of bright blue under the wing and then two turns of claret over the wing |
| *Wing:* | Hackle tips: two hot pink inside two deep claret |
| *Head:* | Black |

## STEELHEAD AKROYD
(John Alevras)

| | |
|---|---|
| *Tag:* | Flat pearlescent tinsel |
| *Tail:* | Fluorescent orange hackle fibers, soft and long |
| *Body:* | Rear half, fluorescent orange SLF dubbing or similar, a joint of fluorescent orange Spey hackle; front half, black dubbing |
| *Ribs:* | Small silver oval |
| *Collar:* | Black Spey hackle followed by two turns of gadwall flank |
| *Wing:* | None |
| *Head:* | Red |

## STEELHEAD AKROYD TUBE FLY
(John Alevras)

| | |
|---|---|
| *Tag:* | Small silver oval |
| *Body:* | 1/2 fluorescent yellow dubbing; 1/2 black dubbing |
| *Rib:* | Small silver oval |
| *Hackle:* | Black Spey hackle through front half |
| *Collar:* | Guinea |

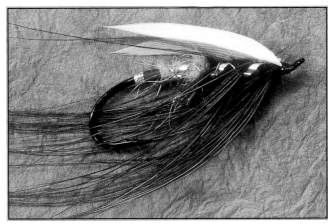

## CADDIS SPEY QUILL-WING
(Marc Danile)

| | |
|---|---|
| *Hook:* | No. 2-4 |
| *Tag:* | Small silver oval and red floss |
| *Body:* | 1/3 green SLF dubbing and 2/3 black Angora dubbing |
| *Ribs:* | Medium flat silver and small gold oval as a counter |
| *Hackle:* | Blue eared pheasant |
| *Wing:* | White goose sections |

## LA BORALDE
(Jean Paul Dessaigne)

| | |
|---|---|
| *Tag:* | Fine silver oval |
| *Body:* | Flat silver tinsel |
| *Rib:* | Gold oval |
| *Hackle:* | Gray |
| *Wing:* | Gray goose shoulder |
| *Cheeks:* | Jungle cock |

## UN-NAMED
(Mark Waslick)

| | |
|---|---|
| *Body:* | Flat gold tinsel, fluorescent flame floss |
| *Rib:* | Fine gold oval through front half |
| *Hackle:* | Yellow schlappen through front half |
| *Throat:* | Tangerine schlappen then blue eared pheasant |
| *Wing:* | Bright yellow hackle tips |
| *Head:* | Red |

## THE CRANE
(dressed by Paul Rossman)

| | |
|---|---|
| ***Tag:*** | Silver tinsel and orange silk |
| ***Tail:*** | Yellow swan |
| ***Butt:*** | Red crewel yarn |
| ***Body:*** | Bright blue silk |
| ***Rib:*** | Silver tinsel |
| ***Hackle:*** | Heron or substitute |
| ***Wing:*** | Two long jungle cock with cuckoo dun hackle over |
| ***Throat:*** | Guinea |

## HALLOWEEN HERON
(John Shewey)

| | |
|---|---|
| ***Hook:*** | Partridge Code N or M, No. 2-4/0 |
| ***Tag:*** | Flat gold tinsel |
| ***Body:*** | 1/3 hot orange silk, 2/3 hot orange dubbing |
| ***Ribs:*** | Wide flat silver and small oval silver; fine gold counter |
| ***Hackle:*** | Black-dyed blue eared pheasant |
| ***Collar:*** | Gadwall or teal flank |
| ***Wing:*** | Orange hackle tips |
| ***Cheeks:*** | Jungle cock |
| ***Topping:*** | Golden-pheasant crest, dyed hot orange (several) |

**Notes:** This and those "Heron variations" that follow are obvious, unabashed knock-offs of the Syd Glasso Orange Heron. Like many other Northwest tiers, I simply began to tie the Orange Heron in different color combinations. Initially I used heron hackles procured through England by Dave McNeese during the 1970s. Thereafter, save a brief infusion of Asian hackles procured by Hareline Dubbin, Inc., I resorted to blue eared pheasant for a substitute. I render these dressings to countless minor variations and thus decided years ago that naming them was of little consequence.

## VARIATION 1
(John Shewey)

| | |
|---|---|
| ***Hook:*** | Partridge Code N, 2-4/0 |
| ***Tag:*** | Silver flat tinsel |
| ***Body:*** | Rear half cerise silk, front half cerise dubbing |
| ***Ribs:*** | Wide flat silver and silver oval; countered with fine gold oval |
| ***Hackle:*** | Claret-dyed heron or substitute |
| ***Collar:*** | Gadwall or falcated teal flank, dyed cerise or claret |
| ***Wing:*** | White hackle tips (or cerise or purple) |
| ***Cheeks:*** | Jungle cock, optional |
| ***Topping:*** | Golden-pheasant crest, dyed cerise or claret; optional |

## VARIATION 2
(John Shewey)

| | |
|---|---|
| ***Hook:*** | Partridge Code N, 2-4/0 or similar |
| ***Body:*** | Rear half purple silk, front half purple dubbing |
| ***Ribs:*** | Wide flat silver and silver oval |
| ***Hackle:*** | Purple |
| ***Collar:*** | 2 turns purple marabou and gadwall |
| ***Wing:*** | White hackle tips (or purple hackle tips) |
| ***Cheeks:*** | Jungle cock, optional |

## VARIATION 3
(John Shewey)

| | |
|---|---|
| **Hook:** | Partridge Code N, 2-4/0 |
| **Tag:** | Silver flat tinsel |
| **Body:** | Rear half light blue silk, front half kingfisher blue dubbing |
| **Ribs:** | Wide flat silver and silver oval; countered with fine silver oval |
| **Hackle:** | Natural blue eared pheasant |
| **Collar:** | Green-wing teal flank |
| **Wing:** | White hackle tips |
| **Cheeks:** | Jungle cock, optional |

**Note:** A variation has kingfisher blue wings or two kingfisher blue hackles inside two purple hackles for wings.

## VARIATION 4
(John Shewey)

| | |
|---|---|
| **Hook:** | Partridge Code N, 2-4/0 |
| **Tag:** | Gold flat tinsel |
| **Body:** | Rear third bright scarlet silk, front 2/3's black dubbing |
| **Ribs:** | Wide flat gold and gold oval; countered with fine gold oval |
| **Hackle:** | Black-dyed blue eared pheasant |
| **Collar:** | Gadwall flank, dyed crimson |
| **Wing:** | Black hackle tips |
| **Cheeks:** | Jungle cock, optional |

## PITCROY FANCY
(dressed by David Barlow)

| | |
|---|---|
| **Tag:** | Flat silver tinsel |
| **Tail:** | A topping and tippet strands |
| **Butt:** | Red wool |
| **Body:** | Flat silver tinsel |
| **Rib:** | Gold oval |
| **Hackle:** | Blue eared pheasant |
| **Throat:** | Guinea |
| **Wing:** | Peacock secondary and golden-pheasant tippets: roof of bronze mallard |
| **Cheeks:** | Jungle cock |
| **Head:** | Red |

## AUTUMN SKIES
(John Shewey)

| | |
|---|---|
| **Tag:** | Silver |
| **Tail:** | Golden-pheasant crest, dyed bright red and topped with fruit crow or substitute |
| **Butt:** | 1/2 orange silk; 1/2 bright red silk, forming one half total body and countered with fine wire |
| **Body:** | 1/2 bright red dubbing; 1/2 purple dubbing |
| **Rib:** | Small oval or flat gold tinsel |
| **Hackle:** | Bright orange Spey hackle with purple at the collar |
| **Wing:** | Goose shoulder, mounted mostly Dee style: purple with two or three bright red fibers married through the center |
| **Head:** | Claret |

**Notes:** In later years I began tying the wing in the vertical, tented style and topping the fly with dyed-red golden-pheasant crest—the version that appeared in print several times thereafter.

## NUMBER ONE
(John Shewey)

| | |
|---|---|
| **Tag:** | Silver and then gold flat tinsel, forming about 1/3 total body and countered with fine wire |
| **Body:** | A tip of orange floss and then hot orange dubbing |
| **Ribs:** | Small gold oval |
| **Hackle:** | Bright orange through body and bright red at the collar (marabou, tip-dyed: orange tipped with red or black; red tipped with black) |
| **Throat:** | Red-dyed guinea (optional) |
| **Wings:** | Paired hooded merganser flank feathers, optionally with jungle cock along the stems |
| **Topping:** | Natural or bright red-dyed golden-pheasant crest (optional) |
| **Head:** | Black, banded with orange |

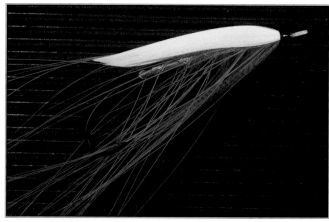

## POLAR SHRIMP SPEY
(John Shewey)

| | |
|---|---|
| **Body:** | A butt of orange silk and orange seal |
| **Rib:** | Wide flat silver, small gold oval and fine silver oval as a counter |
| **Hackle:** | Orange |
| **Collar:** | Mallard, dyed orange |
| **Wing:** | White goose shoulder |

## AUTUMN BRONZE
(John Shewey)

| | |
|---|---|
| **Tag:** | Silver and then gold flat tinsel |
| **Body:** | Orange silk, then fiery brown-orange dubbing |
| **Rib:** | Wide flat gold tinsel and fine silver oval as a counter |
| **Hackle:** | Natural gray blue eared pheasant or heron; from the rear on small patterns or from the mid-point on large hooks |
| **Collar:** | Shoveler duck flank |
| **Wing:** | Bronze mallard |

## CUMMINGS SPECIAL SPEY
(John Shewey)

| | |
|---|---|
| **Tag:** | Flat silver |
| **Butt:** | Yellow silk |
| **Body:** | Claret seal (spun into silk) |
| **Rib:** | Flat gold with fine oval gold counter |
| **Hackle:** | Claret |
| **Collar:** | Gadwall or widgeon flank |
| **Wing:** | Bronze mallard |
| **Head:** | Claret |

**Note:** For the Orange Cummings Spey, substitute bright orange silk for the yellow.

## PURPLE PRISM SPEY
(John Shewey)

| | |
|---|---|
| **Tag:** | Flat silver or none |
| **Body:** | Flat gold tinsel; deep purple dubbing |
| **Rib:** | Silver oval, counter-wrapped |
| **Hackle:** | Bright purple Spey hackle through body |
| **Collar:** | Deep purple Spey hackle and then teal flank |
| **Wing:** | Deep purple goose shoulder and jungle cock |
| **Head:** | Claret |

**Notes:** I prefer to use either dyed blue eared pheasant or tip-dyed marabou with short, black tips; often I use deep purple marabou in two turns for the collar.

## GOLDEN GREED
(John Shewey)

| | |
|---|---|
| **Tag:** | X-fine gold oval and then orange silk |
| **Tail:** | Natural red-tipped golden-pheasant crest |
| **Butt:** | Gold flat tinsel |
| **Body:** | Bright orange dubbing |
| **Rib:** | Medium oval gold |
| **Hackle:** | Orange-dyed marabou with black tips (or similar) and an orange-dyed bustard neck hackle or similar (hand-speckled marabou, for example) |
| **Collar:** | Mallard or pintail, dyed tangerine orange |
| **Wing:** | Orange goose or swan strips, tied vertically |
| **Cheeks:** | Jungle cock, over base of wings |

## ORANGE ANGEL
(John Shewey)

| | |
|---|---|
| **Tag:** | Gold flat tinsel |
| **Butt:** | Orange silk |
| **Ribs:** | Large oval gold tinsel and fine gold oval as a counter |
| **Body:** | Orange dubbing |
| **Hackle:** | Tip-dyed marabou, black-tipped orange or red-tipped orange |
| **Collar:** | Orange-dyed mallard flank |
| **Wing:** | White goose shoulder strips |

## ORANGE EGRET SPEY
(John Shewey)

| | |
|---|---|
| **Tag:** | Silver flat tinsel (optional) |
| **Body:** | Orange floss, hot red-orange floss, hot orange dubbing |
| **Rib:** | Medium oval silver and small silver oval as a counter |
| **Hackle:** | One light tangerine orange and one bright orange Spey hackle, wrapped Spey style through front half of body (bleached and dyed blue eared pheasant or ring-necked pheasant works perfectly) |
| **Wing:** | Bright flame-red hackle tips, rather robust |
| **Collar:** | Tip-dyed marabou: black-tipped hot orange |
| **Head:** | Bright red |

## FIREWEED
(John Shewey)

| | |
|---|---|
| *Tag:* | Fine silver oval and yellow silk floss |
| *Tail:* | A topping |
| *Body:* | Hot pink wool yarn or dubbing |
| *Ribs:* | Flat silver |
| *Counter:* | Fine silver oval |
| *Hackle:* | Blue eared pheasant or similar, dyed claret |
| *Throat:* | Gadwall dyed cerisel |
| *Wing:* | Cerise-dyed goose, turkey or swan, mounted vertical |

## EAGLE ROCK RIACH
(John Shewey)

| | |
|---|---|
| *Body:* | 1/5 orange silk, 1/5 deep orange yarn or similar, 3/5 deep purple yarn |
| *Ribs:* | Wide flat gold tinsel and fine flat gold; silver oval counter |
| *Hackle:* | Purple or black coque or schlappen |
| *Collar:* | Teal |
| *Wings:* | Bronze mallard |

## BLACK RIACH
(John Shewey)

| | |
|---|---|
| *Butt:* | Bright orange wool yarn |
| *Body:* | Back wool yarn |
| *Ribs:* | Wide flat gold, small flat silver & fine gold oval counter |
| *Hackle:* | Black schlappen or coque |
| *Collar:* | Gadwall or green-wing teal flank |
| *Wings:* | Bronze mallard (sometimes dyed hot orange) |

## PURPLE RIACH
(John Shewey)

| | |
|---|---|
| *Butt:* | Hot orange and fluorescent orange yarn or floss, mixed |
| *Body:* | Purple yarn or dubbing |
| *Ribs:* | Wide flat silver and fine flat gold with fine silver oval over hackle stem |
| *Hackle:* | Purple schlappen or coque, one side stripped |
| *Collar:* | Teal or guinea |
| *Wings:* | Bronze mallard (sometimes dyed purple) |

## TRI-COLOR RIACH
(John Shewey)

| | |
|---|---|
| **Butt:** | Light orange and bright red wool strands, mixed |
| **Body:** | Deep claret wool |
| **Ribs:** | Wide flat silver, small flat gold and fine silver oval counter |
| **Hackle:** | Claret-dyed coque or schlappen, one side stripped |
| **Throat:** | Hooded merganser |
| **Wings:** | Bronze mallard |

## BOGUS CREEK RIACH
(John Shewey)

| | |
|---|---|
| **Body:** | Claret and purple wool yarn strands, mixed |
| **Ribs:** | Wide flat gold and fine gold oval |
| **Hackle:** | Black coque or schlappen, one side stripped, reversed under fine oval tinsel |
| **Wings:** | Bronze mallard |

## GEORDIE
(John Shewey)

| | |
|---|---|
| **Body:** | Deep royal blue yarn, thin |
| **Ribs:** | Wide silver oval and fluorescent hot pink silk; counter of fine silver oval |
| **Hackle:** | Gray heron or substitute, dyed purple |
| **Throat:** | Baikal teal or green-wing teal |
| **Wing:** | Bronze mallard dyed purple |

## SILVER JENNY
(John Shewey)

| | |
|---|---|
| **Body:** | A butt of purple silk and then cerise wool yarn |
| **Ribs:** | Wide flat silver and medium silver oval; small silver oval as a counter |
| **Hackle:** | Cerise-dyed coque or schlappen |
| **Collar:** | Purple-dyed golden-pheasant flank |
| **Wings:** | Purple-dyed turkey or goose slips, tied vertical but divided |
| **Head:** | Black |

## PEACOCK SPEY
(John Shewey)

| | |
|---|---|
| *Tag:* | Flat silver tinsel |
| *Tail:* | Peacock sword |
| *Body:* | Peacock herl |
| *Ribs:* | Small silver oval, counter-wrapped |
| *Hackle:* | Blue eared pheasant, dyed claret (or similar) |
| *Collar:* | Mallard flank, dyed cerise |
| *Wings:* | Bronze mallard, dyed cerise or claret |

## SANTIAM SPECTRUM SPEY
(John Shewey)

| | |
|---|---|
| *Tag:* | Silver flat tinsel |
| *Butt:* | Flame red floss |
| *Rib:* | Small gold oval |
| *Counter:* | Fine silver oval |
| *Body:* | Purple dubbing |
| *Hackle:* | Purple Spey hackle |
| *Collar:* | Teal flank |
| *Wing:* | Bronze mallard (optionally dyed purple) |
| *Cheeks:* | Jungle cock (optional) |

## MIDNIGHT CANYON
(John Shewey)

| | |
|---|---|
| *Hook:* | No. 3/0-2 |
| *Tag:* | Gold flat tinsel |
| *Butt:* | Silver flat tinsel |
| *Body:* | Tip of orange floss then black dubbing or yarn |
| *Rib:* | Small oval tinsel, countered over hackles |
| *Hackle:* | Black marabou or similar from rear; tipped-dyed marabou starting at black portion of body (orange with black tips) |
| *Wing:* | Goose shoulder, black with 2 strands of orange married through the center at the bottom edge. Tied vertical and tent-style |
| *Cheeks:* | Jungle cock, angled down |
| *Head:* | Black banded with orange |

## BLACK MAGIC
(John Shewey)

| | |
|---|---|
| *Hook:* | Long shank Dee-style, No. 2-4/0 |
| *Tag:* | Fine silver oval and scarlet silk |
| *Tail:* | Golden-pheasant crest, dyed claret |
| *Body:* | In thirds: claret, deep purple & black dubbing |
| *Rib:* | Wide flat silver and small silver oval |
| *Hackle:* | Black, through front two thirds of body |
| *Throat:* | Teal flank (as a collar) |
| *Wing:* | Purple or black turkey slips, tied Dee-style |
| *Cheeks:* | Jungle cock |

## KIMMEL KING
(John Shewey)

| | |
|---|---|
| **Body:** | A mix of orange and light red yarn |
| **Rib:** | Medium silver oval, reversed over hackle |
| **Hackle:** | Blue eared pheasant dyed claret or similar |
| **Throat:** | Guinea dyed hot orange |
| **Wing:** | Bronze mallard |
| **Head:** | Claret |

# BIBLIOGRAPHY

## Books

Arnold, Bob, *Steelhead & the Floating Line*, 1995.
Ashley-Cooper, John*, The Great Salmon Rivers of Scotland*, 1980, 1987
Bates, Joseph D., jr., *Atlantic Salmon Flies and Fishing*, 1970.
Bates, Joseph D., jr., *The Art of the Atlantic Salmon Fly*, 1987.
Blacker, William, *Art of Fly-Making*, 1842, 1843, 1855.
Blades, William F., *Fishing Flies And Fly Tying*, 1951.
Beckwith, Lady Muriel, *When I Remember*, 1936.
Buckland, John & Oglesby, Arthur, *A Guide To Salmon Flies*, 1990
Burgess, Rosemary & Kinghorn, Robert, *Speyside Railways*, 1988
Combs, Trey, *The Steelhead Trout*, 1971.
Combs, Trey, *Steelhead Fly Fishing and Flies*, 1976.
Combs, Trey, *Steelhead Fly Fishing*, 1991.
Fitzgibbon, Edward (Ephemera), *The Book of the Salmon*, 1850.
Francis, Francis, *A Book on Angling*, 1867, 1872.
Frodin, Mikael, *Classic Salmon Flies*, 1991.
Grimble, Augustus, *The Salmon Rivers of Scotland*, 1899, etc.
Hale, J. H., *How to Tie Salmon Flies*, 1892, 1919.
Hellekson, Terry, *Fish Flies*, Vol. II, 1995.
Jorgenson, Poul, *Salmon Flies: Their Character, Style and Dressing*, 1978.
Kelson, George M., *The Salmon Fly*, 1895, 1978.
Knox, Arthur E., *Autumns on the Spey*, 1872.
Lauder, Sir Thomas Dick, *The Moray Floods* (aka, An Account of the Great Floods. . .), 1873.
Leonard, J. Edson, *Flies*, 1950.
Lingren, Arthur James, *Fly Patterns of British Columbia*, 1996.
Mackintosh, Alexander, *The Driffield Angler*, 1806, 1810, 1821.
Maxwell, Sir Herbert, *British Fresh Water Fish*, 1904.
Maxwell, Sir Herbert, *Salmon and Sea-Trout*, 1898, 1905.
Maxwell, Sir Herbert, *Scottish Land-Names*, 1894.
Meyer, Deke, *Advanced Fly Fishing For Steelhead*, 1992.
Mitchell, Alison, *Pre-1855 Gravestone Inscriptions on Speyside* (spine title: Speyside Gravestones), 1976 by The Scottish Genealogy Society.
Mullens, W.H. and Swann, H. Kirke, *A Bibliography of British Ornithology*, 1917.
Overfield, T. Donald, *Famous Flies and Their Originators*, 1972.
Pryce-Tannatt, T. E., *How to Dress Salmon Flies*, 1914, 1948, 1977.
Radencich, Michael D., *Tying the Classic Salmon Fly*, 1997.
Shipley, William and Fitzgibbon, Edward, *A True Treatise on the Art of Fly Fishing*, 1838.
St. John, Charles, *Wild Sport and Natural History of the Highlands* (aka, *Sporting in the Highlands*; aka, *Short Sketches of the Wild Sport and Natural History of the Highlands.*), 1849, 1882, etc.
Stewart, Dick, and Allen, Farrow, *Flies for Steelhead,* 1992.
Stewart, Dick, and Allen, Farrow, *Flies for Atlantic Salmon*, 1991.
Stoddart, Thomas T., *The Art of Angling as Practised in Scotland*, 1835, 1836.
Stoddart, Thomas T., *The Angler's Companion to the Rivers and Lochs of Scotland*, 1847, 1853.
Sutherland, Douglas and Chance, Jack (eds), *Trout and Salmon Flies*, 1982.
Taverner, Eric, *Salmon Fishing*, 1931
Taverner, Eric, *Fly Tying for Salmon*, 1942
Traherne, John P., *The Habits of the Salmon*, 1889.
Wade, Henry, *Halcyon*, 1861.
Waltham, James, *Classic Salmon Flies*, 1983.

## From Private Correspondence

Walter Johnson
Philip Glendinning
Graeme Wilson
David Burns
Iain Russell
David McNeese

# INDEX